Akhenaten

NEW ASPECTS OF ARCHAEOLOGY

Akhenaten

Pharaoh of Egypt - a new study

Cyril Aldred

17 Colour Plates
120 Monochrome Plates
6 Line Drawings

McGRAW-HILL BOOK COMPANY

NEW YORK · TORONTO · LONDON · SYDNEY

[1969?]

© 1968 Thames and Hudson Ltd.
All Rights Reserved
Library of Congress Catalog Card Number 68-9549
Colour and Monochrome Illustrations Printed in Switzerland
Text Printed and Bound in Germany by Kleins Druck- und Verlagsanstalt, Lengerich
00996

Contents

Part III: Synthesis

General Editor's Preface

To the uninstructed layman there is sometimes, let it be confessed, a certain monotony in the ancient Egyptian achievement, dragging its slow length along through millennium after millennium. Perhaps the operative word should rather be *predictability*, recalling the seasonal predictability of the Nile valley itself. Whether he is depicting a Middle Kingdom pharaoh or a Roman caesar two thousand years later, the Egyptian craftsman may be thought to work with relatively trifling variation between the close limits of an iron-bound tradition. Were it not for written record, we might be at a pardonable loss to distinguish sometimes between one end of the story and the other.

Of course all this is arrant heresy to the professed Egyptologist, his eye trained to critical discernment. But it was a professed Egyptologist who in fact singled out for special remark the hero of the present book as 'the first individual in history'. Few would deny that in the fourteenth century BC this remarkable man (if man he was) at least succeeded in breaking for a few years the reiteration of Egyptian history as we know it; its wars, its intrigues, its laborious sophistication, its raw imperialism, and its miscellaneous cults with their crowding zoology. If he dreamed rather than ruled, that is a part of the marvel. He may be damned as an apostate, as a pusillanimous monarch, as a religious maniac, as a masquerading woman, as a hermaphrodite. Was his parade of family life beside his lovely Nefert-iti amidst a bevy of daughters (no sons) merely compensation and pretence or was it truly a domestic innovation? Was his monotheism an unfulfilled anticipation of history, or was it a mere re-emphasis of previous trends? (Why not both?)

Whatever the substance of his contribution, he bequeathed enough contentious material to attract a varied range of scholarly and less scholarly interpretation—not to mention the playful ingenuity of a novelist. In the Cairo Museum we may pass by a score of pharaohs but his long, intelligent, inbred face, studied by the artist with uncommon sensitivity for all its colossal size, regards us compellingly from his Karnak column, and we pause for speculation.

Mr Cyril Aldred here reproduces the results of a new and prolonged re-investigation of the Akhenaten problem, or rather problems. If universal assent to all his views is in the nature of things unlikely, they are nonetheless full of interest and he presents them amply and fairly to the judgment of the reader.

MORTIMER WHEELER

Foreword

This essay is the outcome of seventeen years of sporadic thought about Amarna and its enigmas. It was in 1950 that I first tried to identify the owner of the Canopic jar illustrated in Plate 67 of this book, and found in the process that current opinions about Akhenaten and the Amarna Period did not stand up well to any rigorous questioning. Since that time I have attempted to investigate some of the problems in greater detail in various articles which have appeared in the specialist journals, but I have lacked the opportunity of presenting a conspectus of my views at greater length. This omission the present book seeks to remedy in some measure.

If the work has not taken the form that I first envisaged with a generous accompaniment of critical footnotes, that is probably all to the good. The experts will be able to recognize the sources from which my information has been culled and to test the authority for my opinions. For the general reader, for whom this work is primarily designed, such a full commentary would be irrelevant as well as tedious. A select bibliography has, however, been provided and a small number of essential notes appended.

I should perhaps emphasize that this is not intended as an exhaustive cultural history of the Amarna Age. I have said little about the art of the period, except incidentally, and even less about the topographical and cultural features of Tell el-Amarna itself. To do so would be to expand the work beyond its proper limits. I have been concerned to discuss only what I believe to have been the proper sequence of events within their cultural context.

No consistency can be claimed for the nomenclature adopted which still remains a matter of choice. Proper names have generally been hyphenated to distinguish their components, but in the interests of clarity even this practice has not been strictly observed (thus Akhenaten, the Pharaoh, but Akhet-Aten his Residence city).

Lastly I would like to pay tribute to my many Egyptological colleagues, some of the most esteemed, alas, now dead, for much help and for photographs and other information willingly given. Their suggestions and criticisms have often helped to form my views for which, however, I must accept the sole responsibility.

INTRODUCTION
The Discovery of Akhenaten

WITH THE POSSIBLE EXCEPTION of Cleopatra, no ruler of Ancient Egypt has provoked a greater flow of ink from the pens of historians, archaeologists, moralists, novelists and plain cranks than the Pharaoh Akhenaten who governed almost half the civilized world for a brief span during the fourteenth century BC. The reason for all this lively interest is not difficult to see. The historian, searching the conscious and unconscious propaganda that masquerades as the official records in Ancient Egypt, is often at a loss to project the personality of the ruler beneath all his trappings of power, the man beneath the divinity. Seldom, except in folk-tales with their element of sardonic ribaldry, is the Pharaoh ever represented as having human foibles. In the official utterances he is larger than life, a mere personification of kingship: only the office has any individuality, and the temporary holder of it is cast always in the same mould.

In the case of Akhenaten, however, there is clearly a departure from the norm. Here is a Pharaoh who ostensibly broke with the sacrosanct traditions of a millennium and a half, and showed hinself as a human being in the intimate circle of his family, dandling his infant daughters, kissing his wife or taking her on his knee, or leading his mother by the hand. Here is a ruler who does not appear as the all-conquering hero of gigantic size slaughtering the foes of Egypt, or as the aloof divine king greeting one of the many deities as an equal. Here was a poet who is credited with having written hymns to his god which anticipate the Psalms of David (see p. 189), and who introduced a new and vital art style of his own conception in which to express his novel ideas. Above all, here is a courageous innovator who abandoned the worship of the multifarious gods of Ancient Egypt in their human and animal forms and substituted for them an austere monotheism with an abstract symbol by which to represent it.

Plates 54, 55, 104

It is small wonder that such an original and revolutionary figure should have aroused the interest of scholars since the early years of the nineteenth century when the pioneer Egyptologists first stumbled upon his peculiar figure carved on the walls of abandoned rock tombs in Middle Egypt.

Plates 103, 105

Since that initial discovery he has been the subject of much enquiry and speculation. He has been identified by one scholar as the Pharaoh of the Oppression, by another as the victim of Exodus. Freud claimed him as the mentor of Moses and the instigator of Jewish monotheism. Glanville's view of him was that as a king he deserved nothing but censure. Breasted hailed him as the first individual in history. To Gardiner he wears a fanatical look and Pendlebury thought he was a religious maniac. Only an exceptional subject could diffract such a wide and vivid spectrum of opinions.

Plates 7, VIII

His chief wife, Queen Nefert-iti, is hardly less celebrated thanks to the famous portrait bust, believed to represent her, which has made an ancient mould of forgotten beauty once more fashionable and perhaps now timeless. Her elegant and earnest figure appears with that of her husband in many a scene of domestic harmony—playing with the children, driving

Plates 54, 55

with her husband in his chariot, pouring wine into his cup—as well as in scenes of more formal ceremonial—shaking her sistrum beside her husband in the worship of the Aten, offering with him before the piled-up altar, assisting in the investiture before the palace Window of Appearances,

Plates 44, 119

holding his hand as they sit side by side on their thrones beneath the great gilded baldachin of state while foreign legates make them fervid vows of loyalty accompanied by precious gifts. We need not jump to conclusions to interpret all this as the true picture of conjugal bliss. Has not Akhenaten

Plate 6

described his wife on the great Boundary Stelae of his city as:

> Fair of Face, Joyous with the Double Plume, Mistress of Happiness, Endowed with Favour, at hearing whose voice one rejoices, Lady of Grace, Great of Love, whose disposition cheers the Lord of the Two Lands.

This devoted pair are seldom represented except in the company of their daughters. The third of whom, Ankhes-en-pa-Aten, became the wife of Akhenaten's successor, Tut-ankh-Amun, whose gold-crammed sepulchre has provided the most spectacular discovery in the annals of archaeology.

Plates 10, 93

Her graceful and, to our eyes perhaps, her wistful figure appears with that of her husband on some of the important treasures of the tomb now in the Cairo Museum and, like her mother Nefert-iti, she too is shown in scenes of affectionate intimacy with her husband. The disarming way in which Akhenaten set a brief fashion in having his family life represented on the monuments has caught the imagination of present-day writers and made him seem the most modern and understandable of the Pharaohs, those remote gods incarnate. Such a man cannot fail to appeal to us across so vast a chasm of time and change and to arouse our sympathy and even that warmer partiality so well expressed among the last generation of Egyptologists by James Henry Breasted, who summed up a classic study of Akhenaten's reign in these words,

'. . . there died with him such a spirit as the world had never seen before —a brave soul, undauntedly facing the momentum of immemorial tradition, and thereby stepping out from the long line of conventional and colourless Pharaohs, that he might disseminate ideas far beyond and above the capacity of his age to understand. Among the Hebrews, seven or eight hundred years later, we look for such men; but the modern world has yet adequately to value or even acquaint itself with this man who, in an age so remote and under conditions so adverse, became not only the world's first idealist and the world's first *individual*, but also the earliest monotheist, and the first prophet of internationalism—the most remarkable figure of the Ancient World before the Hebrews'.

Where so eminent an authority expresses such whole-hearted approval, it would be surprising if less judicious enthusiasts held back; and Weigall for instance, in a study of Akhenaten which has coloured much subsequent work of popularization, has revealed that,

'For once we may look right into the mind of a King of Egypt and may see something of its working and all that is there observed is worthy of admiration.'

In recent years the debunking tendencies of modern historians have cut down Akhenaten to a much less attractive shape. His monotheism has been dismissed as mere henotheism—the belief in one supreme god without any assertion of his unique nature. His social and political innovations have been denied. His pacifism and internationalism have been exploded. The domestic idyll with Nefert-iti and his family has suffered brutal blows. Those thinkers who choose to see modern pressures operating even in the Bronze Age have been eager to assert that the general trend of events would have been no different if Akhenaten had been a mere sack of sawdust. Only his artistic novelties have been left to him, and indeed it is difficult in the face of his weird and disturbing colossi from Karnak to assert that Akhenaten was here following tradition even though the basic Egyptian art conventions are being distorted rather than transcended.

Plates 2–4

But while as a result of fresh information which has come to light in the past few decades Akhenaten now seems a far less revolutionary character than was initially believed, certain assumptions have become so embedded in the history of the reign and have been transmuted into facts, that the picture of the period is in sad need of complete cleaning and restoration. Some of the old discoloured varnish still adheres, the recent re-painting is all too obvious and the retouching needs to be carefully examined. Above all, areas where the paint has completely flaked away need re-defining.

The swing of opinion and the violence of the partisanship among scholars are due largely to matters of interpretation because the ancient records of Akhenaten's reign have come down to us in an even more tenuous form than those of many other kings. The researcher has to contend not only with the chance obliterations of time, but also with deliberate suppressions by man himself. Thus the plain facts upon which any reconstruction of the period must depend are scanty enough, and that they exist at all is due to the ingenuity and industry of generations of Egyptologists who have patiently tracked down and assembled scattered clues after the Ancient Egyptians had deliberately effaced most of Akhenaten's memorials, expunged all mention of him from their official records and done their best to blot out of their consciousness the recollection of a Pharaoh who had apparently not conformed to the centuries-old tradition of repeating the primal pattern of kingship which had come down from the gods.

It was from a deserted site on the east bank of the Nile in Middle Egypt that the early Egyptologists first became aware of the strange nonconformist whose name did not appear on the king-lists. This was at Tell el-Amarna, a modern composite name for an area where tomb-chapels hewn into nearby cliffs were decorated with scenes of the King and his Court. The peculiar style in which these reliefs were carved did not escape their attention, and the figure of the King with his epicene appearance raised doubts in their minds whether the ancient sculptors intended to represent a man or a woman. The figure was certainly that of a queen, but the accompanying titles described a Pharaoh though the name had frequently been cut out and other deliberate damage inflicted. This induced scholars to speculate and some fantastic theories were advanced to account for such an odd state of affairs. Mariette, for instance, with the vivid imagination one would expect of one of the librettists of *Aida*, suggested that while Khu-en-Aten, as his name was at first read, was indeed a man, he had perhaps been taken prisoner while campaigning in the Sudan and

Plates 6, 104

14

castrated, a circumstance which in his view would have explained the King's effeminate appearance, almost like that of a eunuch.

Another French scholar, Lefébure, produced the ingenious theory that Akhenaten was really a woman masquerading as a man, and he pointed to a notable precedent in Hat-shepsut, the queen who had usurped Pharaonic power earlier in the Dynasty and had had herself represented in male attire and even as wearing a beard. In support of his theory he drew attention to a very late tradition which had been briefly mentioned by Manetho, and quoted by Josephus, to the effect that a certain Acencheres who ruled after Orus was the latter's daughter. Lefébure equated Orus with Amenophis III and Acencheres with his successor, Akhenaten. These theories have been generally dismissed or ignored by subsequent scholars, though they require to be weighed as symptomatic of a malaise in the minds of Egyptologists when confronted by the extraordinary monuments of Akhenaten.

Plate 11

Between 1883 and 1893 a French mission cleared the private tombs at Tell el-Amarna where they copied texts and reliefs. They collated the inscriptions on the large stelae that were carved on the cliffs in the vicinity and which apparently marked the boundaries of an ancient township called Akhet-Aten, 'the Horizon (or resting-place) of the Aten'. They also examined the King's tomb, unfortunately not before it had already been uncovered by natives and partly rifled. The Royal Tomb was cut in a deserted wady about four miles from the plain and the drawings that the French made of fragmentary scenes in some of the chambers are now the only record that exists, thanks to subsequent destruction.

Plate 6

Plates 5, 87

But the site did not become the focus of a more intense interest until after 1887 when an old woman digging for *sebakh* (the nitrous compost into which ancient mud-brick decays) among ruins near the modern village of Et-Till at Amarna, lighted upon what we now know were the remains of the Palace Records Office. It was here that she unearthed hundreds of clay tablets inscribed with unfamiliar signs which local dealers and antiquaries dismissed as fakes, and by the time their authenticity had been established, some 350 specimens and fragments were all that remained.

Plates 116–118

The Amarna Letters, as they are generally called, proved to be copies and originals of the diplomatic correspondence, written in cuneiform, that passed between the Egyptian Court on the one side and the rulers of Anatolia, Assyria, Babylonia, Cyprus, Mitanni and the city states of Palestine and Syria on the other. This important archive has thrown a flood of light upon the history, trading relations, social and religious customs, geography and diplomatic protocol of the age. While hints of such a system have survived from an earlier time, the extent and sophistication of relations between the various civilized states of the Near East during the middle of the second millennium BC could hardly have been suspected before the recovery of these sadly damaged lumps of clay.

This sensational discovery brought a number of investigators and antiquity hunters on the scene and in the next decade all the monuments suffered deplorable damage from vandals of various sorts before iron gates were fitted to the tombs and guardians appointed. These measures were unhappily not wholly effective and in subsequent years a painted pavement, uncovered by Petrie during his excavations, was spitefully hacked up and one of the great Boundary Stelae together with its attendant group of sculptures was blown up with gunpowder by Copts who were under the common delusion that it was a doorway in the rocks leading to an Ali Baba's cave full of untold treasure. From 1902 to 1907 the Egypt Exploration Fund commissioned Norman de Garis Davies to copy what was left of the tomb reliefs and Boundary Stelae and his exemplary publications are still a main source for our data about the Amarna monuments.

Plate 47

In the season of 1891–2, Flinders Petrie made the first serious start on retrieving the information concealed below ground when, with his customary flair, he excavated a palace and other official buildings in the centre of the site and a number of houses further south. Although his exploration was little more than a *sondage* he succeeded in one short season in recovering a lot of information that subsequent operations have only confirmed. He was assisted in this work by a youth of nineteen called Howard Carter, who thirty years later was to round off the Amarna investigations by finding at Thebes the virtually intact tomb of Akhenaten's son-in-law and successor, Tut-ankh-Amun. During his only season at Amarna, Petrie also discovered and copied another seven out of the total tally of fourteen of the Boundary Stelae.

Plates 112–115

Plates 1, 7, 84–86

His work of excavation was continued by the Germans from 1907 to 1914, and from 1921 to 1936 by the Egypt Exploration Fund (Society), who between them uncovered the major portion of a city lying beneath the encroaching sands, and including within its confines many private estates, royal palaces, temples, a workmen's village and other constructions. During the course of these campaigns important discoveries were made, such as the excavation by the Germans of a group of workshops containing a number of sculptors' studies and models, including the painted limestone bust of Queen Nefert-iti referred to above.

As the characteristic style of the works of Akhenaten began to be appreciated by archaeologists, monuments of his reign were identified on other sites in Egypt, at Memphis, Asyut, Medamud and Hierakonpolis, but notably at Thebes, where tombs of some officials of his early years were discovered. Of these, the most important is that of Ramose who acted as vizier in the first years of his reign. But there are others, and operations are still being conducted by the Oriental Institute of the University of Chicago in the tomb of Kheruef, an official whose career spanned the later reign of Amenophis III and the earlier years of Akhenaten. Excavations and clearances in the vast temple area of Karnak by various hands over the past century have also brought to light the dismantled parts of a huge temple erected early in the reign and demolished by Akhenaten's successors, In recent years, for instance, several tens of thousands of small sandstone blocks have been recovered from the IInd, IXth and Xth Pylons bearing fragments of gaily coloured relief. As they now lie in their serried ranks near the Opet temple at Karnak they look like a huge jigsaw puzzle with all the pieces tantalizingly jumbled together and over half of them missing or still awaiting discovery.

Plates 42, 43, 75, 76

Plates 38–41

Plate 48

This Karnak haul of dismantled blocks had its counterpart at Hermopolis where in 1939, towards the end of their tenth season, a German expedition uncovered in the foundations of a later construction of Ramesses II over twelve hundred limestone blocks sculptured with reliefs of the Amarna period. Other blocks were brought to light in subsequent years by illicit native diggers, and of these many are now in American collections. It is clear that these reliefs were once part of the temples at Amarna, across the river from Hermopolis, demolished by Ramesses II for building-stone. Their subject-matter and texts have provided fresh material of prime importance for the history of the period, though at the moment of writing their significant inscriptions have not been fully published.

Plates 51, XI

Between 1902 and 1914, the concession for excavating in the Biban el-Moluk, the Valley of the Tombs of the Kings, at Western Thebes was held by Theodore M. Davis, who employed professional Egyptologists like Carter, Quibell and Ayrton to direct operations. As a result of these investigations, an important discovery was made nearly every season including the tomb of Yuya and Tuyu, the maternal grandparents of Akhenaten, which was found in 1905 with its two occupants resting within it and their opulent burial furniture substantially intact. In the season of 1907, Davis succeeded in finding another tomb, now catalogued as No. 55. This was very modest in size and although a dry-stone sealing

Plates 15–17, 28–30, 60–61

Plates 94–97

Plate 98

still blocked its entrance at the moment of its discovery, it proved to have been entered at some time in its past and the burial deliberately desecrated before the sepulchre was sealed up again. The meagre contents were in a wretched state of preservation, though it was clear that the rich burial furnishings had been made for royalty in the Amarna period. The kernel of the deposit was a decayed mummy, reduced to a virtual skeleton, contained within a rotting wooden coffin: but it was found impossible to identify the remains with certainty since the names of the deceased had been excised wherever they had originally appeared on the tomb furniture. Since the time of their discovery, the bones have been examined on four separate occasions and scholarly opinion has oscillated between the view that they are those of Akhenaten himself and the belief that they belong to his ephemeral co-regent Smenkh-ka-Re. We shall have to return to the problems of Tomb No. 55 in a later chapter.

The varied material enumerated above—damaged tomb reliefs, the excavated ruins of an abandoned city, the re-used stone of two temples to the Aten, the decayed Boundary Stelae, a spoliated burial—constitute the bulk of the evidence with which archaeological detectives have had to reconstruct the events of the reign of an execrated Pharaoh, and it is therefore hardly surprising that their interpretations of such material should differ, though of late opinion has tended to revolve around two main poles of thought.

Ill-fortune of a persistent kind has seemed to haunt the recovery of the evidence from the Amarna period and the researcher can only be too conscious of lost opportunities and neglected duties on the part of those who have had the responsibility of uncovering and recording the material remains. If the Amarna Letters, for instance, had been found by a skilled excavator and not native *sebakhin,* or if the blocks recovered from Karnak and Hermopolis had been fully recorded and published, some of the more nagging problems of the reign might now have been solved. As it is, we shall have to give a critical account of what the Amarna monuments reveal in the light of studies which several investigators, the writer among them, have been pursuing of late, but which have not been assimilated into the accepted view of the period.

We would do well, however, to avoid the pitfall of assessing Akhenaten as a man of our time with a contemporary outlook on the world around him, in spite of the modern appearance that so much of his reign seems to wear. If our study is to have any validity, it must consider him strictly within the context of his own time and place; and we shall, therefore, in the next two chapters, attempt to outline the main features of the civilization in which Egypt played a particularly influential role during the middle of the second millennium BC, and which Akhenaten dominated as the god-king of Egypt.

I Egypt in Dynasty XVIII

THE PRESTIGE that Egypt enjoyed among the rest of the civilized world of the Eastern Mediterranean in the second millennium BC derived from the authority of her unified power and resources. The distinctiveness of the land was evident for all to see. Apart from the region bordering the northern coast, it was practically a rainless land independent of the vagaries of the weather for its fertility—a rich straggling oasis in the deserts of North Africa. The inundation of the Nile, with the red silt it carried in suspension, annually watered the fields and fertilized them in the same operation. Except at rare intervals when a series of low Niles brought the 'years of the hyaena when men were hungry', the beneficent river spread its life-giving waters and fertilizing mud over the famished land in an annual miracle of rebirth out of desolation. In the semi-tropical climate large crops could be produced each season. Under a strong centralized government a proportion of the grain harvest could be collected and stored for next year's seed and to meet the needs of non-productive workers. A surplus was sometimes available for lean years, or even for export to other countries suffering from famine.[1]

Among the hungry nations it was the flesh-pots of Egypt that were celebrated. To the wandering Semite driving his flocks and herds from the aridity of the summer pastures in Southern Palestine, after an immemorial custom, the land of Goshen somewhere on the eastern flanks of the Delta, was a promised haven, a land literally flowing with milk and honey, since the flowery pastures of Lower Egypt supported not only a large cattle population but also swarms of bees working the many wild

Plates VII

flowers. The ubiquitous papyrus plant that grew wild in such profusion served a multitude of uses from building-material to food, and also supplied the paper for all kinds of records which were indispensable to Egypt's highly organized government.

Egypt also acted as the principal entrepreneur for the supply of the commodities of tropical Africa to the Mediterranean world either in the raw state or in the work of her supremely skilled craftsmen. Her deserts were equally productive of desirable raw materials such as salt, natron, and other minerals, semi-precious stones, and above all, rich deposits of gold that made her courted by the other nations of antiquity among whom it was proverbial that gold was as dust in the land of Egypt. The demand for it was as insatiable in the Bronze Age as it has been ever since.

It is not difficult, therefore, to see the immense prestige and influence that the god-king who ruled over such a unified and wealthy state exercised in the ancient world, and we shall have more to say about this aspect later. But what of the subjects of Pharaoh whose toil and ingenuity exploited the six hundred-mile long tract of the Nile Valley? The vast majority of the Ancient Egyptians were farmers diligently cultivating the rich Nile alluvium and steadily winning fresh land by draining the marshy rush-grown tracts that bordered the river. The labour, though well-rewarded, was onerous, and almost continuous, except during the inundation, and was largely concerned with irrigation—the building of dams to hold back the flood-water in shallow basins so that silt could settle on the fields and the ground become thoroughly soaked, or the piercing of dykes to allow water to flow from one area to another as the river receded. In spring and summer the higher-lying fields had to be laboriously watered by means of the *shaduf* or from jars slung on a yoke. The fertile soil bore at least one crop a season; and in favoured localities where artificial irrigation was possible, a second summer crop could be gathered. Nor does the harvest appear to have been blighted by those vagaries of the weather that in more temperate zones can suddenly produce disaster. Nevertheless, the present-day pests of the Near East were no less active in ancient times; and the satirist in describing the lot of the farmer draws an exaggerated picture of him contending with the depredations of field-mice, birds, grubs and locusts.

Besides its arable farms, Egypt had a large population of domestic animals such as oxen, sheep, goats, pigs and donkeys and, in the New Kingdom, the horse. The cattle-breeders and herdsmen led a freer and more nomadic existence in the natural habitat of such animals—the marshlands, with their lush pasturage and thickets of rush. Here they camped under their portable reed shelters tending the cattle and snaring birds and fish during their leisure hours. They probably evaded much of the forced labour that fell to the lot of the settled cultivators, as did the hunters and prospectors who roved the deserts and wadys on the verges of the Nile, trapping animals and birds for their skins, feathers and eggs and trafficking in aromatic woods, resins, hardstones and minerals. Such nomads, not entered on the census lists, represented only a small proportion of the population. The vast majority of the Egyptians were committed to the cultivation of the land as much by predeliction as of necessity. They were deeply attached to the soil and unhappy away from their Valley.

The basic social unit of the agricultural community, as of other classes, was the family, several families forming village settlements under the rule of a headman or mayor. Some of the farmers were veteran soldiers, often foreign mercenaries, who had been given land by the Pharaoh as a reward for service in his armies. While some cultivators were nominal owners of the fields they worked, others were tenants of land-owning institutions, chiefly the great temples of Memphis, Heliopolis and Thebes, but also the more modest local temples and such secular departments as the Treasury and the Royal Harims. The majority followed a hereditary calling and the whole family, women as well as men, shared in the work: small children too young to plant or draw water were able to scare birds from the growing crops or to glean the stubble fields.

The average peasant almost certainly led an isolated life within his village, unaware of much that went on beyond the immediate environs. Disputes with his neighbours and similar local affairs would be settled in the *kenbet* or village council that consisted of the headman and the elders of the communities. But this self-contained and circumscribed existence could be drastically impinged upon by the Central State in two ways.

Plates 28–30, 73

The period of the inundation, when for three months the fields were under water and the peasantry was largely unemployed, had resulted in the institution of a corvée or national labour force which could be drafted in an unskilled capacity to large public works such as the clearing of choked irrigation channels, the erection of moles and dykes, the hauling of building-stone from the quarry to the site, the making of bricks, and similar large-scale operations.

Plate 31

The State also made its presence felt in another way. As soon as the crops had reached a critical stage in their growth, officials appeared to measure the fields under cultivation and assess their yield for taxation purposes. At harvest time, a few months later, the officials would arrive to collect the revenues which were paid either by the owning institution or by the cultivators as they were liable; and such levies went into the state granaries.

The control of this illiterate toiling mass of Egyptians was vested in an elite class of officials whose prime qualification was that they could read and write. The business of the Egyptian state in the Late Bronze Age was conducted by paper-work of a volume and complexity that it would be hard to match until recent times. Egypt was ruled in the name of the Pharaoh by a hereditary bureaucracy that was well aware of its privileges. 'The scribe directs the work of all people. There are no taxes for him: he pays his dues in writing', wrote one. 'It is the scribe who reckons every-thing there is and makes the accounts. All the army depends upon him. It is he who conducts the magistrates before Pharaoh and assigns his position to each man. It is he who administers the land in its entirety and every affair is under his direction,' claimed another.

Plate 56

It was the scribal class who organized and carried out in all its detail the business of state, either directly as servants of Pharaoh, or indirectly as servants of those beneficiaries, such as certain institutions (*e.g.* temples great and small), or functionaries (*e.g.* the King's Son of Kush, the Vizier) to whom Pharaoh had delegated some of his powers. Not only had these bureaucrats to read and write, they also had to acquire a special knowledge of other branches of learning, such as agriculture, building science, arts and crafts, foreign affairs, according to the position they were destined to fill. The King's Scribes occupied such high offices of state as the Vizierate and Treasury. The army had its own staff of scribes; and important officials had subordinate ranks of scribes to assist them.

There is no doubt that it was this literate bureaucracy which, in spite of all the drawbacks of such a system, was responsible for the development of a highly organized civilization in Ancient Egypt. Whenever the control of this central administrative machine began to weaken, Egypt plunged into doubt, anarchy, civil war, invasion and famine.

The entire Egyptian nation from the Pharaoh downwards followed an hereditary calling, according to the native ideal of appointing the son to the place of his father. The sons of craftsmen became craftsmen, the scribe taught letters and learning to his sons; the farmer's children learnt hus-bandry in helping their father in the work of the fields. Among the educated classes, the younger sons though trained as scribes, sometimes secured a position in a cognate sphere of activity when their father's post was not open to them.

Only the army in the New Kingdom provided the uneducated man with an opportunity of stepping outside his caste and achieving a position of importance and affluence. From field officers who had risen in their profession by meritorious service were chosen the police officials, sports instructors to the royal princes and even major-domos of the princesses, besides the holders of other Court sinecures. This way of advancement was something new in Egypt and owed much to a novel social system that had sprung up with the introduction of the horse-drawn chariot by Ayran peoples about the eighteenth century BC. The warrior society that is so familiar to us from *The Iliad* with its aristocracy of armoured chariot-fighters expert in the use of the javelin and the new composite bow, and with its emphasis upon athletic contests and the management of horses had spread all over the Near East forming a class of *maryannu* or professional fighters to replace levies of conscribed peasants. These *maryannu* established feudal states in Syria and Palestine among the petty rulers who found the service of such formidable condottieri acceptable in their own tribal wars. During the anarchy that followed the fall of the Middle Kingdom in Egypt, they may well have taken service with Semitic immigrants, the so-called Hyksos, who in the face of ineffectual rule by the native kings were gradually able to bring Lower Egypt under their sway and to be recognized as the legitimate successors of the Pharaohs. In expelling their Hyksos overlords, the Theban princes in the sixteenth century BC had to adopt all the new weapons of their foes; and they seem to have taken over with them the military organization and the social structure that were their concomitants. It is probable that mercenary *maryannu* fought with the Theban forces and were rewarded by their successful leaders with estates in Egypt.

The Pharaohs of the New Kingdom showed the impact of these new ideas. To the old traditional garb of the prehistoric pastoral chieftain, they added a new crown, the Blue Crown, or war helmet of Asiatic origin. The scimitar replaced the old club with which they slaughtered their foes and was even added to the traditional 'flail' and crook sceptres. They are often shown mounted in a war-chariot charging into the thick of the foe and their prowess as athletes, archers and sportsmen was vaunted as truly superhuman (see p. 44). For the king himself now took the field in person at the head of his armies often with his sons on his staff even when they were mere infants: and it is as a divine war-lord, the incarnation of Mont, Baal or Reshep that he appears.

This novel militancy, however, merely overlaid the former character of kingship. The entire land of Egypt and all that was in it, men, animals, and resources, belonged to the Pharaoh, who was a god incarnate. He is always represented on a heroic scale, greater in stature than mere mortals and able to confront the gods on equal terms. He is the intermediary between gods and men and is represented in each sanctuary as the sole officiant. It is he who founds the temple and dedicates it to the gods since it was by his donations of land and revenues that it existed.

Plates 23, 42, 74
Fig. 3

Plates 13, XV

Plates 12, VII

In return for what Pharaoh gave the gods, they accorded him universal dominion, for he was not only the ruler of Egypt but the lord of the contiguous nations as well, having overcome both by his divine right. He had the power of life and death over all humanity. He could give 'the breath of life to their nostrils' from the *ankh*-sign he held in his hand when in the presence of mortals, and it was he who confirmed a sentence of death. He also assured the yearly rise of the Nile during the proper time; and was believed to make rain fall even in the distant land of the Hittites, as was accredited to Ramesses II. Even Akhenaten, the sun-worshipper, is apostrophized by his courtiers as 'this myriad of Niles' . . . 'a Nile which flows daily giving life to Egypt.'

Plates 38, 40

The king was the personification of *maet*, a word which we translate as 'truth' or 'justice', but which has the extended meaning of the proper cosmic order at the time of its establishment by the Creator. For it was believed that the gods had first ruled Egypt after creating it perfect, and it was their son and avatar who continued to govern it at every reincarnation. The essential novelty of this brave old world is seen in the Egyptian practice of dating. The years were numbered from the accession of a new king up to the moment of his death, when the system began again from the start of his successor's reign. Pharaoh established the rule of *maet* by his 'omniscient percipience' and his 'creative utterance' which had the inherent power of compelling obedience. His pronouncements were therefore oracular and however young the king might be his words had all the weight of superhuman thought and judgement for 'the god sits upon his lips.'

Such was the theory of kingship. Pharaoh was the 'Good God' who ruled for the benefit of Egypt, who could do no wrong and whose utterance was holy writ. He was 'born to rule while yet in the egg' and destined to be absorbed in the godhead at his death when as a falcon he flew away to the horizon. In practice, of course, such an ideal was modified by expediency and the course of history. He delegated power to his officials. Private property was created when he donated land, goods and people to institutions or individuals. Privileges were created when he exempted estates and persons from the operation of State exactions. In theory the king could annul at any time every liberty or privilege since the law was his pronouncement. The fact that this was not done, that institutions and individuals continued to enjoy their income, that private possessions were bought or hired and bequeathed to others was due to a heavy weight of precedence which necessarily formed the body of *maet*, for once an innovation under one god-king was accepted, it tended to become an indivisible part of *maet* thereafter. The king did not rule arbitrarily despite the fiction that he needed to consult only his own heart, or sometimes take heed of the oracle of a god. Precedents were frequently consulted and his life in all its minutiae was strictly regulated.

Events had also modified the pristine ideals of kingship. In archaic times, the Pharaoh was regarded as an incarnation of Horus, 'the remote one,' a supreme universal sky-god manifest as a giant falcon whose wings spanned the heavens. Two of the names in the Pharaonic titulary expressed that identification. Horus was the Great or Greatest God whose title is conferred upon the king himself, 'the Living Horus.' This idea reached its fullest development in the early Old Kingdom, and probably the Step Pyramid at Sakkara and the great stone pyramids at Meydum, Dahshur and Giza stand as the memorials of an age when the entire nation undertook the tremendous activity involved in raising and equipping these giant monuments to ensure the persistence of their greatest divinity.

By the end of this period, however, under the influence of the theologians of Heliopolis, the centre of the worship of the sun-god Re-Atum, new ideas were introduced. The Pharaoh was then regarded as the son of Re, who had ruled Egypt in primeval times and there was a subtle shift of emphasis from the view that the king was the incarnation of the supreme god, to the idea that he was his son. He was still Horus, as his titles declare, but he was also the Son of Re, theogamously created. An early legend recounts how Re fathered the first kings of Dynasty V upon the wife of a mere High Priest of Heliopolis, and this idea is given concrete representation in Dynasty XVIII, both by Queen Hat-shepsut at Deir el-Bahri and Amenophis III at Luxor, though the iconography is known to be much earlier. In both series of reliefs the various sequences are the same—the God takes the form of the Pharaoh and fills the Chief Queen with the spirit of life; the Annunciation is made to her by the Messenger of the Gods: an infant king is fashioned on the potter's wheel by the Creator; the infant is born and presented to the Gods; and his name is inscribed in the imperishable annals.

Towards the end of the Old Kingdom and during the First Intermediate Period and the earlier half of the Middle Kingdom, the political power of the Pharaoh suffered a severe diminution through the rise of feudalism, when his unique nature and powers were claimed by a multiplicity of local governors. At the same time he shared his special privilege of apotheosis on death. Much of the reverence for the Pharaoh as the greater-god-to-be passed to a king-like deity, Osiris, with whom the dead Pharaoh became identified. The advantages conferred by royal burial were arrogated by all Pharaoh's subjects who could afford a proper interment. His funerary liturgy was pirated and adapted, and his exclusive dress, crowns, sceptres and even his uraeus were usurped for the burials of his subjects who considered themselves as Osiris in death, whatever their position had been in life.

In the New Kingdom, however, the fighting Pharaohs who had liberated Egypt from the Hyksos domination and went on by their aggressive momentum to extend their sway over Asia, Nubia and the Sudan, recovered much of the old prestige and authority of the Crown. Their leadership was a resounding success and brought victories, dominion, wealth and unparalleled economic expansion to Egypt. The Pharaoh ruled the Two Lands with the same organization that had made such an efficient fighting machine of his armies. He could call to his aid able officials who were only too ready to accord divinity to the power who had advanced them. Akhenaten's henchmen refer to their king as 'the god who made them'; and the Vizier Rekh-mi-Re declares that Tuthmosis III was 'a god by whose guidance men live, the father and mother of mankind, unique, peerless.' The superhuman stature of these kings is symbolized by the colossal statues of themselves that they erected on the main sites and some of which even had their own cults like the kings they represented. This progression to grandeur rises to a peak with Amenophis III (see p. 58).

Plate V

Indeed everything conspired to set the king apart from mere mortals. The tabus that operated in the case of his subjects did not apply to him. He kept several large harims in the manner of Oriental potentates, but he was also expected to contract an incestuous marriage with his sisters, a common feature of all such ideas of divine kingship. The eldest son of the Pharaoh by his principal queen became his heir and the eldest daughter by the same queen the Royal Heiress, whose dowry evidently comprised the actual throne, itself an object of great sanctity as elsewhere in Africa today. It was therefore usual for the Crown Prince to marry the Royal Heiress so as to consolidate his claims and keep the divine essence they inherited undiluted. Owing to the high rate of infant mortality in Ancient Egypt even among royalty, the full brother-sister marriage was not always achieved and it was often the son by a secondary wife or concubine who married the Heiress. In such cases, however, the appointment as Heir-Apparent was usually confirmed by the oracle of a god as in the cases of

Tuthmosis III, Tuthmosis IV and Har-em-hab. As whoever married the Heiress became king, it would seem that it was not until the throne was vacant, as on the death of Tut-ankh-Amun (see p. 252), that such marriages were contracted. Nevertheless, marriages between the Heiress and the Crown Prince did take place before the death of the reigning Pharaoh, and this fact brings to the fore one of the most vexatious and controversial aspects of the Egyptian monarchy—the institution of co-regency.

It appears highly paradoxical that the unique god incarnate, the Living Horus, should share his rule with another, but that is what several Pharaohs tolerated and the evidence is incontrovertible. The generally accepted theory of kingship as it had developed by the end of the Old Kingdom is that the Pharaoh was Horus incarnate and only relinquished that im-

Plate XVII

manence to his son on his death, when he became assimilated to Osiris the progenitor of Horus. The eminent scholar, Gardiner, has pointed out that an act of association which resulted in two Horuses functioning simultaneously makes nonsense of such a doctrine. Despite this objection, however, there is a curious logic beneath the inherent contradiction. Representations of the theogamous birth of the Pharaoh, and other texts, make it clear that like Horus he was born a god, destined to rule, even while he was 'yet in the egg'. From the moment that the Heir Apparent arrived there were two Horuses in the land, and to have a young Horus ruling with an Osiris-to-be is no more ambiguous than to have a Horus ruling with a younger Horus-to-be. The relationship, Horus the Son, Ruler of the Living, and Osiris, the Father, Ruler of the Dead, must be regarded as a complete entity, 'God-the-Father-and-God-the-Son', or as the Egyptians phrased it, 'Horus in the arms of his father Osiris.'

The junior co-regent seems to have been shown to the people and nominated to the kingship at his birth, but the moment when he was crowned varies from reign to reign though it seems ideally to have taken place when he officially reached manhood, apparently at sixteen. Many princes, however, became co-regents at a later date, an elder brother having held office for a time and having died before his father. The question of co-regency will prove to be of critical importance in our examination of the Amarna Period and will de dealt with more fully in Chapter VII.

The transfiguration of a king *de jure* into one *de facto* was accomplished by the mystical rite of coronation. Here it will not be necessary to describe the various episodes in detail. The ceremonies can be divided into two parts, the private and public. During the first, the king toured his domains and was recognized by the gods of the important cult-centres as their true heir. He was baptized, anointed, and assumed various crowns and sceptres in the national shrines of Upper and Lower Egypt. At the public part of the ceremonies, he seated himself upon the throne and received the homage of his people, both native and foreign, who came bearing gifts like the Magi on their famous journey to a new King. As a damaged text of a later date describes it, 'God caused the King to seat himself upon the Throne; and mankind, the patricians, the common folk, and all who are upon earth brought gifts of homage and the princes of all foreign lands came to do obeisance.'

Plate 44

This scene is frequently represented on the walls of the tomb chapels of Dynasty XVIII though it has been invariably misinterpreted as the presentation of annual tribute or the spoils of war. The presence among the tribute-bearers of delegates from the 'Isles of the Mediterranean' whom the Pharaoh never reached tends, however, to upset the orthodox view. This coronation *durbar* was the occasion when the Pharaoh installed the viziers and other high officials, appointing his own nominees to the more important posts, if he did not confirm the former incumbents in their offices, and addressing to each a homily on the duties of the position he was about to assume. Hence the importance of this scene in the *cursus vitae* which the courtiers had represented on the walls of their tomb-chapels, and several examples mostly survive damaged.

Another *rite de passage* which all Pharaohs hoped to observe, though few actually did so, was the Feast of the Sed, or jubilee, when their powers were rejuvenated. The Sed Festival is rendered in the Greek portion of the Rosetta Stone as 'the Thirty-Year Feast,' from whence it has been assumed that the first celebration of the jubilee was held thirty years after the nomination of the Pharaoh to the throne. There are, however, certain cases which seem notable exceptions to this rule, though if our documentation were more complete it might be seen that such anomalies are due to the fact that it is the jubilee of the senior co-regent that is being celebrated and not that of the king in question, since the eldest son had an important role to play in the jubilee ceremonies. Certainly by the time of Dynasty XII it was only those Pharaohs who reigned for thirty years or more who celebrated Sed Festivals, and this practice appears to have been followed in the New Kingdom despite certain ambiguities. After the first jubilee had been held, a Pharaoh might observe others at three or four year intervals: thus Ramesses II was able to celebrate thirteen at least in his sixty-seven years of rule.

Plates 38, 91

Plate 49

In origin, the Sed Festival may have been a sublimation of a prehistoric rite whereby the divine king was slain when his powers began to wane, as Osiris was traditionally believed to have been murdered and parts of his corpse buried in various towns of Egypt for its greater fertility. In historic times, however, this savage practice had been replaced by a magic ceremonial whereby the office of kingship was renewed. Though the Sed Festival was celebrated at Memphis, some of its rites may have been repeated in other great cult centres. Amenophis III, for instance, repeated the event in his palace at Thebes. A Festival Hall and Court were built in which the ceremonies took place, including a re-enactment of the coronation ritual. The king generally wore for the occasion a short cloak

Plate 91

with a stand-off collar and the fealty of his high officials, both native and foreign, was renewed. He also gave and received gifts in abundance.

The ceremonies were traditionally supposed to start on the first day of the first month of Winter. The official who played a leading part in these initial proceedings was the Crown Prince who wore the same archaic

Plate 49

short cloak as the king himself and who in early times was associated with the archaic canine god Sed, the first-born or Opener-of-the-Womb, equated with the falcon Horus, the heir of the gods. In the reign of Amenophis III, however, it was the falcon-headed god of death and resurrection, Sokar, who appears to have played a cardinal role. His seat was believed to be on the fringes of the desert at Memphis, where his festival took place a few days before the New Year, at the beginning of Winter, which was the canonical day for the coronation of the Pharaoh.

The rites of the Sokar Festival enshrine very ancient beliefs in which the king made a circuit of the walls of Memphis, an onion around his neck, like the garlanded sacrificial cattle that in other years were driven in a similar circuit, ploughing the earth as they went. It was probably at this moment in prehistoric times that the king himself was sacrificed and dismembered, his blood fertilizing the ground. At the jubilee ceremonies, however, the hacking-up of the earth was in preparation for the burial of Osiris, that deification of kingship, which took place four

Plate 38

days after the Sokar Festival. During these rites, a *Djed*-pillar, the fetish of Osiris in his Delta town of *Djedu*, was raised up to symbolize the resurrection of the dead god in his form of Horus, the living god, whose incarnation, the Pharaoh, was crowned on the succeeding day, the first of the New Year. Thus the king, identified first as Sokar suffers death, is resurrected as Osiris, and reigns again as the rejuvenated Horus at the season of the renewal of the cultivation.

The celebration of the jubilees of Amenophis III, however, appears to have extended over a period of several months within each year, probably because the repetition of the festival, at Thebes for instance, had to be observed at different dates from the canonical times. We shall refer to the jubilees of this king in greater detail later, as they are important for the sequence of events during the Amarna Period.

I   Statue of Akhenaten in yellow steatite (ht. 65 cm), acquired by Henry Salt about 1826 probably in the ruins of a building at Thebes dating to the late XVIII Dynasty. Originally the King was represented seated upon a cushioned throne with his Queen whose figure has been broken away except for her left arm which clasps his waist. The part below the knees is also missing. In the absence of any inscription, the sitter has been identified by some as Smenkh-ka-Re, but wrongly in view of the latter's reconstructed physiognomy (see p. 147). The face in profile with its over-grown jaw and long nose corresponds to portraits of Akhenaten on certain sculptors' model reliefs belonging to the latter part of the reign (cf. Plate 68). The slack pose, with the prominent breasts and pendulous paunch, faithfully reveals the peculiar physique of Akhenaten, but in the idealizing style of his later years

II   Cartouche-shaped burial chamber in the tomb of Tuthmosis III in the Biban el-Moluk, show-ing the painted quartzite sarcophagus and the walls decorated as though an ancient papyrus had been unrolled against them. It bears a cursive linear rendering of the magical texts of the Book of What is in the Underworld (see p. 165)

III   Painted red granite sarcophagus of Har-em-hab in situ in his tomb in the Biban el-Moluk, resembling in its design those of Tut-ankh-Amun and Ay. These in turn appear to have been influenced by the Amarna sarcophagi, judging from the fragments which have survived, except that the figures of their guardian goddesses at the corners have replaced that of Queen Nefert-iti. They also bear different texts. In this view, the scorpion goddess Selkit stretches protec-tive winged arms at the south-west corner, with Neith on her right and Nephthys on her left. Between her and the latter stand three funerary deities. Invocations to the gods of burial and the goddesses of the four quarters are inscribed on the outer surfaces

II

III

II

The Approach to Amarna

IT WAS IN THE MIDDLE of the sixteenth century BC that the Thebans began their revolt against the overlordship of the Hyksos Pharaohs, which because it eventually prospered was not afterwards called treason. The Theban forces with their Madjoi auxiliaries from the deserts of Nubia were imbued with a zest for conquest that after years of fighting took their tenacious leader Amosis from the uneasy control of the southern provinces to the position of Pharaoh of a reunited Egypt and the greatest prince of his age. Although he was a direct descendant of the Theban line of local rulers classified by Manetho as Dynasty XVII, he was evidently recognized as the initiator of a new dynasty. With him the Second Intermediate Period ends and the New Kingdom begins. By the end of his reign his family was firmly on the throne, the Hyksos were no more, all rivals had been eliminated, Nubia with all its wealth had been recovered and Egyptian traditional claims in Palestine and Syria re-stated with new force.

In place of the armies of former times, with their small nuclei of royal household troops supported by local levies, the New Kingdom Pharaohs deployed standing armies of considerable size, manned by soldiers who had chosen the army as a career, and officered by professionals who had a more sophisticated idea of warfare than the mere clash of armed bodies in a general mêlée. It was this fighting machine that reconquered Nubia and pushed the southern boundary of Egypt as far as Napata (Gebel Barkal) below the Fourth Cataract. Under successive Pharaohs this region became completely Egyptianized, and while its inhabitants liked to wear their own native dress on State occasions, they bore Egyptian names, acquired Egyptian trade-goods, worshipped gods of Egyptian origin and wrote in the Egyptian language. Nubians and Sudanis formed the backbone of the Egyptian armies and the Madjoi peoples of the Nubian deserts gave their name to the Egyptian police force. With the recovery of the southern lands the Pharaohs got once more into their hands the wealth of tropical Africa, notably gold, which was so powerful an instrument of policy in their dealings with other rulers of the Near East.

By his capture of Sharuhen, a key town of Southern Palestine, Amosis had served notice on the Asiatics that his new Egypt was reviving vigorously its claim to a region which it had long regarded as its legitimate sphere of interest. There had been, however, a change in the political situation since the Middle Kingdom Pharaohs had sought to make the Asiatics 'come to heel like dogs.' The Hurrians, a people living around Lake Van in Armenia, had pressed southwards and established a feudal state, Mitanni, between the Upper Tigris and Euphrates, ruled by an Indo-European military aristocracy speaking an Aryan language. They had brought into their orbit the Amorites of North Syria. To the west of Mitanni and the north of Syria was Hatti, the land of the Hittites, a mixed people occupying most of Anatolia also ruled by an Indo-European caste speaking a tongue akin to Greek and Latin. These two powers challenged Egyptian pretensions in Asia, though in the earlier part of the Dynasty the more serious threat came from Mitanni.

The geographical and political conditions in Palestine and Syria assisted the Egyptians in holding this large tract of empire in their grip. The Semitic population was small and largely concentrated in the coastal plains and uplands and in the Jordan Valley. In these more fertile areas the inhabitants lived mostly around the townships and were largely detribalized: elsewhere they were still nomadic. The tribal settlement of the region was evident in the many little states each governed by a ruler, the vassal of the Pharaoh, who often bears an Indo-European name. These princes and their aristocracy of *maryannu* were often the descendants of Aryan and Hurrian adventurers who had brought their new weapons and methods of warfare into Syria and Palestine during Hyksos times.

Such petty states were in constant conflict with each other. Occasionally, under the leadership of a prince more energetic and crafty than his fellows, a coalition of states would win some temporary ascendancy, but the federation would all too quickly dissolve and reform in another direction. The proximity of Egypt, Hatti and Mitanni exerted a magnetic effect upon these princes drawing them into the orbit of the Great Power that lay nearest to hand and whose assistance could be sought in promoting their own local ambitions. What the vassals required of the Pharaoh (and doubtless of the Kings of Hatti and Mitanni, too) were his troops to assist them in their squabbles and jockeyings for power; and they therefore set up a constant clamour for armed help from Pharaoh to save them from an impending or actual attack from some villain of a neighbour. Assurances that unless such aid was sent immediately they would be overrun and the town or state they were so valiantly holding for the king would be lost for ever, were combined with protestations of their own loyalty and honesty, and the treason and chicanery of their rivals. Very often their accusations were contradictory; and included in their censure are the commissioners who were supposed to be carrying out Pharaoh's orders. There is more than a suspicion that the Egyptian governors on the spot were taking advantage of the local rivalries in order to prevent any one state from becoming too powerful. 'Divide and rule' was as much their motto as that of Machiavelli. Such is the state of affairs revealed by the Amarna Letters (see pp. 15–16).

The situation was further complicated by the presence of the traditional *Shasu* bedouin who were always ready to swoop out of their desert places to raid unprotected settlements and caravans. There was also a more mysterious people the 'Sa Gaz' of the cuneiform tablets who are identical with the Hapiru and who appear in Egyptian texts as the *apiru*, a name applied to foreign unskilled labourers and slaves evidently captured in war. The Hapiru seem to have been displaced persons of different ethnic origins and speech who wandered about Palestine and Syria, living by rapine and mercenary service. In origin the majority of them appear to have been donkey caravaneers obliged to give up their mercantile occupation during the troubled times that began in the eighteenth century BC. They took employment as viticulturists, soldiers of fortune, or brigands according to their opportunities. Sometimes bands of Hapiru were employed as mercenaries by the local dynasts to aid them in their petty wars, and they even appear to have been hired on occasions by the Egyptian commanders. Whether they were the ancestors of the Israelites of Joshua is still debated.

The successors of Amosis all sustained the age-old Egyptian pretensions in Asia. Tuthmosis I led an expedition in a sweep through Palestine and Syria which culminated in his crossing the Euphrates and setting up a commemorative stela in Naharin, the territory of Mitanni. During the regency of his daughter Queen Hat-shepsut, however, a less aggressive policy appears to have been adopted, and the absence of any show of force encouraged the more independent vassals to secede from the Egyptian orbit and come under the influence of Mitanni. By the time that Tuthmosis III came into his own, it required fourteen campaigns in Asia to overthrow a coalition of rebellious states, settle disputes and replace dissident governors and princelings with loyal collaborators. Above all, Mitanni, the arch-fomenter of trouble and the most serious rival to Egyptian amibtions in Asia at this time, had to be confronted and contained, if

Plate 11

not defeated. The stability so achieved lasted for three or four generations until the expansionist aims of Hatti upset the balance of power in Syria and allowed the local dynasts to indulge once more their hopes of independence and their dreams of wider dominion.

Plate 12

In after years the Egyptians looked back to the long and prosperous reign of the dynamic Tuthmosis III as a golden age in which their arms had been everywhere successful from Napata in the Sudan to Naharin beyond the Euphrates. The material wealth in tribute and slave labour that poured into Egypt as a result of these campaigns stimulated all kinds of enterprises, notably grandiose and widespread temple building in every centre in Egypt but particularly at Thebes. The early kings of the Dynasty had distributed lands in the Delta among their families, including the rich vineyards along the course of the western branch of the Nile, but their first loyalty was to their birthplace, Thebes, and its god Amun who had brought them success and prosperity. Its oracles had induced them to challenge the Hyksos Pharaohs and had sustained them throughout their long struggle. They now showed their gratitude by lavishing treasure upon the god who had sponsored them. Each king sought to outdo his predecessor in the size and richness of his constructions, and the wealth of his endowments. Brick and limestone and simple cedar-wood gave way to massive sandstone, quartzite and granites. Gold and silver and various coloured bronzes were expended on temple fittings. The tribute of Asia and Africa was diverted to the treasury of Amun whose image was inlaid with lapis lazuli from Babylon and whose pylons were graced with the tallest cedar flagpoles from Lebanon, besides the gold, ivory and ebony furnishings of Nubia and Kush. The immense size and profusion

Plate IV

of the monuments still standing among the extensive ruins of Thebes have given Egyptologists of a former generation the impression that the city was the great centre of the Egyptian 'empire' in the New Kingdom; but it is now clearer that the northern capital Memphis never lost its importance as the principal seat of government. In the reign of Tuthmosis I a great estate was founded there in whose precincts subsequent Pharaohs build their main palaces. It is doubtful in fact whether the Pharaohs visited Thebes except during the more important of its annual festivals. Thebes takes on the character more of a holy city, the centre of an influential Amun cult, and the resting-place to which the Pharaohs were brought

Plates II, III

after death for interment in decorated tombs hewn in the flanks of a lonely valley on the Western Bank, the Biban el-Moluk. The mortuary temples dedicated to the cult of Amun and that of the dead king were erected on the verge of the cultivated plain over a mile south-east of the Biban from Deir el-Bahri (temple of Hat-shepsut) to Medinet Habu (temple of Amenophis III), and overlooked by the foothills in which deserving officials were granted tombs. It is the painted chapels of these private tombs that have contributed so much to our impressions of the character and progress of the Dynasty.

Plate V

Plates 31, 32, VI

The former barons who in the feudal age had governed the various provinces of Upper and Lower Egypt had been replaced in the later Middle Kingdom by officials bearing the same titles who were no more than mayors or headmen of the chief towns. Their jurisdiction extended to the harbours of the Nile and the cultivation in the vicinity. Their main function was the collection and transport of taxes, mostly in grain, but also in other products, and they accounted for the proper discharge of these duties to the viziers. But while in its simplified organization the administration of Egypt during the New Kingdom may have been modelled on the lines of the army with its division into distinct classes of society, and while important local officials may have been ex-army officers, the management of affairs was still very much in the hands of the scribal class who alone could deal with all the paper-work of a government which was meticulously organized. While many of these scribes belonged to the palace administration, such as the Treasury and the Vizierate, the greater body were attached to the various religious foundations, such as the temples of the gods in the chief towns, through which much of the business of state was carried on at one remove, since the king had delegated responsibility and authority to them.

Plates 19, 20

Despite the many wives, including foreign princesses, that the Pharaohs maintained in their harims, the line of succession was often in danger of petering out and few of the heirs-apparent lived long enough to ascend the throne. The claims of Tuthmosis I to succeed Amenophis I are by no means clear and he appears to have come from a collateral branch of the Royal Family. Tuthmosis II nominated as his co-regent a son (afterwards Tuthmosis III) by a concubine in default of heirs by his Chief Queen Hat-shepsut. The choice was approved by the oracle of Amun while the young prince officiated as a neophyte in the temple at Karnak. If we are to believe the account that Tuthmosis III later gave of the event, he was recognized by the god as the successor of Tuthmosis II on an occasion when his father was actually sacrificing to Amun in the temple, and promptly crowned within the sanctuary. Thereafter he ruled as co-regent to his father who, however, died after a short joint reign of little more than a year. It was then that the Heiress Queen Hat-shepsut usurped the supreme power as regent of the entire land and made it labour with bowed head for her. Her daughter Nefru-Re appears to have been married to Tuthmosis III, both being mere children at the time. Hat-shepsut claimed that her father had appointed her his co-regent and in the presence of the entire Court declared her to be his successor. It is generally agreed by Egyptologists that this *post hoc* justification of her seizure of power is wholly fictitious. Nevertheless, it must have been suggested by a real event of orthodox character, and there seems little doubt that what she was describing was the appointment of the co-regent Tuthmosis II to whom she was married as an infant during the coronation ceremonies, and whose part in her career she subsequently ignored.[2] She evidently thought her claims superior to those of her young step-son, and had

Plate 11

herself represented in all the trappings and titulary of a male Pharaoh. Some twenty years after her death, Tuthmosis III had all mention of her expunged from the records and altered her monuments so as to suppress her name.[3] It was not appropriate that the Living Horus should be a female, though several queens in Egypt's history attempted to usurp male prerogatives.

Plate 14

Tuthmosis IV, too, although a son of Amenophis II, was not the heir-apparent but came to the throne by a twist of fortune, probably on the death of an elder brother. He hints as much when he relates on an incomplete stela how as a young prince without prospects, while he rested from the hunt in the shadow of the Great Sphinx at Giza, the sun-god Re-Herakhty came to him in a dream and promised him the kingdom if he would clear the encroaching sands from the huge image which was his embodiment. Manetho accredits him with a reign of nine years eight months and this figure is confirmed by the paucity of his monuments, there being few private tombs at Thebes which belong exclusively to his reign.

The examination of his remains which came to light in 1898 when Victor Loret discovered a cache of royal mummies in the tomb of Amenophis II in the Biban el-Moluk, showed that he was little more than twenty-five years old when he died, suggesting that he came to the throne when he reached official manhood at sixteen, two years earlier than the age attained by his father at his accession.

III

The Reign of Amenophis III - The Historical Outline

NEB-MAET-RE, Amun-hotpe hek-Wase, came to the throne on the early death of his father Tuthmosis IV. His mother was Mut-em-wiya, and if she had indeed been the Hereditary Princess that he claims she was on a large stone votive bark in the British Museum, she should have been a sister or half-sister of her husband Tuthmosis IV. She is nowhere dignified, however, with the titles of 'King's Daughter' and 'King's Sister'. This ambiguity about her exact parentage has led some scholars to suggest that she was the daughter of the Mitannian King Artatama, who was given an Egyptian name on her marriage to Tuthmosis IV, and that her son, Amen-ophis III, was therefore only half Egyptian. But if there is any truth in the Mitannian assertion that Tuthmosis IV had to ask seven times for the hand of the princess, it is fairly certain that she can have entered his harim only towards the end of his brief reign, in which case Amun-hotpe, if he were her son, would have been but a few month's old when he came to the throne.

There is no evidence, therefore, for identifying Mut-em-wiya with the daughter of Artatama, and her importance derives from the circum-stance that she had borne the King's eldest son, Amun-hotpe. She pre-sumably had a proper claim to the title of 'Chief Wife of a King' in addi-tion to that of 'Mother of a King' bestowed upon her by Amenophis III during his reign. Whether she was also the mother of Amun-em-het, A-kheperu-Re and other sons of Tuthmosis IV who all appear to have died young is unknown. We shall offer some opinions on her familiy connec-tions later (see pp.88–89).

Amenophis III is usually dismissed as the typical oriental potentate, uxorious and indolent, with a taste for luxury and opulence, pursuing diplomacy abroad more by the lavish expenditure of gold than the ener-getic exercise of arms. At home he has been regarded as largely under the dominance of his Chief Wife, Tiye, a woman of non-royal birth whose saturnine features have induced some Egyptologists to see in her a capable manager of imperious temper. Such viewpoints, based, of course, on the most subjective of opinions do scant justice to the character of Amenophis

Plates 21, 22

III whose reign reveals novel features not found before his time or afterwards.

Plate 20

In truth it is probable that the innovations of the period owed less to the King himself than to his advisers and high officials of whom one, Amenophis-son-of-Hapu, left behind him such a reputation that he was deified in Ptolemaic times as a great sage. The guidance of such wise men was certainly needed at the King's advent for it has been generally overlooked that on his accession Amenophis must have been no more than a mere child. The anatomist Elliot Smith who examined his badly damaged mummy was unable to form any precise estimate of his age at death and left open the question whether he was nearer forty or fifty years of age. Since Amenophis III ruled for thirty-eight years at least, he cannot have been even adolescent at his accession. It is, however, almost certain that he was less than nine years old, since his father reigned for little more than nine years and could hardly have received a harim before he came to the throne at fifteen or sixteen years of age. Certainly the Brooklyn statue-head of Amenophis III shows those who are familiar with the conventions of Egyptian sculpture the chubby features of a very young boy. In the tomb of one of his tutors he is shown seated under the coronation baldachin with his mother supporting him. No wife is in attendance at this representation, but the chief consort, Tiye, soon puts in an appearance and is thereafter closely associated with her husband in representations and inscriptions throughout their reign.

Plate 23

The first mention of Tiye occurs in a novel manner which is peculiar to the reign. During the first twelve years of his rule, Amenophis III issued a series of five large scarabs, just as a modern ruler might strike medals, commemorating the important events of his times. They were despatched to all quarters of his realms and specimens have been found as far afield as Ras Shamra in Syria, Ain Shems in Palestine and Wady Halfa in the Sudan.

Plates 24, 26

The first of the series provides the only undated example, but the fact that it bears the full titulary of the new king and defines the boundaries of his dominions suggests that it was issued at his accession as a rescript to apprise his officials of the correct mode of addressing him, similar to an announcement made at the accession of Tuthmosis I, and probably of every king. The text is as follows:

Live the *Horus*, Strong-Bull-Appearing-as-Justice; *He of the Two Ladies*, Establishing-Laws-and-Causing-the-Two-Lands-to-be-Pacified; *Horus of Gold*, Mighty-of-Arm-when-He-Smites-the-Asiatics; *King of Upper and Lower Egypt*, Neb-maet-Re (Lord of Truth like Re); *Son of Re*, Amun-hotpe (Amun-is-pleased), Hek Wase (Ruler of Thebes), Given Life: and his *Chief Wife*, Tiye, May she Live! The name of her father is Yuya; the name of her mother is Tuyu. She is the wife of a mighty king whose southern boundary is at Karoy (near Gebel Barkal) and whose northern is at Naharin (Mitanni).

The fact that the parents of Queen Tiye bear no titles that would indicate that they were of royal stock has led to their being classed as 'commoners' and we shall have more to say about this later. Any romantic notion that the royal marriage was the result of a 'love-match' is best dismissed. Amenophis III was too young to have exercised much choice in the matter and it is probable that Tiye was even younger, perhaps not more than four years old. Traditionally the new king should have married as his chief consort a sister or half-sister in order to confirm his rights to the throne, and the fact that he did not, suggests either that no heiress daughter of Tuthmosis IV was surviving at her father's death, or other considerations were operating.[4]

Yuya was the King's Lieutenant of Chariotry and Master of the Horse. As such, of course, he carried high military rank and almost certainly was the chief instructor of the young king in horsemanship and the arts of war, although Amenophis had other tutors to teach him writing and all the ancillary knowledge of a properly educated scribe. Tuyu bore the title of Royal Ornament which in her case probably means that she was brought up and educated in the harims of Amenophis II and Tuthmosis IV as a lady-in-waiting and given to Yuya in marriage as a special mark of favour. She was also the Superior of the Harim of Amun and held a like office in the cult of Min, posts that would give her charge of female temple-singers of those gods in Akhmim and Thebes.

In the season of 1903, J. E. Quibell, excavating for Theodore M. Davis found near the mouth of a branch of the Eastern Valley of the Biban el-Moluk a small tomb (No. 46) which served as the last resting-place of Yuya and Tuyu. It is possible that they had originally been buried elsewhere and transferred to the royal necropolis at a later date.[5] The inevitable robbers had found the tomb and tumbled its occupants out of their nests of coffins and rifled their corpses, but evidently had been interrupted in their pillaging, for the sepulchre was still crammed with most of its opulent funerary equipment, the gift of Yuya's son-in-law. Yuya proved to be a

Plates 60, 61

Plate 72

Plates 15–17, 28–30

43

Plates 60, 61

man of striking appearance, fairly tall for an Egyptian with a head of long, wavy, white hair, a large beaky nose and prominent lips. His unusual physiognomy and the various spellings of his name, which was probably a pet form of a more orthodox name, have induced some scholars to accredit him with a foreign origin. Tuyu's appearance, in contrast to that of her husband, was typically Egyptian, and she closely resembled the fellah women of today.

The second series of commemorative scarabs is dated to the King's second regnal year, where following the full titularies of Amenophis and Tiye we are told of 'a wonder which happened to His Majesty.' It was reported that wild cattle had been seen in the Wady Keneh[6] near Koptos, whereupon His Majesty sailed downstream, presumably from Thebes, in the royal barge at evening and making good progress arrived at Keneh in the morning. He then appeared in a chariot (the text says 'on a horse') followed by his entire military entourage who were told to keep a watch on the cattle. The King ordered that the beasts should be surrounded with a rampart and a ditch and counted. They were found to number one hundred and seventy. In the first day's hunt, fifty-six of the herd were brought to the King, who then rested for four days in order to invigorate the horses when the hunt was resumed. The total number of cattle caught in this way amounted to ninety-six.

The presence of the King so early in his reign at such a dangerous recreation induced an earlier generation of Egyptologists to believe that Amenophis must have been quite mature when he came to the throne; but there is nothing in the inscription to say that he actually killed any of the animals. They were merely brought to him, whether dead or captured by the lasso, is not revealed. He was probably no more than eight or nine at the time and the fact that Yuya would almost certainly have been present in charge of the chariotry, with other experienced officers to command the soldiers and beaters is carefully omitted to give the King the sole glory that befitted his divinity.

Plate 24

The King's prowess in the chase, however, is more specifically celebrated in the third issue of scarabs concerned with his lion hunts. These scarabs, which are the most numerous, record the total bag of 102 wild lions brought in during the first ten years of his reign; and explicitly state that they were shot by the King with his own arrows. Probably only a little more credence is to be placed in this feat of arms than in the later

Plate XV

painting on the lid of a box showing Tut-ankh-Amun unerringly slaying a pride of lions in the Eastern Desert. In these hunting exploits, both kings were conforming to the sporting tradition set by their immediate predecessors with their elephant hunts in the North Syrian district of Niy and elsewhere.

The fourth series of scarabs commemorated the marriage of Amenophis to Gilukhipa the daughter of Shuttarna, King of Mitanni, who had succeeded Artatama, and is dated to the tenth regnal year, probably when the King reached official manhood. After the customary full titulary of Amenophis and Tiye, we read, 'Marvels brought to His Majesty: Gilukhipa, the daughter of Shuttarna, the Prince of Naharin, with the chief part of her retinue, consisting of 317 women.' This is the first mention of a number of dynastic marriages which the King was to contract during the remainder of his reign. The foreign princesses entered the harim of the King together with their entourages and are seldom heard of again.

The last issue of scarabs is perhaps the most interesting. Owing to a misinterpretation in their translation, they have for long been known as the 'Pleasure Lake' or 'Lake' scarabs. They are precisely dated to the first day of the third month of Inundation, Year 11, and state how His Majesty ordered that a 'basin' (rather than 'a lake') should be made for Queen Tiye in her town of Djarukha, its length being 3700 cubits, and its breadth 700 cubits. The inscription goes on to say that His Majesty performed the ceremony of Piercing the Dykes on the sixteenth day of the same month, rowing in his State barge, 'The Aten is Resplendent.'

Djarukha was in the Ahkmim district from which the parents of Tiye had originated, and where a relic of her presence still survives in the name of the modern town of Tahta, which is a corruption of the Ancient Egyptian expression for 'The walled village of Queen Tiye.'[7] The meaning of the text, therefore, is that early in October 1395 BC Amenophis ordered that an irrigation basin should be made for his Chief Queen in Djarukha by closing the breaches in various dykes so as to keep back the waters of the inundation for sixteen days in a sort of shallow lake, and allow the area to become fully saturated and silt to be deposited. The King performed the important annual ceremony of Opening the Basins that year at Djarukha by sailing into the artificial lake as soon as the dykes had been pierced to allow the waters to return eventually to the river as it fell. Two or three weeks later when the vast basin was empty, peasants would have planted seed in the fertile mud; and at the following harvest, officials would have come to measure the yield and carry off for the Queen the revenues of a domain which measured nearly 190 acres.

Plate 26

Plate 31

45

Although the King was to rule for a further twenty-seven or more years, no other 'historical' scarabs were issued, or if they were, examples have not survived; and for reports of events during the rest of the reign we are dependent upon other sources. Several fragmentary inscriptions describe with characteristic bombast a campaign that the King fought in his fifth regnal year in Nubia where his forces evidently penetrated as far as his southern boundary at Karoy. Little trust need be placed in the assurance that Amenophis, who was probably not yet a youth, was responsible for the plan and fighting that resulted in the inevitable victory. The totals of 312 of the enemy killed and 740 taken prisoner show that it was a small-scale action, doubtless against those bands of warlike nomads who have threatened the peaceful settlements of the river banks in Nubia and the Sudan since earliest times.

If other records of the King's campaigns have not survived, it may well be because in his case he left such duties to his generals and district commissioners, though it would appear that he made some kind of expedition to Sidon in the earlier part of his reign. For further evidence of foreign relations at this time we have to consult documents other than those pronunciamentos which give the official viewpoint, and we are fortunate

Plates 116–118

in this respect thanks to the spectacular find of the Amarna Letters referred to above (pp. 36–37). This archive reveals that in the literate world of Amenophis III, messengers travelled from one Court to another bearing despatches by which kings, queens, and even their high officials communicated with their opposite numbers in other states. By such means, marriage-alliances were arranged, trade-goods exchanged, treaties negotiated, extradition requested, protests submitted, demands made, warnings administered, aid solicited—all the features, in fact, of a well-established system of international relations which compares favourably with that functioning in Europe in recent times.

The messengers, part couriers, part ambassadors, both Egyptians and foreigners, who carried these despatches were important functionaries in their own countries and evidently enjoyed some kind of diplomatic immunity, for a passport has survived (Kn. No. 30)[8] which was issued by a North Syrian ruler to allow his envoy to pass safely through Canaan on his way to attend a state funeral, probably of Amenophis III himself. In time of war, the journeyings of these envoys were particularly hazardous. Amenophis II boasts of having captured in the Plain of Sharon a messenger of the King of Mitanni with a cuneiform tablet 'at his neck,' where presumably it was carried in a satchel. Even in times of peace such ambassadors could sometimes encounter a cool reception and be detained in the country of their hosts as a sign of the king's displeasure with their masters. Kadashman-Enlil of Babylon had to complain that one of his messengers hade been detained in Egypt for no less than six years. On the other hand, envoys who brought good news could expect to be well entertained by their hosts, being allowed to sit in the presence of the king, even to dine with him, and to receive rich gifts.

The kings of Egypt, Babylon, Mitanni, Assyria and other great powers who regarded themselves as equals, address each other as 'brother' and accompany their letters with valuable presents, lapis lazuli, gold, silver, chariots, horses, worked garments and the like. Tushratta of Mitanni whose relations with Egypt were especially close was lavish with such gifts to which on one occasion he added a boy and girl from booty he had captured from the Hittites. At another time he included thirty women who were doubtless skilled in weaving, embroidery and other Asiatic arts. It was probably such immigrants and such gifts which were boastfully referred to in the official texts as tribute exacted by Pharaoh from the 'Chiefs of Retenu.'

A more aloof and even peremptory tone is employed by the Pharaoh when writing to his vassal kings in Palestine and Syria. The preamble is brief and the ending often contains an implied threat with the assurance that the king is mighty and his chariots many and ready. The reply of the vassals is couched in a suitably servile form and invariably refers to the Pharaoh as their 'sun,' their 'god' even while rebellion was being actively fomented.

Plate 77

The picture that these fragmentary records give us of the world that lay to the north of the Egyptian border is confused in its details. We shall discuss in Chapter XI some of the problems of historical interpretation that the Amarna Letters have bequeathed us; here we shall content ourselves with sketching the broad outlines of the story which are rather clearer. While Egypt was too remote for its living-space to be seriously threatened by the struggle for dominance that was being waged between Mitanni and the Hittites, with the Assyrians waiting to intervene and the Babylonians staking their own claims, these nations were concerned to keep her from engaging in their dynastic wars on the side of their foes. Burnaburiash of Babylon was sensitive to any favours that an Assyrian deputation might have received at the Egyptian Court and reminds Pharaoh that in the reign of his father, when the Canaanites sought his help in invading Egyptian territory, he warned them off by invoking his alliance with Egypt. He expected a similar reaction by the Egyptians to any Assyrian mission. The King of Alashia, thought to be Cyprus, or Enkomi in Cyprus, also requests that Pharaoh shall not make a treaty with the Hittites and North Syrians.

The few surviving drafts of letters which the Pharaoh addressed to his fellow monarchs are mostly concerned with negotiations for his marriage to their daughters. The ambition of Amenophis III, like an earlier Solomon, to fill his harim with foreign princesses, was not just to satisfy the recherché tastes of a lascivious despot. The custom was of long standing: both Tuthmosis III and Tuthmosis IV had contracted marriages with daughters of foreign kings and their cases cannot have been isolated. Amenophis III espoused Gilukhipa of Mitanni in his tenth regnal year and later in the reign wedded her niece Tadukhipa, probably on her death. Such marriages were a tangible expression of a diplomatic alliance, and the negotiations that preceded the despatch of the bride and her retinue were often protracted. The extent and nature of her dowry had first to be agreed; and then the Pharaoh himself had to offer a bride-price which gave a further excellent chance for haggling. The inventories which have survived of the trousseaux of these princesses read like a catalogue of the contents of a state treasury of the time—gold, jewels, gold and silver vessels, horses, chariots, weapons, bedsteads, chests and other furniture overlaid with gold, mirrors and braziers of bronze, bronze vessels and instruments, elaborately embroidered clothing, bed-clothes, stone vessels full of oils, spices, and so forth. The retinues were considerable as we have learnt from the commemorative scarab (see p. 45) and must have included many skilled needlewomen and musicians and a powerful armed escort. The weight of gold and silver used in the manufacture and embellishing of the various items is always carefully stated, just as it is in the case of other royal gifts, perhaps to ensure that a proper bargain will be struck, but also doubtless to insure against pilfering *en route*.

In return, the Pharaoh sent similar gifts, particularly ebony furniture overlaid with gold and silver and inlaid with coloured stones and opaque glass, objects in ivory, stone vessels, oils, gold and silver statues, clothing, fine linen and above all the gold in worked and bullion form for which Egypt was so renowned. These marriages, which were negotiated not only with the Hittites, Babylonians and Mitannians, but also with local dynasts, were in the nature of important state trading enterprises at a time of autarky when private commerce could only have been sparse and marginal.

The foreign kings write to their brother in Egypt to request that good relations should be maintained between them or to complain of misdemeanours committed against their nationals in the territories subject to Pharaoh. Thus Burnaburiash had to complain twice that caravans had been plundered and their merchants slain on Egyptian-held lands. He asked that Pharaoh should make good the loss and punish the culprits. The King of Alashia asked for the price of a consignment of wood which was taken from his people by Egyptians. He also requested that the possessions of one of his subjects who had died in Egypt should be sent back by the hand of his messenger since the man's wife and child were still in Alashia. Ashuruballit of Assyria was vexed to hear that Pharaoh's messengers had been molested by bedouin in his territories and did not rest until he had pursued and captured the miscreants.

But the one demand which all these foreign rulers alike make of the Pharaoh is for gold. 'Send gold, quickly, in very great quantities, so that I may finish a work I am undertaking; for gold is as dust in the land of my Brother'—this is the burden of nearly all their letters: and when they are not begging for gold, they are complaining about the niggardly quantity which has been sent, or about its quality which was not up to expectations when assayed. It is clear that the large deposits of gold which Egypt could mine in her Eastern Desert, in Nubia and the Sudan, made her respected and courted by the nations of the Near East.

As far as can be judged from the Amarna Letters, the Great Powers were cordial enough in their relations with Egypt in the later years of Amenophis III. The vassal princes appear to be in their usual state of endemic bickering and intrigue. A display of force had been deemed advisable earlier in the reign when Pharaoh had visited Sidon; and he also despatched troops to help Ribaddi of Byblos against his rival Abdi-ashirta of Amurru. Notorious trouble-makers, like the latter, were violently removed from the scene when admonitions had failed to check them in their interminable conspiracies. As soon as they disappeared, however, new dissidents took their places; but the general impression left by the Letters is that if the mutual accusations of perfidy, rapine, menace and mayhem are not accepted at their face value from the vassal princes, the King's commissioners, with the aid of Egyptian troops from the garrison towns and local loyalists, were able to keep the situation in hand, and by playing off one ruler against his rival to keep both in check.

IV   The temple of Luxor, view of the court of Amenophis III from the north-west with its double peristyle of papyriform columns of clustered-bud type. From the open courts in brilliant sunshine the procession that brought the great state barge of Amun from Karnak during the Feast of Opet in the second month of Inundation passed into the increasing gloom of the hypostyle hall and vestibules to reach the sanctuary in virtual darkness. Here the bark was brought to rest upon a podium before a statue of the Theban triad, Amun, Mut and Khons

V   The Colossi of Memnon, hewn originally from single blocks of quartzite sandstone, but repaired with smaller stones in later ages, stood before the now vanished mortuary temple of Amenophis III on the plain at Western Thebes. On either side of the legs of the seated Pharaoh is a standing figure of his mother, Mut-em-wiya, or his chief wife, Tiye; and between the knees was a figure probably of a daughter. The colossus on the left was the more important in antiquity, being known as the 'Prince of Princes' and having its own cult and priesthood; but by the early days of Imperial Rome its companion enjoyed the greater favour, being thought to represent the Homeric Memnon and to sing at sunrise

VI   Orchestra and dancers, fragment of the painted wall of the tomb of Neb-Amun from Thebes. This part of a larger scene of feasting and entertainment displays the characteristics of drawing in the reign of Amenophis III at their most sophisticated, with its fluid line, looser and more naturalistic poses and sense of movement—features which are so often considered to be the sole discovery of the Amarna Age. Two of the women are rendered in a novel fashion, their faces and breasts being shown from the front (*cf.* Plate XI)

VII   Scene painted on mud plaster on the right-hand side of the rear wall of the sanctuary of a small rock-temple at the Wady es-Sebua in Nubia. King Amenophis III, right, makes an offering to a seated figure of Amun-Re. Behind the god is an unusual scene of the epiphany of the demiurge alighting in the form of a bird (falcon or vulture) on the primeval marsh (*see* p. 164)

IV

V

VI

VII

The Reign of Amenophis III - The Cultural Outline

THE REIGNS of the Tuthmosides with their aggressive foreign policies and their genius for organization promoted a steady increase in the power and prosperity of Egypt. By the time Amenophis III came to the throne, this growth had reached its culmination. To Memphis and Thebes flocked the clever artisans of the Near East and Africa, the lapidaries, metal-workers, embroideresses and musicians, as well as the unskilled labourers, the refugees and prisoners of war who were employed as gardeners, temple-serfs and in other menial capacities. Larger opportunities for a better life in Egypt were avidly seized by the spearmen and charioteers of Palestine and Syria, the infantry of Libya, the shock-troops and police of Nubia and the Sudan. Exotic raw materials were imported into Egypt in much greater quantity as a result of tribute or state-trading, the horses, cattle, fine woods, lapis lazuli, silver and bronze of Asia; the oxen of Libya; the hides, pelts, ostrich feathers, ebony, ivory, apes, incense, gums and resins, minerals and gold of Africa. The finished products of these lands were just as valuable, the iron dagger-blades and red and purple coloured gold of Mitanni; the lapis lazuli jewellery of Babylon; the gold and silver rhytons, ewers and bowls of the Aegean; the metal-work, ivory oil-horns

Fig. 1

Plate 44

I *Escort of Egyptian, Syrian, Libyan and Negro outrunners for the King's chariot, Tomb of Ahmose, Amarna (cf. Plate 55)*

and combs, the embroidered garments, leather-work and chariots of Syria; the weapons, ebony furniture and ivory implements of Kush.

All this wealth pouring into a cosmopolitan society which followed the fashions of the Court with its large entourage of foreign princesses and their suites, had its effect upon the traditional Egyptian culture, loosening its classical, tight-lipped utterances, softening lines, intensifying colours and injecting a new and nervous vitality. The completely different surface that Egyptian culture wears in the New Kingdom must owe nearly everything to its wider and more intimate contacts with the world of the Amorites, Hurrians, Indo-Europeans and Pre-Hellenes during the Late Bronze Age. After the Hyksos Period, Egyptian civilization lost many of its home-grown features and adopted those of other East Mediterranean lands. The god-king became something of a Homeric champion, an athlete and chariot-fighter as well as a leader of his people in war and peace. His paladins and courtiers take on the character of the new class of *maryannu* that dominated society in Asia. Foreign wives, slaves, and even officials brought their influence to bear at the very centre of government and probably account for that 'pagan' delight in personal greatness and pride in worldly success which are such novel features of the age and are so attractively expressed in the painted scenes of former glory on the walls of the Theban tomb-chapels.

The reign of Tuthmosis IV followed by the long and settled reign of Amenophis III, with its sophisticated patronage by the King and his officals, encouraged the emergence of two or three generations of painters, sculptors, architects and craftsmen whose technical abilities were fully equal to the demands that were now placed upon them. At no other period of Egyptian history is so consistently high a standard achieved in artistic expression from colossal statues to minutely carved jewels; from the ubiquitous stone statuary to the small figurines in wood and ivory; from the sublimity of the Luxor temple at one extreme, to the fresh charm of the little painted mud shrine at the Wady es-Sebua, at the other. A widespread zest for luxury, no doubt stimulated by the tastes of civilized Asia, is just as evident in the applied arts of the period, in the products of glass and faience makers, ivory carvers, bronze-workers, lapidaries and weavers. If some descriptive tag has to be tied to this era of 'Amenophis the Magnificent', then 'The Age of Opulence', seems to be the most appropriate.

The Cattle-Hunt Scarab suggests that the King may have been living in Upper Egypt in his second regnal year, probably at Western Thebes

Plate 13

Plate VI

Plates V, IX, XIII

Plates 58, 59

Plate IV

Plate VII

Plates 89–91, X

Plates 36, 72

where later in his reign he certainly had an enormous palace at Medinet Habu, the modern name of which may enshrine some echo of that of his great minister Amenophis-son-of-Hapu. The site of this vast structure, more in the nature of a town or compound than a single building, covers about eighty acres and has been dug over by various excavators, besides generations of local natives grubbing for what they could pick up. The Metropolitan Museum Expedition has explored enough of the ruins to show that the palace, which first bore the name of 'The-House-of-Neb-maet-Re-shines-like-Aten,' but which was also called 'The-House-of-Rejoicing' from the time of the King's First Jubilee, is but the nucleus of an aggregation of rambling constructions facing vast courts and built as occasion demanded without any relation to each other except propinquity.

All the buildings in this palace city were constructed largely of sun-dried mud-brick. The roofs were made of wooden rafters, to the underside of which matting was attached and plastered with straw-bound mud. In the larger rooms, which like those at Amarna doubtless rose above the general roof-level, the ceilings were supported on wooden columns resting on limestone bases. Some of the door-sills were also of stone as were the draining slabs in the bathrooms with their stone-lined dados to prevent damage by splashing. Ceilings, walls and even floors of the more important rooms were decorated with painted scenes on thin washes of lime plaster in a freer, more sketchy and lively style than that employed in the contemporary tomb paintings.

Some imagination is necessary to see these scanty and devastated ruins as they would have appeared in their heyday; but when complete, the gaily painted mud-brick rooms would have had wooden fittings in the form of doors, door-frames and window-grilles, mostly painted, but some gilded and doubtless inlaid with coloured faience to give the name and titles of the King and his principal Queen. With gilded ebony and cedarwood chests, beds, stools and chairs, rush-work stands decorated with floral bouquets, leather cushions in blue and red chequer-work, and their other furnishings, the interiors must have been a flickering glow of many intense colours, softened by the subdued light from the clerestory windows. Of this oriental splendour all that has survived in quantity are fragments of table-ware. But an idea of what the contents of these palaces once were like can be gleaned from a study of the articles of domestic furniture which were buried with Yuya and Tuyu and Tut-ankh-Amun, all close relatives of the King, who must have spent some part of their lives within the precincts of the Malkata Palace.

Plate 34

Plates 114, 115

Plate 33
Plate 34
Plate VI

Plates 10, 17, XV

Besides this 'House of Rejoicing' at Thebes, it is almost certain that Amenophis had another and perhaps more important palace at Memphis and subsidiary residences, such as a hunting lodge at Medinet el-Ghurab in the Faiyum. The Theban palace was connected by a causeway to a funerary temple, dedicated to Amun and the King's mortuary cult, which rose about a mile to the north and must have been much the largest in the row of such monuments that by now fringed the cultivation on the west of Thebes. It was first used as a convenient quarry a century and a half after its founder's death, thus making a mockery of his boast that it was 'established for ever and to all eternity.' Almost all that now is left of it are the two lonely quartzite colossi of the King which originally measured nearly seventy feet in height and flanked the entrance to the temple.

Plate V

In 1896 Petrie excavating in the ruins of the near-by funerary temple of Mineptah of the following dynasty (1338–1319 BC), found a grey granite stela over ten feet high which had been installed originally in the temple of Amenophis III but usurped by the later king. It gave a description of some of the mighty works that Amenophis had made for Amun-Re in Thebes and Nubia, including the mortuary temple at Medinet Habu, the Third Pylon of the Temple of Amun at Karnak, the Luxor temple, a *maru* or 'viewing' temple at Western Thebes, and a temple at Sulb some fifty miles north of the Third Cataract of the Nile. The description of the mortuary temple in this stela must also serve to give some idea of the appearance of the other structures enumerated. It was built, we read, in fine white sandstone, embellished with gold throughout. The floor of its sanctuary was covered with silver, and all its portals with electrum. It was made very broad and long, and adorned with a great stela embellished with gold and coloured stones. In it were numerous statues of the King in excellently worked granite of Elephantine, in hard red quartzite and every fine stone. They rose in their height more than the heavens and were beautiful to the sight like the Aten, or Disk of the Sun, at its rising. Its flagstaves were plated with electrum. Its sacred lake was filled by the Nile. Its offices were staffed with servitors both male and female, together with foreign captives, and its store-rooms were full of countless treasures.

At Karnak, while Amenophis added little apart from a great triumphal gate, the Third Pylon, to the temple of Amun, he built on an ancient foundation a temple to the older Theban god Mont in precincts to the north of the Amun complex; but of this little now remains except the ground-plan. Another ruined edifice, dedicated by Amenophis to Mut the consort of Amun, lies a quarter of a mile to the south in the region around a crescent-shaped lake known as Ashru ('the pool of the lion'?). Here Mut took the form of the Memphite lion-headed goddess of war, Sekhmet, and was represented by hundreds of granite statues showing her seated as well as standing. Many of these large statues, usurped by later kings have survived, and nearly every Egyptian collection has an example.

The most impressive of the Theban monuments of Amenophis III, however, must be sought not at Karnak but in the 'Southern Sanctuary,' the ancient name for Luxor. Here rises the great temple to the Theban Plate IV trinity, Amun, Mut and their offspring, the child Khons, which the King's architect, another Amun-hotpe, was still building in Year 35. Around its sanctuary were rooms for storing the emblems, garments, vessels and offerings used in the cult; and in a columned hall flanking the vestibule is a representation of thet heogamy or divine birth of the King in which appear all the elements seen in the better preserved reliefs of Hatshepsut in her mortuary temple at Deir el-Bahri. In this case, however, Amun enacts the part of Tuthmosis IV and it is the King's mother Mutem-wiya who is led by Isis and Khnum to the birth-chamber. The temple was once gorgeously decorated with gold, silver, lapis lazuli and coloured opaque glasses and furnished with sculptures in hard and soft stones; but only a few dispersed and usurped examples of the statuary bear some witness to its former magnificence. Despite its ruinous state, however, and the alterations it has suffered, its grandeur is still impressive particularly at sun-rise, the moment of the temple's awakening, when the Theban luminescence gives an almost translucent effect to the stone. The contrast between the rows of clustered papyrus-bud columns where the diagonal shadows fall thick, and the broad areas of light in the open courts, the nice balance of the proportions between the main structure and the soaring colonnade with its huge campaniform capitals, make it evident that within the rigid requirements of the Egyptian temple as cosmological myth translated into stone, Amenophis III has been able to call upon the services of a great architect whose work, however, was left unfinished in the next reign when he was disgraced for reasons which we can only surmise.

Besides these works at Thebes, great buildings were erected in most of the larger centres of Egypt during the long reign of Amenophis III. At Memphis he founded a second mortuary temple for his posthumous cult as a northern pendant to the vast structure at Medinet Habu. He also built temples at Athribis and Bubastis in the Delta, and a charming peripteral kiosk for his Second Jubilee on the Island of Elephantine as the traditions of his Dynasty demanded. The ruins of his temple at Sulb, an outpost of his empire in the Sudan, are still considerable. Nearby is a companion temple at Sedeinga built for Queen Tiye who is identified here with the goddess Hat-Hor.

All these works were notable for the lavish use of opulent materials, the exceptional quality of the workmanship and their huge size. It is in his reign that statuary on a really enormous scale in great quantities makes its appearance. Whether all this urge towards the colossal expresses the King's own personal desires, or whether it was but a manifestation by his architects and artists and officials of their pride in the power and importance of Egypt of which their Pharaoh was lord, must be left to the psychologists; but that there is an insistence upon the divinity of the Pharaoh during the reign of Amenophis III is obvious. The theogamic nature of his birth has other precedents and can be over-stressed, but there is little doubt he was worshipped in the form of a statue at Sulb, Memphis, Hierakonpolis and Thebes during his own lifetime. At Sulb even he adores his own image. At Sedeinga, Queen Tiye was worshipped as the local patroness; and this increase in the aura of majesty may have been indebted to antiquarian research, to a harking back to a remoter past when the Pharaoh had been the Egyptians' greatest god. But it also surely owed much to the steady growth during the Dynasty of the idea of a single universal and supreme divinity of which the king was at once the offspring and the incarnation.

Throughout the reign of Amenophis III, the position of Queen Tiye as the Chief Wife of the King was never challenged, despite the host of other queens, probably because she had borne several sons, including the heir-apparent. Her name frequently accompanies her husband's in ceremonial inscriptions and her figure, albeit usually on a smaller scale, attends his on many of his statues and reliefs. After the death of Amenophis III, King Tushratta of Mitanni addressed a letter to her (Kn. no. 26) asking that the good relations that had existed between Egypt and his country during the reign of her husband should be continued under her son. She was given the title of Heiress, which normally was claimed only by the eldest surviving daughters of Pharaohs by their Chief Consorts. Apart from her deification at Sedeinga during her lifetime, her cult was maintained for many years after her death. A funerary estate of hers at Thebes was administered by an influential priesthood in Ramesside times and another estate in Middle Egypt by the tenth century BC at least. Not only does her name survive today in the name of the town of Tahta (see p. 45 above) but also in that of the village of Adaya near Sedeinga.

Plate V

Plates V, IX

Plate 66

Amenophis III had other native and foreign wives but their names exist only in one or two instances. Queens Henut and Nebet-nuhe, and Princess Tia-ha are known from fragments of their Canopic jars which appeared on the market about the turn of this century and may be dated to his reign. Such was the mortality-rate of the Ancient World, however, that fifteen years after the King's death it would appear that no direct descendants remained from his vast progeny.

Plate 39

During his reign Amenophis III was served by loyal and competent officials whom he rewarded with valuable gifts, including gold decorations and magnificent tombs in Western Thebes. Foremost among his henchmen was Amenophis son of a certain Hapu, a man of no account, so we are asked to believe, from the Delta town of Athribis, whose relatives were destined to rise to great power in Thebes and Memphis.

Plate 20

Closely related to him, and also hailing from the Delta, was the King's High Steward in Memphis, another Amun-hotpe, who held several important offices including Controller of Works in Memphis, Treasurer and Overseer of the Double Granary of Egypt. He, too, claims that his parents were relatively humble in origin, but he studied as a scribe and his proficiency led to his appointment as one of the personal secretaries of the King. Like his name-sake and near-relation, he served as a scribe of the elite troops, a post which resulted in his appointment as a treasurer, steward and architect. In the latter capacity he was responsible for the erection of the mortuary temple of Amenophis III in Memphis, which doubtless was an impressive and splendid structure, though nothing of it can be identified today. His half brother, Ramose, who held the position of Vizier of Upper Egypt, has a tomb at Thebes which is one of the show-places for tourists since its restoration by Sir Robert Mond in 1923–6. He was present at the King's First Jubilee but his short official career belongs more properly to the next reign and will be considered below.

Plates 19, 75

Plates 75, 76, *Fig. 2*

Another Memphite, also called Amun-hotpe, was the Northern Vizier and ran for a time in double harness with Ramose, but our knowledge of the Court of Amenophis III and Queen Tiye, sketchy as it is, derives mostly from the Theban necropolis where still survive tombs of the southern officials, and some of the northern officials too, such as Men-kheper the Mayor of Memphis. Of these, the most important are the elegantly sculptured chapels of the Overseer of the Granaries of Upper and Lower Egypt, Kha-em-het and his wife named Tiye after the Queen, the Chief Steward, Amun-em-het called Surero, and Kheruef who was the Queen's High Steward. In all these tomb-chapels appears a represen-

Plate 50

Plates 38–41

tation of the owner re-living his finest hour on earth in the royal presence during the festivities that marked the King's jubilees.[9]

Plate 75

All the reliefs in these tombs and in others of the same period are notable for their exquisite drawing and detail, and their precise and accomplished carving. To our eyes they are suffused with the bloom of a ripeness that trembles on the verge of decay, since with our hind-sight we can see them as the last development of their kind in the Theban necropolis. The same sunset glow plays over the paintings in glue-tempera that decorate the walls of contemporary tomb-chapels which in the light of what is to follow seem to express a nostalgic joy in the earthly life which is past rather than an acceptance of the eternity which is to come. They show the same assured drawing as the reliefs but are gay with bright yet harmonious colour. The fragments of a magnificent tomb, thought to belong to a certain Neb-Amun and now in the British Museum, and the tombs of the Two Sculptors and the Overseer of Crown Lands, Menna show these features at their best. There are, however, other painted tomb-chapels which though even more badly damaged have left some memorials of the reign and it is from these and stray monuments that we are able to glean a little idea of the careers of the King's officials.

Plates 31, 32

Plate VI

Plate 31

Plate 32

The great events during the last decade of the reign were the King's three jubilees held in regnal years 30, 34 and 37. The Festival of the Sed, or the Jubilee, in its essentials rejuvenated the ageing king and confirmed him in his tenure of the throne (see pp. 29-30). The locus of the event, like that of the coronation, was at Memphis and was closely bound up with the Festival of the falcon death-god Sokar. Some of the rites are represented in the tomb of Kheruef where a text suggests that special research was undertaken to enact the ritual in its proper form. In other ceremonies, which a text informs us were held on the west of Thebes, Amenophis III and Tiye were towed in a bark along a canal like the sun through the underworld regions in the last hours of night towards a rebirth at dawn and a triumphal re-coronation. It needs to be mentioned here that such scenes of the King in this mystery play of death and resurrection during his jubilees have been interpreted, wrongly in the writer's opinion, as revealing that Amenophis is shown actually dead and deified (see p. 109).

Plate 91

Plate 38

Plate 40

Apart from such mysterious rites, there were other ceremonies in which the King had to take part during his jubilees, and a great deal of preparation had to be made for these events. New statues of the King and Queen had to be fashioned for all the sanctuaries in which such royal sculpture had a proper place in the cult, and we can see a large collection of these awaiting

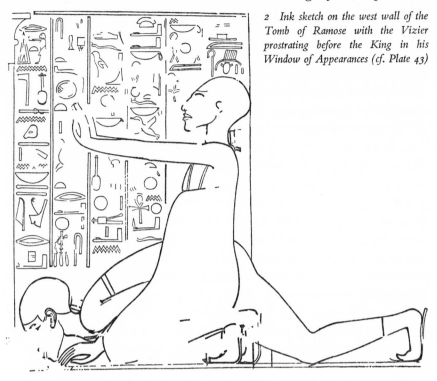

2 Ink sketch on the west wall of the Tomb of Ramose with the Vizier prostrating before the King in his Window of Appearances (cf. Plate 43)

consecration in the damaged reliefs of Surero. New clothes, jewellery and other equipment also had to be specially made. At the re-enactment of his coronation, the King received the homage of his peoples from Egypt and from the lands of Africa and Asia who came bearing rich gifts. Obelisks were erected at Sulb where the temple was decorated with scenes of the First Jubilee. At Thebes, in the precincts of his palace, and at Elephantine, special peripteral temples were built to commemorate the Second Jubilee. As tradition demanded, not only were images of the various gods brought from their cult centres to Memphis to attend the jubilee rites, accompanied by priests and officials, but the King also began a grand tour of his dominions to hold celebrations in the more important towns. These functions involved the distribution of enormous quantities of consecrated food and we are fortunate in having some record of the provisions supplied at Thebes from the mass of fragmentary pottery vessels, which contained meat, drink and unguents, found in the midden heaps and among the ruins of the Malkata Palace. The dockets, written on these despised fragments of pottery, have thrown considerable light on the events of the last years of the reign. We learn from them that the King

Plates 89–91

Plate 37

lived to the last few weeks of his thirty-eighth regnal year at least, and probably entered his thirty-ninth before he died. They also show which of his officials were active in the various years, and the relative importance of the three jubilees.

Work on the sepulchre of the King must have started early in his reign: indeed, it would seem that it had been initiated while he was still Crown Prince since the foundation deposits outside the entrance bore the name of Tuthmosis IV. For his tomb, a site was chosen in the then untouched gorge which forms the Western Branch of the Biban el-Moluk. In this remote and desolate spot a hypogeum was hewn which resembled in design that of his predecessor but in which the burial chambers lay south of their approach corridor, so penetrating further into the hill-side. The first corridor is cut in three lengths which slope rapidly down to reach a 'well-chamber.' This has its walls painted with scenes of the King in the presence of various gods. Once the well has been bridged, a two-pillared hall is entered in the floor of which a steep stair leads by way of another corridor and an ante-chamber to the large, pillared burial-chamber with its painted astronomical ceiling and side-halls. Only the broken sarcophagus-lid of red granite remains in this chamber and the rest of the tomb is a sad wreck of its former splendour though it does not appear to have been completed. Its most remarkable features are the two large, pillared halls, each with a subsidiary chamber, which lead from the main funerary hall and which some scholars have suggested were for the burials of Queen Tiye and Sit-Amun. The tomb was rediscovered by two engineers of Napoleon's Egyptian Expedition in 1799, and since then various rummagers

Plates 89–91

have recovered from the ruined chambers meagre wreckage of what was probably the most opulent burial ever to be deposited in the Valley.

The mummy of Amenophis III was discovered in the tomb of his grandfather Amenophis II in 1898 and found to have been severely damaged in antiquity by robbers who had hacked it in pieces in order to retrieve the precious amulets which protected it. Nearly all the soft tissues of the head had disappeared but enough data remained to show that the King was about five feet two inches in height and was almost completely bald at death, having only scanty hair on his temples. He had lost his upper incisors some time before death and another tooth just before he died. There was also evidence of alveolar abscesses and it is clear that in the last years of his life he must have suffered miserably from toothache and dental disorders. It has been inferred that his health was poor towards the end of his reign because in Year 36 Tushratta of Mitanni despatched a statue of Ishtar of Nineveh on what was described as her second visit 'to Egypt the land which she loves.' It has been presumed that this was a prophylactic statue sent to cure the Pharaoh of some malady, but the evidence for this is very slender. What his mummy does reveal, however, is that special measures were taken by the embalmers to restore to his corpse some of the semblance of his appearance in life by packing a mixture of resin and natron under the skin, an innovation which is not repeated until four centuries later, when other sorts of stuffing were used to plump out the mummies of the ruling house at Thebes in Dynasty XXI (1080–945 BC). The embalmers who mummified Amenophis III may have taken such exceptional measures because the king at death was grossly obese. Several statues and a relief of him in his last years show him as corpulent and elderly, though, with the traditional idealism of Egyptian Court art, such portraits are discreet and restrained.

Plate 116

Plates 58, 59, 80

V

The Reign of Akhenaten and its Sequel

Part I

IN OUR FIRST CHAPTER we have outlined the sources which scholars have been obliged to use for their knowledge of events during the Amarna Period; and we have pointed out that the interpretation of the incomplete and patchy evidence has produced a conflict of opinion about the character of Akhenaten and the history of his times. One of the difficulties in the way of charting the proper sequence of events during his reign has been the paucity of dated monuments, since all records of the period were either obliterated or doctored in Ramesside times. Nevertheless, a few items have escaped destruction or falsification. A contemporary letter written on papyrus and dated to the King's fifth regnal year has come to light at Ghurab and still names him as Amenophis, thus giving the latest date by which he is known to have used this form of *nomen*. On three of the greatly damaged Boundary Stelae at Amarna the date 'Year 4' has been read with difficulty and reservations. The rest are dated to Year 6 and two have a codicil dated to Year 8. An event depicted in two tombs at Amarna, where the reception of foreign tribute is represented, is dated to Year 12.

Plate 6

Plate 44

These nodal dates allow us to see that between Years 5 and 6 the King and Queen changed their names; and between Years 8 and 12 they altered the didactic name of their god, the Aten. Suggestions for more precise dates when these events took place will be offered below. The various changes of name have allowed monuments to be sorted approximately into their proper sequence in the reign, but the system has to be used with discretion since inscriptions with early versions of the names have sometimes been altered to show the later forms. In the past, therefore, Egyptologists have been tempted to sort the monuments into some kind of order by the number of princesses that accompany the Royal Pair on them. Nefert-iti bore six known daughters and as three only are depicted on the Boundary Stelae of Year 8, and all six are shown in a representation of Year 12, it would seem that a rough time-scale could be constructed from such an equation.

Plates 46, 49

Unfortunately, this argument overlooks the way the Ancient Egyptian craftsman worked, particularly at Amarna, where the frantic haste in which the immense building projects were carried out and the obvious shortage of skilled workmen and efficient supervisors led to anachronisms being perpetrated. It conformed to Egyptian practice if a certain number of accepted subjects for representation in relief and painting were in stock from the earlier years of the reign and only tardily and incompletely revised by the workmen, whose instinct would be to prefer a pattern which they had perfected by constant copying. Thus, although one scene of the reception of foreign tribute in Year 12 shows six princesses in attendance, another version of the same subject shows only three, and some scenes of the Royal Family worshipping the Aten with the late form of its name show only one daughter in their retinue. The number of daughters therefore accompanying their parents in any Amarna scene can give no certain indication of its date.

Plate 44

Before discussing in the next section of this book the problems that the Amarna Period has bequeathed us, we shall present in this chapter an orthodox view of the reign, largely based upon J.H. Breasted's chapter in the first edition of the *Cambridge Ancient History*, since the appropriate chapter in the revised edition is not available as we write; and we shall supplement it with additional information which has won some tacit acceptance in recent years. This interpretation of the age has influenced a number of non-Egyptological writers and thinkers who have helped to consolidate still further the received view of Akhenaten, the Amarna Period and its aftermath.

Part II

At his accession, Amenophis IV, the young and inexperienced son of Amenophis III and his Chief Queen Tiye, inherited a difficult situation. The Kingdom of Mitanni, now an ally of Egypt, was under pressure from a resurgent Hatti who was fomenting trouble among the treacherous vassal states of Syria, while nomadic bands of Hapiru freebooters were creating unrest in Palestine. The times demanded a strong king like the conquering Pharaohs of the earlier half of the Dynasty who had marched at the head of their armies into Asia and put down insurrection and petty squabbles alike with exemplary severity. Instead, the new King appointed as his advisors his mother Tiye, his Chief Queen Nefert-iti, perhaps a woman of Asiatic birth, and a favourite priest Ay, the husband of her nurse. Instead of coming to the aid of his ally, Mitanni, the young King immersed himself deeply in the philosophizing theology of the time; and in such contemplations he steadily developed ideals and purposes which make him

Plate VIII
Plate 62

the most remarkable of all the Pharaohs and the first *individual* in human history.

The expansion of Egypt during Dynasty XVIII into a world empire had brought about a new concept in Egyptian thought and the idea was born of a unique universal god, the Sun, who surveyed the whole earth and was lord of all countries, not merely Egypt. Already under Amenophis III, an old name of the material sun, the Aten, or Disk, had come into prominent use; and under his son the cult of this god was rapidly expanded until it became not only the supreme deity, but the sole one as well. A new

Plates 5, 43, 47

symbol depicted the Aten as a sun-disk from which diverging beams radiated, each ray ending in a human hand, some of them bringing the symbol of life to the nostrils of the King and Queen, thus suggesting a power issuing from its celestial source and putting its hand upon the world and the affairs of men. This outward symbol could have universal significance in the foreign dominions of Egypt in a way which the old anthropomorphic or zoomorphic gods entirely lacked; and to indicate the imperial power of the Aten, the god's expanded or didactic name was

Plate 105

enclosed within two cartouches like those of a Pharaoh, thus suggesting a supreme heavenly king.

The zeal of the young Pharaoh for the new cult was evident from the very first. A mighty temple to the Aten was erected at Karnak; and Thebes was now called 'the City of the Radiance of Aten' instead of 'the City of Amun.' The priesthood of Amun, the old god of Thebes, whose power and wealth had greatly increased during the Dynasty could not view these measures with complacency. The priests of Amun had installed the great conqueror Tuthmosis III as king (see p. 39), and they could have supplanted with one of their own nominees the young dreamer who now held the throne if Amenophis IV had not possessed remarkable force of character and come of an illustrious line of rulers too strong to be set aside even by so powerful a priesthood. A bitter conflict then ensued in which the issue was sharply drawn between Aten and the old gods. It rendered Thebes intolerable to the King and he decided to break with the old cults and make Aten the sole god, in fact as well as thought. The priests were dispossessed, the official temple worship of the gods throughout the land was terminated, and their names were erased from the monuments, even

Plate 58

the plural form of the word for 'god' was obliterated. The persecution of Amun was particularly severe. Even the cartouche of the King's father which contained the name of the hated god was not respected during this orgy of excision; and the name of the young Pharaoh was changed from

Amenophis to Akhenaten. Thebes as a Residence was abandoned and a new capital, Akhet-Aten, 'The Resting-Place of the Aten' founded at what is now Tell el-Amarna in Middle Egypt.

Plate 112

In his sixth regnal year, and shortly after changing his name, Akhenaten took up residence in his new town which he vowed never to leave. Large palaces and temples were erected for the King, Nefert-iti, Tiye and other members of the Royal Family. The Great Temple of the Sun's Disk, the centre of the new Aten worship all over the world was built within a huge enclosure. A royal sepulchre was hewn in the wady that bisected the semi-circle of cliffs enclosing the site on the east. The same lavish provision was made for Akhenaten's officials whose estates were laid out on a generous scale and whose tombs were cut in the foothills to the south and in the cliffs to the north. These courtiers were not drawn from the old governing families, but were new men who claimed that they owed their advancement entirely to the Pharaoh himself. It is to their tomb-chapels, decorated with reliefs and containing texts in praise of the Aten and Akhenaten that we owe our knowledge of the King's new teaching.

Plate 113

Plate 115

Plates 103–105, 119

One hymn, in particular, which appears in the tomb of the priest Ay is generally regarded as having been written by Akhenaten himself. In it the universalism of the Egyptian empire finds full expression with the royal poet projecting a world faith to displace the nationalism that had preceded it for twenty centuries. He based the universal rule of god upon his fatherly care of all men alike, irrespective of race or nationality, and he calls Aten, 'the father and mother of all that he had made'. Akhenaten thus grasped the idea of a world lord as the Creator of Nature, but he likewise saw and revealed the Creator's beneficent purpose (see pp. 187–189 below).

Plate 120

There is in Akhenaten's teaching a constant emphasis upon *maet*, 'truth', such as is not found before or afterwards. The King always attached his name to the phrase 'Living in Truth', and that this is not meaningless is evident in the delight he took in displaying his family life in public. He was represented with his queen and daughters on all possible occasions enjoying the most familiar and unaffected intercourse with them, and they were shown also participating in the temple services. His Chief Sculptor, Bek, claims that he was taught by the King himself, and the artists of his Court were instructed to express what they actually saw. The result was a new and simple, but beautiful realism. They caught the instantaneous postures of animal life, the running hound, the fleeing quarry, the wild bull leaping in the papyrus thicket, for all these belonged to the 'truth' in which Akhenaten lived. The King's person was not exempted from the

Plates 5, 47

Plates 54, 55, 105

Plate 79

Plates 35, X

Plates 2, 47

laws of the new art; the artists represented Akhenaten as they saw him, not idealistically, but as he appeared to their eyes, with all his bodily deformities.

Immersed in his exalted religious ideas, and absorbed by his extensive building schemes at Amarna, Akhenaten allowed the affairs of empire to fall into neglect and did not realize until it was too late the necessity for drastic action. The Hittites and their collaborators had steadily eroded Egyptian influence in Syria, and a similar situation developed further south in Palestine, until the Egyptian empire in Asia in effect ceased to exist. The tribute of Asia and Kush was received at Akhet-Aten as usual

Plate 44

in Year 12 and the Pharaoh and Nefert-iti and their six daughters are shown receiving it in gorgeous state; but no further imposts are recorded.

Plates 103, 104

It appears to be in this same year that Queen Tiye paid a state visit to Akhet-Aten, and may have been instrumental in bringing home to her son the disastrous condition in which affairs at home and abroad outside the little world of Akhet-Aten were drifting as a result of his policies, or lack of them. The people were resentful of the suppression of their old gods, and a powerful priestly party openly or covertly did all in its power to subvert his doctrines. In addition, there was unrest in the army as a result of his pacifist management of foreign affairs and the loss of the Asiatic territories. But it was only when the ever-deepening crisis had become really severe that the King was forced to face realities. A young

Plate 9

prince, Smenkh-ka-Re, perhaps a younger brother, was married to the eldest daughter, Meryt-Aten, made co-regent, and sent off to Thebes to patch up the quarrel with the priests of Amun. Nefert-iti, however, appears to have been unconvinced of the need for a change in policy and retired to a palace at the north end of Akhet-Aten, taking with her another young prince, Tut-ankh-Aten, who was married to the second surviving daughter, Ankhes-en-pa-Aten. Within two years, however, Akhenaten had died in his seventeenth regnal year, the highest recorded on wine-jar dockets found at Akhet-Aten. Smenkh-ka-Re had probably predeceased him. Tut-Ankh-Aten then reigned alone for a year or so under the influence of Nefert-iti, until with her death the Amarna revolution came to an abrupt end and the way was clear for a triumphant return to orthodoxy.

Part III
We know from his mummy that Tut-ankh-Aten could not have been

Plate 74

more than nine years old at his accession, and such a mere child must have

1 Head in plaster of Akhenaten, excavated by the Deutsche Orient-Gesellschaft in the ruins of sculptors' workshops at Amarna, 1913–14. It is probably the cast of a clay or wax model which gave the official master-portrait for copying by lesser sculptors engaged upon works of the King. It shows the characteristics of his peculiar physiognomy, particularly the long nose, hanging chin and thick lips, but with the restraint and idealization of his later portraits

2-4 Fragments of painted sandstone colossi of Akhenaten from the destroyed Aten temple at Karnak, excavated by the Egyptian Antiquities Service, 1926–32. The King is shown standing with feet together and wearing different crowns and dress. These statues are carved in the extreme revolutionary style that erupted after the first year or so of the King's reign (*cf.* Plate 47). The design can only have been produced by the Chief Sculptor, probably Bek (*see* Plate 79) at the insistence of Akhenaten himself. These statues have an unusual coherence, the sculptural masses of the body enhance the management of the features in a rare unity of form and feeling, like that achieved in the best of primitive African carvings. It should be noted that in Plate 2, the King is shown entirely naked without any genitalia (*see* p. 133)

5,6 *Above*, a limestone relief excavated in the Royal Tomb at Amarna by the Egyptian Antiquities Service 1891, and probably intended as a model for workmen carving the chapel walls. The design is squared-up ready for transfer to another surface. Akhenaten, wearing the Blue Crown, and the Queen with disk, horns and feathers above her coronet of uraei, place flower-offerings on altars under the rayed symbol of the Aten. A similar design appears on Boundary Stela 'S', *opposite*, hewn in the cliffs at Amarna where an opposed scene shows the King and Queen raising their hands in adoration of the Aten while their two eldest daughters shake sistra. Both reliefs are carved in the extreme style of the early years of the reign (*cf.* Plate 47)

7 Front view of the painted bust of Nefert-iti illustrated in Plate VIII. The soft limestone in which it is carved has encouraged a more idealistic treatment of the features than is evident in the head opposite. The pupil of the left eye has not been painted in and the neck has been elongated to balance the heavy mass of the cap. The Queen is shown wearing an elaborate collar which in reality consisted of beads, flower-petals, leaves and mandrake fruits sewn to a papyrus backing, or a jewelled version of such a collar (*cf.* Plates 9, 10, 93, 109)

8 Head in yellow quartzite excavated by the University of Pennsylvania at Memphis 1915, beneath the foundations of a palace of Mineptah (1237–1219 BC). This head is often improperly identified as representing Smenkh-ka-Re, and is usually photographed incorrectly posed so that the jaw is thrust forward and over-emphasized. It undoubtedly represents Nefert-iti, though the features are rather more realistically modelled in the gem-hard stone than in the bust illustrated opposite. It is part of a composite statue made in various coloured stones, characteristic of the Amarna Period (cf. Plates 21, 84, 85). The eyes and brows were originally inlaid, probably in opaque glass

9　Painted limestone relief, 24 cm. high, carved with the figure of a king leaning upon his staff and smelling a bouquet held out to him by his queen (*cf.* Plate 93). The Amarna breeze blows through the scene, fluttering the streamers on the king's dress. Since Newberry's identification, the pair are generally taken to be Smenkh-ka-Re and Meryt-Aten. The features of the king are similar to those of Akhenaten but far less exaggerated. The plump cheeks, small mouth and un-arched neck distinguish the appearance of this king quite sharply from that of Akhenaten (*cf.* Plate 68). This relief was bought at Giza and probably came from the Memphis area

10 Back panel of a throne of Tut-ankh-Amun in wood overlaid with gesso and gold and silver foil and inlaid with coloured glass and faience. It shows the King wearing the elaborate triple Atef Crown of his coronation, and being anointed by his wife, Ankhes-en-Amun who also wears her great crown. The rayed sun-disk of the Aten indicates that this object belongs to his earlier years as King. His slack pose (*cf.* Plate 80), the pronounced paunch (*cf.* Plate 9) and the domestic nature of the scene even on a state throne are wholly in the Amarna tradition. The *nomen* of the King appears in both its Amun and Aten versions

11-13 Three predecessors of Amenophis III. *Below*, Queen Hat-shepsut in the costume of a Pharaoh kneeling to have her crown affixed by the god Amun; represented as a seated man wearing a cap surmounted by tall plumes to signify his mastery over the invisible air. His figure and name were hammered out by Akhenaten but restored by Sethos I. This relief is on the pyramidion of a fallen granite obelisk at Karnak. *Above right*, King Tuthmosis III is represented on a heroic scale grasping the traditional northern foes of Egypt by their topknots and smiting them with his upraised mace. This colossal relief is on the south wall of the west tower of the King's VIIth Pylon at Karnak. The counterpart on the opposite tower shows the King smiting negroes and other southern foes. *Below right*, King Amenophis II is charging in his chariot and shooting his arrows through a wooden target and a copper ingot like some Homeric champion. This granite stela has been assembled from broken fragments found in the IIIrd Pylon erected by his grandson at Karnak

14   King Tuthmosis IV sits with his left arm around his mother Queen > Tia, the wife of Amenophis II. This black granite statue was probably one of the series made at the King's coronation (*cf.* Plate 57). Although he is represented as a man of athletic build, the King was little more than fifteen years old at his advent. The name of Amun has been re-worked (*cf.* Plate 11). This pair-statue was found in 1903 by the Egyptian Antiquities Service, buried below ground level in the vestibule of the sanctuary of Amun at Karnak (*see* Plate XVI)

15-17 Objects from the tomb of Yuya and
Tuyu, the maternal grandparents of Akhenaten (*see also* Plates 28–30, 60, 61), one of
the richest deposits to be uncovered at
Thebes. While the more portable valuables
had been stolen, the coffins covered with
gold and silver leaf and inlaid with coloured
opaque glass were virtually untouched.
Above left, the upper part of the fourth
coffin of Yuya, showing the inlaid broad
collar and vulture pectoral. *Above right*, the
upper part of the second coffin of Tuyu, his
wife, with the vulture replaced by a figure
of the sky-goddess Nut. An inscription on
this coffin naming her son Anen (*see* Plate 18)
suggests that he was commissioned to
provide his parents' burial equipment at the
expense of Amenophis III, and took the
opportunity to have himself associated with
his mother in her funerary prayers. *Right*, a
chair, made of red wood belonging to the
Royal Heiress, Sit-Amun, and contributed
by her to her grandparents' burial furniture.
The back-panel shows her seated on a throne
receiving from a handmaid the gift of a 'gold
collar of the South'

18–20 Three high officials of Amenophis III. *Left*, a black granite statue of Anen, a son of Yuya and brother of Queen Tiye, who held the offices of Second Prophet of Amun and Greatest of Seers of the sun-god, Re-Atum. The first post embraced responsibilities for religious and secular works at Thebes while the latter implies that he wielded great influence at a time when the solar cult was expanding widely. *Below left*, a grey granite squatting statue of the High Steward Amun-hotpe, excavated at Abydos where he superintended the King's additions to the temple of Osiris. Amun-hotpe was primarily a man of Memphis, in which town he held his highest appointments. His greatly damaged tomb was found at Sakkara early in the last century and its contents dispersed among half-a-dozen collections. *Below right*, a grey granite statue of the Master of Works and Scribe of Recruits, Amenophis-son-of-Hapu, representing the sage in his old age. It was found at Karnak in 1901 before the VIIth Pylon (*see* Plate 12) near where it had been installed by favour of Amenophis III, who also endowed for him a mortuary temple in the row of royal monuments at Western Thebes. His tomb at Thebes has not been identified

21 A head in dark red quartzite, half life-size, from a sculptor's studio at Amarna and intended to fit onto a body of white stone representing the colour of linen garments, while the head-dress would be of a darker stone or faience. The eyes and brows were inlaid, probably with coloured glass (*cf.* Plate 8). This head has been identified as of Smenkh-ka-Re as well as of Akhenaten. It is, however, of a woman and almost certainly represents Queen Tiye who played an important role at Amarna. Many statues of her are represented as standing in the colonnades and sanctuary of her sun-shade temple at Amarna (*cf.* Plate 104), and the studio of her chief sculptor Yuti is represented in the tomb of Huya as within the precincts of Tiye's palace. This head is carved in such a way as to show that it was to be completed by a woman's wig similar to the one shown below (Plate 22). The small feminine chin is far removed from Akhenaten's overgrown mandible while the pouting lips and morose expression are characteristic of Queen Tiye in her more realistic representations

22 A head of Queen Tiye from a statuette in green schistose stone excavated in 1904 by the Egypt Exploration Fund in the temple of Serabit el-Khadim, Sinai. This is a precious document for the identification of Tiye's portraits. The face with the delicate but pronounced chin, unfortunately chipped however, the small pouting lips with their down-turned medial line, the furrows running from the alae of the nose to the corners of the mouth. are all characteristic features and are seen also in the head illustrated above (Plate 21). Her name appears on the coronet between two winged cobras. The two crowned uraei on her brow are also usually found in her representations. A stela of Amenophis III, dated to year 36, in the same temple, and records of some of his officials there, suggest that he was active in Sinai towards the end of his reign. This head of Tiye, therefore, probably represents a more realistic portrait of the queen produced under the impact of the contemporary Amarna style, like the example above, and should be compared with the earlier official mode as exemplified in Plate IX

23   Black basalt statue-head of Amenophis III, over twice life size. This is a masterpiece of stylized portraiture, the complementary masses of the head and Blue Crown being integrated by a surface-play of such applied ornament as the coils of the uraeus, the line of the diadem, the appliqués of the arched eyebrows, the large almond eyes and lips prinked into a benign smile. Despite this stylization, doubtless encouraged by the colossal scale, the features are undoubtedly those of Amenophis III. The pattern of the Blue Crown and the chubby features reveal that this statue-head was made very early in the reign, probably for the series produced for the King's coronation. It clearly reveals that at his advent he was still an infant (*cf.* Plate 59)

24–26   Commemorative scarabs of Dynasty XVIII. Most scarab-shaped amulets were made of glazed steatite on a small scale, some carrying mottoes and good wishes written in an abbreviated style. Royal scarabs of this type bearing terse obscure inscriptions of a semi-historical nature are rare and mostly confined to the reign of Tuthmosis III. *Centre* a large scarab (L.5 cm.) of Tuthmosis IV bears a longer text, evidently commemorating the reception of gifts from Mitanni, perhaps on the marriage of its princess to the Pharaoh, and speaks of the king fighting with Aten before him and bringing the foreigners under the rule of the god. Large scarabs more than 7 cm. in length inscribed with accounts of dated events appear only in the first decade of Amenophis III. *Left*, a 'Lion Hunt' scarab of Year 10; *right*, a 'Lake' scarab of Year 11

27–30   Funerary figurines (shawabtis) and model tools. *Left*, an alabaster shawabti of the Master of the Horse and King's Father-in-law, Yey; probably reign of Tuthmosis IV: *centre*, painted and gilded wooden shawabti of the Master of the Horse and King's Father-in-law, Yuya; reign of Amenophis III. *Right*, a model hoe and basket from the tomb of Yuya. Such magic figurines and equipment were designed to exempt the deceased from forced labour in the Elysian Fields. They belong essentially to the agricultural concept of an after-life held by the Osirian religion

been under the influence of powerful advisers, first Nefert-iti, and then, on her death, the priest Ay, who from being the husband of Nefert-iti's nurse and Master of the Horse had advanced to the position of Vizier and virtual ruler of Egypt. It was doubtless by his persuasion that Akhet-Aten was abandoned as the Residence, and the Court moved back to Thebes where the priests of Amun recovered their former ascendancy. The royal pair were obliged to change their names to Tut-ankh-Amun and Ankhes-en-Amun and to undertake a heavy programme of restoration of the monuments and endowments of the old gods, particularly Amun. The Aten faith was abandoned and Akhet-Aten allowed to decay, first to a town of squatters and then to a derelict area. A docket on a wine-jar found in his tomb and dated to his regnal year 10, shows that Tut-ankh-Amun ruled for a full nine years. He strove to return to the *status quo* as it had existed in the time of Amenophis III, but died of unknown causes before the work of restoration was far advanced. None of his monuments at Karnak and on most other sites above ground has come down to us bearing his own name; and he would have remained one of the more ephemeral Pharaohs, if the discovery of his tomb, the only royal burial in the Biban el-Moluk to have survived virtually intact and crammed with treasure, had not brought him a world-wide posthumous fame. He left no sons to carry on the dynastic succession and it was at this juncture that his widow wrote to Suppiluliumas, the Hittite King, as we learn from the tablets excavated at the Hittite capital near modern Boghaz Keui in Anatolia, asking him to send one of his sons whom she would marry and so make Pharaoh of Egypt. The Hittite King hesitated over this unprecedented request, but eventually despatched the Prince Zennanza who was murdered on his way to Egypt; whereupon Suppiluliumas attacked and defeated Egyptian forces in the Amki region between Lebanon and Anti-Lebanon.

Fig. 3

Plate XVI

3 *Piece of gold foil embossed with the scene of Ay and Ankhes-en-Amun raising hands in adoration of Tut-ankh-Amun, who slaughters a traditional foe with a scimitar*

85

Plate XVII

Plate 56

Plate 57

In the meantime Ay had seized the throne of Egypt and as the new Pharaoh is represented in the wall-paintings in the tomb of Tut-ankh-Amun performing the last rites for his predecessor, for whose burial he must have been responsible. King Ay ruled for a short period only and was succeeded by the General Har-em-hab who had risen to great authority under Tut-ankh-Amun, being appointed the King's Deputy. He had the support not only of the army but of the priesthood of Amun as well, and he had only to appear in Thebes to be recognized by the city god as the legitimate heir and crowned King, while his wife, a certain Mut-nodjme was made Queen.

The ability which Har-em-hab brought to the administration of public affairs was evident in his unflagging efforts to restore order and prosperity to the State. An edict which he issued, but which has survived only in a greatly damaged state, shows that he was concerned to put down abuses which had appeared in central and local government during the preoccupation of Akhenaten with religious reforms, and which had resulted in the oppression of the populace, particularly the poor, and the commandeering of their goods and services under all kinds of pretexts. The arbitrary exactions, which had also impoverished the State coffers, are enumerated and savage penalties prescribed in each case for breaches of the law. At the same time he took steps to stamp out corruption in the judiciary and collusion between dishonest inspectors and rapacious tax-collectors.

These measures must have gone far to restore material prosperity to Egypt and authority to the Crown; but he also undertook works for improving the morale of the people riven by religious dispute, whose troubles would seem to them as much due to alienated gods as to greedy and dishonest men. Har-em-hab repaired and refurbished the temples in the entire land, re-consecrating them, re-establishing their daily offerings and endowments, equipping them with gold and silver vessels and appointing priests and temple officials from reliable army men. The populace were thus able to resume the public worship of their gods. In all this he probably did no

Plate XVI

more than carry on the policy of his two predecessors. But he also usurped all the monuments they had erected as apostates of the Aten religion; and excluded their names from the official king-lists so that on them Har-em-hab appears as the immediate successor of Amenophis III.

Stone-masons were sent throughout the land continuing the work of restoration that Tut-ankh-Amun had initiated, and razing to the ground the monuments of Akhenaten. The city of Akhet-Aten was visited and its

buildings demolished and the stone carted off for use elsewhere. The
Royal Tomb in the central wady was wrecked, its funeral furniture was
smashed, even such solid objects as stone Canopic chests and sarcophagi;
and the reliefs were hacked out of the walls. Similar destruction was
wrought in the tomb-chapels of Akhenaten's adherents, so that one of
the most recent writers on the period, with a fine melodramatic turn of
phrase has called this imputed vindictiveness, 'the Vengeance of Har-em-
hab'. The vast temple of the Aten at Karnak was also dismantled and its
scores of thousands of stone blocks used as foundations and fill for three
pylons and other works in the temple of Amun. All effort was made to
wipe out any mention of Akhenaten who, if a reference was unavoidable,
was designated as 'that criminal of Akhet-Aten' or simply 'that Criminal'.

Har-em-hab reigned for at least twenty-seven years and was able to
prepare for himself a large tomb in the Biban, the extensive decoration
of which, however was incomplete at his death. It was found in 1908 by
Theodore M. Davis in one of his clearance campaigns in the Valley, but
although the King's red granite sarcophagus, similar in design to those
of Tut-ankh-Amun and Ay, was found *in situ*, the mortal remains of
Har-em-hab were not recovered, and the rifled chambers showed all too
clearly that it had suffered the inevitable plundering. A few fragments of
his funerary equipment survived to show that it was similar in design to
Tut-ankh-Amun's but less rich.

Such is the orthodox picture in its main outlines which historians paint
of the Amarna Revolution and its aftermath. In the next section of this
book we shall have to see how far it conforms to evidence which has
survived.

Plate 112

Plate 110

Plates 45, 46, 48

Plate III

VI The Familial Relationships

Plate 14

THE PATTERN of inheritance in Dynasty XVIII was interrupted and changed by the early death of Tuthmosis IV after a reign of only nine years. His eldest son can have been but a mere child at his succession, as we have already argued. Other children had probably pre-deceased their father: one son, Amun-em-het, was buried with the king in his tomb in the Biban el-Moluk at Thebes, where a daughter Tent-Amun was also interred. It is in fact virtually certain, bearing in mind the high infant mortality rate of ancient times, that Tuthmosis left behind him no heiress daughter by whom the rights to the throne could have been transmitted to his son, and in these straits the young Amenophis was married to Tiye the daughter of Yuya and Tuyu.

Yuya appears to have originated from Akhmim, the capital of the Ninth Province of Upper Egypt, where he doubtless possessed estates and whose chief god Min he served as a Prophet and Superintendent of Cattle. He also held an important position at Court, being the King's

Plate 28

Lieutenant of Chariotry and Master of the Horse. It may therefore be that as the daughter of a distinguished and influential *maryannu*, Tiye was regarded as the proper consort of such a war-lord as the Pharaoh. On the other hand, she may have been some collateral of her husband, her father being a relative of the King's mother, Mut-em-wiya. In the Metropolitan Museum in New York there are two shawabti-figures inscribed for a 'Father of the God, and Master of the Horse, Yey'. The first title, which

Plate 27

was also applied to Yuya in preference to any other, almost certainly indicates at this period that Yey's daughter had married a Pharaoh. The second title was also borne by Yuya and both men have similar-sounding names. Thus Yey may well have been Yuya's father since the shawabtis in question are made in the familiar style of the middle reigns of Dynasty XVIII. It is also not without significance that names compounded with that of the goddess Mut, whose cult received for the first time immense favour in the reign of Amenophis III, often appear among the womenfolk of the family[10]. Queen Mut-em-wiya who held an influential position in the early years of her son's reign may indeed have been a close relative of Yuya, his sister in fact. Although she is described as an 'heiress' in inscriptions, which all date to her son's reign and not her husband's, she is nowhere described as a King's Daughter, or King's Sister, like her contemporary, Queen Yaret.

Tiye was not the only child of Yuya and Tuyu. She had a brother, Anen, who held a high position in the hierarchy at Thebes, being the Second of the Four Chief Prophets of Amun, and the Greatest of Seers in the Temple of Re-Atum. He held office during most of the reign of Amenophis III, being present in his official capacity at many of the ceremonies attended by his royal brother-in-law. But he also had private access to the King at any time and it was doubtless Amenophis III who honoured him with the gift of a tomb in the hill of the Sheikh Abd el-Qurna at Western Thebes. Despite Anen's prominence, with the reserve characteristic of all officials in similar positions, he makes no admission of his kinship with the royal family. His relationship to Tiye in fact would not be known were it not that an inscription on their mother's coffin names him as her son.

It is extremely unlikely that this important family, so closely connected with royalty for two generations at least, did not have another son to carry on the tradition of arms which they professed, since Anen had evidently deserted a military calling for a sacerdotal one. We do not in fact have to look far for such a successor. In the next generation at the Court of Akhenaten we find a Divisional Commander Ay holding most of the titles and offices claimed by Yuya under Amenophis III. Both men were Fathers of the God and Masters of the Horse; both referred to themselves as 'one trusted by the Good God (the King) in the entire land', as 'foremost of the companions of the King' and 'Praised by the Good God'. We regard these titles as merely honorific, but they may have conveyed discreetly some degree of consanguinity to the ruler. In addition, Ay was a 'Fan-Bearer on the Right of the King', and 'King's Own Scribe' or personal secretary. It is also noteworthy that Ay bears a name that approximates to that of Yuya, which could be rendered in one of its many variants as Aya. As has been already stated, this family had a predilection for one or two similar-sounding names, and Yey, Yuya, Aya and Ay are certainly suggestive of some relationship between the owners[11].

There is also another connection between these two men. Yuya came from the Akhmim region where he held important offices, and where his daughter Tiye had extensive estates. Ay also had a connection with Akhmim, later building a rock-chapel there to its local god Min, presumably because it was his birthplace or family seat. It is noteworthy that

Plate 18

Plate 32

Plate 16

Plate 62

references to Min and names compounded with Min become common in Court circles at the time of Ay's greatest influence. It is surely no coincidence that two near-contemporaries whose titles and careers offer such close parallels as those of Yuya and Ay and who both hail from a small provincial city should have a connection with each other. The evidence that Ay was a son of Yuya, appointed to his father's place in the time-honoured Egyptian tradition is thus strongly circumstantial.

Plates 60–63

There is, moreover, a close physical resemblance between these two men. It is true that we lack the mummy of Ay from which to draw comparisons, but the colossus at Berlin with its highly individualized features, a rather unusual cast of countenance for an Egyptian in fact, bears a striking likeness to the mummy of Yuya described by the anatomist Elliot Smith as having a peculiar and most un-Egyptian appearance.

Plate 120

Ay's important position at the Court of Amenophis III and his successors must have owed much to his being a brother of Queen Tiye and an uncle of Akhenaten, but he had other connections as well. The title that Ay uses in preference to all others is 'Father of the God', which he also incorporated into one of his names when he became King. This title usually denotes the holder of a priestly office, and most historians have referred to Ay as 'the Priest Ay'; and he has been accredited with some of the religious thinking behind the Aten heresy, largely because the much-quoted hymn to the Aten appears *in extenso* in his tomb at Amarna (see p. p. 187). But Ay was primarily a soldier and held no priestly offices at Amarna, where Pinhasy, Penthu and Meryre II officiated as Chief Servitors and High Priest of the Aten respectively. Moreover, Ay is the only dignitary at Amarna to bear the title of 'Father of the God'. Over sixty years ago the German scholar Borchardt showed that in some circumstances this could mean 'the Father-in-law of Pharaoh', and this is particularly the case with Yuya, who is known to be the father of Queen Tiye from the Marriage Scarabs, and is referred to most commonly on his funerary equipment as 'Father of the God', that title in fact being used in preference to any other where there is no space for other epithets. It would appear, therefore, that Ay, too, must have been the father-in-law of a king, though Akhenaten was the king he served. In that case, Ay's daughter must have been a wife of Pharaoh and probably his Chief Wife. Such a person can only have been Nefert-iti.

Queen Nefert-iti's parentage has been the subject of much speculation. As the Chief Wife of Akhenaten, she should in theory have been an heiress princess, the daughter of Amenophis III and Tiye; and that is the line of descent that has been postulated for her by some scholars. But she nowhere lays claim to the title of 'King's Daughter' or 'King's Sister' which she would certainly have done if her father had been a Pharaoh. She has also been identified as the Tadukhipa who, as we learn from the Amarna Letters, was sent by Tushratta of Mitanni as a bride for Amenophis III towards the end of that monarch's lifetime and afterwards entered the harim of his successor. The supporters of this idea point to her 'foreign' type of countenance and the significance of her name, 'A Beautiful Woman has Come', to sustain their argument. Of late years this theory has lost favour. Opinions about the alleged 'un-Egyptian' cast of her features are too subjective to carry much weight. Moreover, it seems reasonably clear that marriages between the Pharaohs and foreign princesses were arranged purely for diplomatic reasons and there is nothing to show that at this time these foreign women egyptianized their names and assumed positions of importance. On the contrary, the evidence is all against such assumptions. A Babylonian princess, for instance, a wife of Amenophis III lived in such retirement that envoys from her father had difficulty in hearing anything of her: and several queens are known with un-Egyptian names during this Dynasty[12].

Plate VIII

If Nefert-iti was not the daughter of either an Egyptian or a foreign king, it is only reasonable to suppose that her father was a man of some importance in the entourage of Akhenaten. Ay fills such a part better than anyone else. He was one of the four 'sole companions' who carried the fan on the right of the King and the unique title of 'Father of the God' is applied to him exactly as it was to Yuya, and not as a concomitant of other titles. Moreover, his large and imposing tomb, which was probably the first to be hewn at Amarna, and obviously intended as the finest in the whole necropolis would not have been bestowed on anyone except a near relative of the King.

Plates 62, 119, 120

If Ay were the father of Nefert-iti, it would normally follow that his wife, Tey, would have been her mother; but here we encounter a difficulty. Tey is not called, as Tuyu was, 'the Mother of the King's Chief Wife', but merely her 'nurse' and 'tutor'. This has been an insuperable obstacle to some scholars who have refused to accept that because Tey is not categorically described as the mother of Nefert-iti, her husband Ay could have been the father of the Queen. In most genealogies, however, in Ancient Egypt, the mother's name is given preference, and if the mother of Nefert-iti is not stated, it can only be because she was dead at the time Ay's tomb was decorated. We must presume, therefore, that the mother

4 Mut-nodjme

Plate 57

Plate 73

Plates 64, 65

of Nefert-iti died at some time after giving birth to her daughter, an assumption surely not over-bold in the case of Ancient Egypt where the infant and maternal mortality rates even among royalty were very high. The orphaned Nefert-iti would have been brought up by the next wife of Ay, and it is perhaps as 'step-mother' rather than 'wet-nurse' and 'tutor' that Tey's titles would best be rendered.

In some of the earlier tomb reliefs at Amarna there appears the figure of a lady-in-waiting who is given rather more prominence than the other women in the Queen's retinue and is often accompanied by two dwarfs as attendants. She is described as the Queen's Sister, Mut-nodjme, and the fact that she lays no claim to the title of 'King's Daughter' is another indication of the non-royal parentage of Nefert-iti. Her father must also have been Ay, particularly as it is in his tomb that she figures most prominently as well as in others whose decoration was influenced by it. She is shown in those reliefs where the detail has survived as wearing her hair arranged with a side-lock and appears to be a little older than her eldest niece Meryt-Aten. She was therefore probably a younger sister of Nefert-iti, but we do not know whether she was a full sister, or as a daughter of Tey, only a half-sister. Mut-nodjme disappears from view as the reign wears on and is not represented in the later tombs at Amarna. It is a curious fact, however, that the wife of King Har-em-hab was called Mut-nodjme, a somewhat rare name at this period, and appears on his coronation statue at Turin equal to him in stature. Elsewhere she bears the title of 'Heiress', and it may have been through her claims that her husband came to the throne on the death of Ay. From the days of the German scholar Brugsch, therefore, historians have been disposed to identify the Chief Wife of Har-em-hab as the sister of Nefert-iti; the idea has recently returned to favour, as philological objections to the equation have been removed[13].

Whether Ay and Tey had other children besides Nefert-iti and Mut-nodjme is not known for certain, but there is a strong presumption that the General Nakht-Min who contributed shawabtis to the burial equipment of Tut-ankh-Amun was some close relative and may have been a son of Ay. On a very fine but badly damaged statue of himself and his wife in the Cairo Museum he bears the title, 'a King's Son of . . .', but whether it is to be completed 'his loins' or 'Kush' is a subject of speculation, though the writer regards the former alternative as more likely[14]. This funerary statue indicates that Nakht-Min had died a little before King Ay, if the latter were indeed his father: otherwise he would have succeeded him on the throne.

That the name of Nakht-Min was not unknown in the family of Ay is seen from a recently acquired block-statue at the Brooklyn Museum which is dated by the cartouche-marks borne by the owner to the reign of Ay. This represents a Second Prophet of Amun and a Chief Prophet of Mut, also called Ay, who was the son of Mut-em-nub, a sister of Queen Tey, by a certain Nakht-Min. The inscription on this statue shows clearly some of the ramifications of this powerful family, the important positions it held and its attachment to one or two constantly recurring names.

Plate 66

Dockets from the Malkata Palace show that Amenophis III survived to the last days of his thirty-eighth regnal year at least, and suggest that he may have entered his thirty-ninth before he died at the age of about forty-five. It is almost certain that his Chief Wife Tiye was younger than he since a scene represented in one of the later tombs at Amarna shows her as a widow, accompanied by her daughter Beket-Aten, visiting her son at Akhet-Aten, where she and her daughter had residences. A dated scene in the tomb suggests that this visit took place in Year 12, or at least after Year 9, of Akhenaten. Beket-Aten by her dress is still shown as a minor, hardly older than the eldest Princess Meryt-Aten; and she must therefore have been born posthumously or at the very end of the old King's reign (see, however, p. 99) when her mother was still of an age to bear children.

Plate 37

Plates 103, 104

Besides Beket-Aten, Tiye and Amenophis III had other daughters, the most important of whom was the eldest princess, Sit-Amun. This great lady occupied a palace of her own in the vast Malkata complex at Thebes. She contributed supplies to the celebration of her father's first jubilee in his regnal year 30, and a docket on a jar-fragment from the Malkata site shows that she was still alive in his year 37, so she probably survived him. She sometimes bears the additional title of 'King's Chief Wife', and since this appears on objects also inscribed with her father's names the conclusion is inescapable that Amenophis III married his own daughter. This corollary is accepted only with the greatest reluctance by some Egyptologists, such as Gardiner, to whom incestuous relationships among the gods incarnate of Ancient Egypt are less acceptable than those prevailing upon the Olympus of Ancient Greece. There is no doubt, however, that even by Egyptian standards, this marriage between father and daughter must have been unusual, for the eldest daughter should by long tradition have been married to the heir-apparent on his ascending the throne. Such a signal departure from the norm will require further comment later.

Plate 17

Plate 36

The sons of Amenophis III and Tiye are less well known and documented. There is a Prince Tuthmose who has left some monuments in the Memphis area where he served as High Priest of Ptah, an office that was customarily filled by the heir-apparent. He presumably died prematurely, like so many of the first-born of Egypt, and it may be his whip inscribed for 'the King's Son and Captain of the Troops, Tuthmose' that was included among the heirlooms buried in the tomb of Tut-ankh-Amun. On the death of Tuthmose, the position of heir-apparent was filled by Prince Amun-hotpe who later ascended the throne as Nefer-kheperu-Re Amenophis (IV) and later changed his name to Akhenaten. He almost certainly had younger brothers, but their identification will prove a difficult problem which is best left until the end of this chapter.

The daughters of Nefert-iti are known from their many representations. Six surviving girls are recorded and are represented in the scanty remains of a wall-painting from the King's House at Amarna which shows the Royal Family in a remarkable conversation-piece. Nefert-iti and Akhenaten are seated on low stools facing each other with their three eldest children disposed between them, the two younger children playing with each other beside their mother's feet, and the youngest sitting on her lap. This composition includes the name of the Aten in its earlier form showing that all six had been born by regnal year 9[15]. They all reappear together, a little older, in the tomb of the Steward Mery-Re at Amarna, in a relief showing the reception of foreign tribute at the great *durbar* at Aket-Aten in Year 12, ranged behind the King and Queen under the royal baldachin.

Plate 44

This is the last glimpse we have of a united family, thereafter their fates diverge. Nefert-iti disappears from the scene about a year later and her place is taken by her eldest daughter Meryt-Aten (the Mayati of the Amarna Letters) whose features and name replace those of her mother on some of her monuments, a usurpation which has been held to mark the fall of Nefert-iti from favour and her retirement to a northern palace at Amarna. In our view, however, Nefert-iti was not disgraced, but died about this time (see p. 242). Her place was taken by Meryt-Aten who was married to the young prince Smenkh-ka-Re on his appointment as the co-regent of Akhenaten. An unpublished inscription on a block from Hermopolis mentions a baby princess called Meryt-Aten-ta-sherit (Meryt-Aten-the-Less) who is presumably her daughter, but nothing more is known of this child. We hear little more of Meryt-Aten either. She is shown as the consort of Smenkh-ka-Re, with her name in a cartouche as the King's Chief Wife, in a rough ink-sketch on a wall of the tomb of the Steward Mery-Re at Amarna. Thereafter, she too leaves a troubled scene and presumably died before her husband.

Plate 68

Plate 9

Meket-Aten died soon after Year 12 when she had been in attendance at the *durbar*. She was apparently buried in the Royal Tomb at Amarna for a subsidiary suite of rooms leading off its main corridor is decorated with scenes concerning her death. An unusual relief, unique in fact for a royal tomb, shows the King and Queen weeping over the bier of the dead princess. The presence of Nefert-iti in this scene of mourning must surely indicate that Meket-Aten died before her. A princess or nurse-maid holding a babe in her arms and followed by a fan-bearer to show the importance of the child or its nurse appears outside the death-chamber as though she had just left it. This nurse and her charge have excited some attention from Egyptologists. One scholar has sought to recognise the infant as a recently-born daughter of Nefert-iti. Another has postulated that it is the baby of Meket-Aten who has died in childbirth: yet another has identified it as the daughter of Meryt-Aten. In the absence of an inscription any choice can only be arbitrary.

Plate 44

Plate 87

The third daughter, Ankhes-en-pa-Aten, had a career which is more fully documented than that of her sisters though we still know all too little about it. She, too, appears to have given birth to a daughter while she was still a princess, for blocks from Hermopolis associate her name with that of a child who was called after her, Ankhes-en-pa-Aten-ta-sherit. The presence of the cartouche of Akhenaten in this greatly incomplete text has led a number of scholars to restore it so as to make Akhenaten the father of his daughter's child, though Gardiner, who holds such mixture to be a stain, has categorically denied the possibility.

Ankhes-en-pa-Aten then fades from our view until she re-appears as the Queen of Tut-ankh-Aten. Her graceful figure is represented on some of the objects from her husband's tomb. She followed Tut-ankh-Amun in changing her name so as to honour the god who had brought their dynasty so much good fortune, and as Ankhes-en-Amun her name is linked with his on many of his tomb furnishings. It is presumably she who was the mother of two still-born premature children whose mummies were buried with Tut-ankh-Amun. Each had been enclosed in a set of miniature gilded coffins like any royalty, but under their father's name, since they had not come into this world as living beings. On the death of Tut-ankh-Amun, their mother, as we have already mentioned, attempted to make a dynastic marriage with the son of the Hittite King, but when that move failed, she appears to have wedded Ay, her own grandfather, who thus secured the throne. This marriage which was doubtless purely a formality, has been denied by some scholars, but such a marriage of

Plates 10, 93

Plates 62, 119

convenience is most probable, since it could have been the only way that Ay could have gained the throne except by blatant usurpation backed by force of arms, in which case he would have dismissed his predecessor as illegitimate and certainly not have buried him with so much pomp and treasure. No more is heard of Ankhes-en-Amun and the queen represented in the tomb of Ay in the Biban el-Moluk is Tey, who is shown at Amarna with her husband making obeisance to Akhenaten.

Of the three youngest daughters of Nefert-iti, who were the interested onlookers at the *durbar* in Year 12, nothing is known. The excavations at Ras-Shamra (Ugarit) on the North Syrian coast have unearthed fragments of a stone vessel engraved with a scene in the Egyptian style showing a princess or concubine making a libation to the King of Ugarit, or pouring wine into his cup. The woman has been identified on no certain grounds as an Amarna princess, but this is extremely unlikely. When the King of Babylon wrote to Amenophis III asking for his daughter in marriage, he received a haughty reply to the effect that as of old it had never been the custom for Egyptian princesses to be married to foreign royalty. There was, of course, good reason for this exclusiveness: the daughters of Pharaoh carried with them rights to the throne of Egypt, and it is therefore virtually certain that no woman of the royal family at Amarna would have been given in marriage to a foreigner, particularly to such a minor potentate as the King of Ugarit.

It has long been postulated that two of the Amarna Pharaohs owed their rights to the throne entirely through marriages of this kind to the heiress daughters of Akhenaten and Nefert-iti. The kings in question are Smenkh-ka-Re, the husband of Meryt-Aten and Tut-ankh-Amun, the husband of Ankhes-en-Amun. Indeed, earlier Egyptologists regarded these two kings as influential nobles who had in turn assumed the crown by making an advantageous marriage. The discovery of the tomb of Tut-ankh-Amun has effectively destroyed this idea, in his case at least, since an anatomical examination of his body has shown that he died at the age of at least eighteen. As his highest regnal year was 10, it seems quite implausible that a child of eight or nine would have been sufficiently influential to secure the throne by marriage unless he had strong rights of his own. In fact, on a granite lion in the British Museum which he found still rough-hewn in the quarry at his accession and which he completed as a companion for another in the temple of Amenophis III at Sulb, Tut-ankh-Amun explicitly calls that king 'his father', a declaration which has seldom been taken seriously in modern times. 'Father' is here either translated as 'forefather' or Tut-ankh-Amun is credited with claiming a distinguished ancestor to whom he had no right. If the normal pattern of kingship, however, was followed in the case of Smenkh-ka-Re and Tut-ankh-Amun, it is certain that they had royal blood in their veins and were near-relations of their wives, perhaps even full or half brothers.

That this is the case with Tut-ankh-Amun admits of little doubt since an unpublished inscription written at the time when he was still a mere prince makes it clear that he was begotten of a king and was not an adopted son. What was true of Tut-ankh-Amun must be equally the case with Smenkh-ka-Ra. There is every reason to believe that the body of the latter has survived (see p. 147) and proves to be that of a young man who died at the age of at least nineteen. It would therefore appear that he must have been appointed co-regent of Akhenaten when Tut-ankh-Amun was aged about six or seven, and would never have been elevated to the throne in preference to the younger claimant unless he, too, was the son of a king. Smenkh-ka-Re and Tut-ankh-Amun have lately come to be regarded as brothers and their mortal remains show remarkable affinities, particularly in the similar measurements of their rather exceptional platy-cephalic skulls. Indeed, their close family resemblance can only have come from their having the same parents, since Smenkh-ka-Re was not old enough at the birth of Tut-ankh-Amun to have been his father.

The question remains, who was the father of these two brothers? He must have been a king and the obvious candidate is Akhenaten whose sons would normally be expected to succeed him in turn if the elder died without issue. There are, however, some obstacles in the way of accepting Akhenaten as their father. In the first place, the close fraternal resemblance between them suggests that they were sons of the same queen by the same king; and such a woman as the mother of the heir-apparent would have been a very important person at the Court of Akhenaten, probably taking precedence over the other royal wives. Such a queen cannot have been Nefert-iti who in the many intimate scenes with her husband is never shown with sons but only daughters. If she had borne live sons, it seems likely that they would have been paraded with all that lack of reticence that marks the representation of the private life of the Royal Family at Amarna. No other queen of Akhenaten is represented at Amarna though it is known that he had an extensive harim as befitted his majesty: and it seems clear that he also accepted responsibility for his father's harim on his death. Kia, a secondary wife of Akhenaten, is known from a calcite pot in New York and a fragment in London that was once part of the furnishings of her unknown tomb; but she is given no additional title to that of 'King's Wife' and her name is not enclosed within a cartouche. If she were the mother of the royal princes, her name was not honoured either by her husband at Amarna, nor by her sons when they came to the throne, judging by what little evidence has survived.

There is another impediment in the way of identifying Akhenaten as the father of his two immediate successors. Smenkh-ka-Re is believed to have died before Akhenaten or at best to have had little more than one year of sole rule[16]. As Akhenaten died in his seventeenth regnal year and Smenkh-ka-Re was aged nineteen or more at death, it follows that the latter must have been born before the former came to the throne. Now those who follow the conventional line in thinking that Akhenaten was so immature at his accession that his mother had to guide him in state-craft (see pp. 65, 209) can hardly also accept that he was already the father of a son at least two years old. The author takes a different view, believing that where the normal pattern of succession was observed in Dynasty XVIII, and there is no reason to think that it was otherwise in the case of Akhenaten, the king's eldest surviving son was appointed co-regent on reaching manhood, supplied with a harim and married to the royal heiress. If he came to the throne before reaching his majority, he was married to the heiress on accession and procreated offspring thereafter, as soon as he reached the age of puberty. Akhenaten cannot have been the father of Smenkh-ka-Re unless he had been made co-regent of Amenophis III before his first regnal year; but as the tradition in Dynasty XVIII was for the co-regent to count his regnal years from moment of his appointment, it is impossible that Smenkh-ka-Re could have been born to him. If Smenkh-ka-Re was not a son of Akhenaten, neither can Tut-ankh-Amun have been, since the son of a ruling king would not have been passed over in preference to another and more distant relative at the induction of a co-regent.

The father of Smenkh-ka-Re and Tut-ankh-Amun on this basis can only have been that king whom the latter claimed as his parent on the granite lion from Sulb, namely Amenophis III. This paternity has long been urged by a number of scholars who have seen a physical resemblance between the two kings[17]. Tut-ankh-Amun had a number of personal objects bearing the name of Amenophis III included in his tomb furnishings, notably a little gold statue of the King worn on a chain and treated with great reverence as a family heirloom, being enclosed and sealed within two miniature coffins.

Plates 71, XIII

The mother of Smenkh-ka-Re and Tut-ankh-Amun is even less certain in the absence of any categorical statement of affiliation, but the inference can only be that she must have been an important queen of Amenophis III. Two candidates have been suggested, Sit-Amun and Tiye. Sit-Amun appears to have married her father about his regnal year 30, probably in year 28; and if this date should prove to be correct and not an approximation, she is unlikely to have been the mother of Smenkh-ka-Re who must have been born about regnal year 24 according to the author's calculations. No objects bearing the name of Sit-Amun have been published among the material found in the tomb of Tut-ankh-Amun, a somewhat notable lack if she had been his mother. On the other hand, a number of articles belonging to Tiye were found in the tomb, including, most significantly, a plaited lock of her auburn hair, anointed and enclosed in a coffinette with the same care as the statuette of Amenophis III had been treated. That Tut-ankh-Amun and Smenkh-ka-Re should have been younger brothers of Akhenaten who succeeded to the throne in turn in the absence of any male issue by their predecessor is what might be expected. But although a close resemblance has been noted between an ebony head generally identified as Tiye and the gold portrait-mask of Tut-ankh-Amun, the nearest relationship that has been regarded as possible is that of grandmother and grandson. The fact, however, that Tiye was evidently the mother of Beket-Aten who is represented as a young girl after year 9 at the Court of Akhenaten, shows that Tiye was still of child-bearing age at the very end of her husband's reign unless there was a long period of joint rule between Amenophis III and Akhenaten. There is no reason therefore why she should not have borne Tut-ankh-Amun before Amenophis III died. Bearing in mind, however, the length of his reign and his age at death, Tut-ankh-Amun must also have been born about regnal year 7 or 8 of Akhenaten, and it follows, if our affiliation is correct, that there must have been a long co-regency between Amenophis III and Akhenaten, and to this vexatious problem we shall devote our next chapter.

Plate 71

Plates 69, 70

Plate 53

VII

The Case for a Co-regency

WE HAVE REFERRED in an earlier chapter to the curious institution of co-regency in Ancient Egypt whereby the eldest surviving son of the king became his father's co-regent on reaching manhood and assumed the more dynamic role. We have also pointed out that this did not necessarily lead to the premature eclipse of the older partner, since the high mortality rate in the Ancient World ensured that the elder sons often died before they reached maturity, or the co-regent died after a very brief reign, leaving his father to make other arrangements.

Many Egyptologists find co-regency a difficult concept to admit and would like to deny its existence, but unfortunately the evidence is too much against them, particularly during Dynasty XII when every king, with one possible exception, co-opted his eldest surviving son on the throne with him and double datings exist to prove the fact. Some of these co-regents ran in double harness with their fathers for some time, as much as ten years in the case of Sesostris I. But not every relevant date during these co-regencies is given in a dual form; and the kings of Dynasty XII appear in their use of these occasional double datings to depart from the practice generally in force in earlier and subsequent periods.

During the Middle Kingdom it seems to have been the practice for co-regents to be appointed on New Year's Day, or to date each advent as though it had been made on such a day, thus bringing dates in the regnal year and those in the civil year into step. Double dates therefore can be harmonized, and a month and day in the regnal year of a co-regent corresponds with the same month and day in that of his senior partner. In the New Kingdom, however, a different system was introduced by the self-glorious kings of Dynasty XVIII whereby each regnal year was reckoned from accession day to accession day without reference to the civil calendar; and although Hat-shepsut, for instance, said of her father Tuthmosis I that he knew the virtue of an accession on New Year's Day, not one king's advent during this Dynasty fell on that particular day. The result is that the regnal year can change at any point in the calendrical year on the anniversary of the king's accession, whereas the civil year began on

New Year's Day, or the first day of the first month of Inundation. Since 'the civil calendar continued to be used for the business of everyday life, one could never be quite sure that this or that day of a given month really preceded that which its number seemed to demand should immediately follow it.'[18] This circumstance could, of course, lead to difficulties when a scribe for instance sought to place in proper sequence a series of dated documents, and when two such systems had to be co-ordinated the complications must have been the greater. It was doubtless for this reason that double datings were avoided during the New Kingdom, and the scribes adhered to one system or the other without trying to reconcile them. Those Egyptologists, therefore, who will not accept co-regencies in Dynasty XVIII until double datings are found are demanding what does not exist.

The dating system, however, for all its ambiguity, has produced evidence of a co-regency in one case at least. Tuthmosis III is said, in the biography of one of his henchmen, to have died in his fifty-fourth regnal year on the last day of the seventh month, and his son Amenophis II at the next dawn, as custom demanded, was established on the throne of his father. It is known, however, from another inscription, that the accession day of Amenophis II was not the first day of the eighth month, but the first day of the fourth month; and even the extreme sceptics have been prepared to accept that this discrepancy can only be explained by the probability that Amenophis II had been associated on the throne with Tuthmosis III for exactly four months before the latter's death. Others, of course, have added years to this four-month period of joint rule.[19]

Co-regencies during Dynasty XVIII have in fact been suggested by different Egyptologists in the case of nearly every Pharaoh. The only points at issue have been the choice of kings who ruled with co-regents and the length of each period of co-regency. Some historians have tried to avoid all the implications by postulating that each co-regent ruled with the older Pharaoh for a very brief period only, as though the exact time of the death of the senior partner had been nicely calculated in fixing the moment for the appointment of his co-regent. However much prescience may have entered into such matters, there seem to have been instances when the old king, so far from conveniently dying soon afterwards, outlived his young partner, and a new co-regent had to be appointed.

From the New Kingdom there have survived three accounts of the appointment of Pharaohs as the co-regents of their fathers. We have already mentioned the elevation of Tuthmosis III to the throne while his father was actually officiating in the temple of Amun at Karnak (see p. 39 above). Another account is that of Hat-shepsut where she claims that her father, as part of the coronation ceremonies, presented her to the assembled dignitaries of his Court and declared:

> This is my daughter, Hat-shepsut. May she live! I have placed her upon my throne. She it is who shall sit within my exalted baldachin. She shall direct the people in every office of the palace. She it is who shall lead you. You shall proclaim her words and be united under her command.

Both these accounts are now taken to be fictitious, and there is little doubt that the latter one is wholly so. But if the sovereigns concerned subsequently wished to legitimize their assumption of supreme power, they would hardly have chosen to relate a means that was not orthodox and familiar. A third account is that given by Ramesses II of Dynasty XIX when he discloses how his father, Sethos I, promoted him from the time he was a child until he became king:

> When my father made his state appearance before the people, I being a child in his lap, he said referring to me: 'Crown him as King that I may see his qualities while I am still living.' And he ordered the chamberlains to place the Double Crown upon my brow. 'Let him administer this land: let him show himself to the people'—so spake he through his great love of me.

Ramesses goes on to relate how he was provided with household women and a royal harim, so he evidently telescoped into one occasion a series of events when he was proclaimed heir, probably at the advent of Sethos I himself, appointed a commander of the armed forces while still an infant, and at the age of manhood crowned as co-regent, given a separate household and provided with a Chief Wife and concubines.

This memoir by Ramesses II has also been discounted, but on insufficient grounds, and is accepted, for instance, by so convinced a sceptic as Gardiner. The objection has been raised that it, like the accounts of Tuthmosis III and Hat-shepsut, was recorded long after the event and is therefore suspect. But the very nature of the record ensures that it could hardly be contemporary with the event, and there is no reason to think that it is any more inaccurate than other declarations by the Pharaohs. The accounts of these appointments to kingship may be enhanced and give a favourable gloss to the situation, but they can hardly be complete fabrications relating a unique happening. The memoir by Ramesses II in fact serves to show the various stages in the appointment of a co-regent—the presentation of the heir-apparent to the people or the Court usually at his birth, his promotion to high military office, which would entail athletic exercises and weapon training, his elevation to a post in the administration, which would require the education of a scribe, and on reaching manhood his coronation as the co-regent of his father.

The existence of two Courts each with its Pharaoh ruling at the same time has proved a severe stumbling-block for most critics; but *The Story of Sinuhe*, a novel about Sesostris I, shows the system functioning in Dynasty XII without any apparent difficulty. The junior partner in each case from the time of his appointment was properly consecrated at his coronation with appropriate pomp, being granted a full titulary and regalia, a harim and the privileges of appointing his nominees to office and dating events to his own years of rule. From then on he became the more important member of the duumvirate, although foreign potentates, whose ideas of kingship were quite different, held to what they understood and continued to correspond with the older Pharaoh until death removed him from their ken.

On his installation as co-regent, the new Pharaoh appointed his own men to office, and these would almost certainly be the young companions and followers who had been brought up with him as a kind of shadow Court. They were nearly all sons of the senior officials who duplicated their fathers' posts and would in due course succeed them according to the Egyptian ideal of appointing the son to the place of his father. It is quite evident that whole dynasties of officials existed side by side with the dynasties of kings whom they served, though it is not always easy to trace lines of descent from the ambiguous and incomplete genealogies that have been vouchsafed us. The entourage of the elder Pharaoh continued to serve him for as long as he lived and ignored, for the most part completely, the establishments of the younger co-regent. The appointment of the son to a parallel post to that of his father, therefore, appears to be no more than the prudent taking of 'a staff of old age', as the Egyptian expression describes it, since on the death of the senior Pharaoh the majority of his officials retire without trace, a phenomenon which is perhaps a faint echo of the prehistoric custom of sacrificing the followers of the chieftain and his servants at the moment of his burial. On the other hand, some of the former incumbents in office, particularly the experienced military commanders, were transferred to the new Court on the appointment of the co-regent as a special mark of favour, the presumption being that the older king would not be taking the field at the head of his armies, but would leave such active service to the younger and more energetic partner. This is certainly the arrangement described in the opening passages of *The Story of Sinuhe*, as the young Sesostris I leads home his triumphant forces from Libya to learn of the death of his father at the Residence; and a similar situation seems to have prevailed in the declining years of Tuthmosis III when Amenophis II took the Egyptian armies into North Syria.

It has often been maintained that the time-honoured custom of appointing sons to their fathers' posts was abandoned in the reign of Akhenaten since he surrounded himself with upstarts or new men, free from the old prejudices and influences, in conformity with his revolutionary and heretical opinions. It is true that a number of his henchmen, like those of some earlier kings, pay him extravagant compliments by describing themselves as mere nobodies whom the king made great and whose career he advanced; but for the most part these must be examples of gross flattery made to enhance the graciousness of their Pharaoh. It is extremely doubtful if Akhenaten, in the absence of a system of universal education, could have found any cadre of educated and trained officials outside the old scribal families to carry on the business of state. Nor is there anything to show that these members of the old families would have been any less loyal than new men, since both equally would have owed their prosperity entirely to the favour of the reigning sovereign. There are a number of cases in which it is evident that the son under Akhenaten succeeded to the office of his father under Amenophis III. Thus Ipy, the Chief Steward of Memphis in the reign of Akhenaten, was the son of Amun-hotpe who held the same post under Amenophis III. We have already suggested that Ay played the same role under Akhenaten that his putative father Yuya had under Amenophis III. Akhenaten's Chief Sculptor Bek was the son of Men, the Chief Sculptor of Amenophis III. Akhenaten's butler, Pa-ren-nefer, was also his chief craftsman, and a like office was held by the latter's father, Apuia, under Amenophis III. It is to be suspected that other close relationships lurk under non-committal names and titles devoid of their affiliations.

On the face of it, therefore, a co-regency between Amenophis III and his son Akhenaten is only to be expected, especially as the former Pharaoh had a long reign and conditions during his latter years, when he celebrated no less than three jubilees and his health may have been indifferent, would have been conducive to the appointment of a junior partner. Historians,

Plate 105
Plate 19

Plate 79

nevertheless, have until recently taken the view that Akhenaten succeeded his father only on his death and ruled for his full span of seventeen years alone. In truth, there is much to recommend this view which is still firmly held by an influential body of opinion. Such scholars find it difficult to accept that what they regard as the revolutionary ideas in religion and art introduced by Akhenaten could exist side by side with the orthodoxy of Amenophis III. To them it is impossible that one Court at Akhet-Aten was, so they think, execrating Amun and all his works, while another Court at Thebes was providing lavishly for the very same god. Again, they point out, at least two of the Amarna Letters addressed to Akhenaten, which obviously from their context are among the first received at Akhet-Aten, refer to the recent death of Amenophis III, or to his funeral; and this, they declare, shows that Akhenaten succeeded only after the death of his father. They are evidently unwilling to admit that a foreign king would continue to correspond with the same Pharaoh and only to write to his successor after the death of the elder partner. They also draw attention to another of the Letters from Tushratta in which he recommends Akhenaten to consult his mother, Tiye. They argue that this is ample proof of the king's immaturity at his accession and his need for his mother's guidance in state-craft (see, however, p. 209). They also point to the fact that one of the letters (Kn. No. 27) from Tushratta, which must have been the first to have reached Akhenaten after the death of his father, since it speaks of the ceremony of mourning, is inscribed with a docket dated to regnal year 2 and mentions the place of residence of the King as a palace at Thebes. This, they believe, must refer to the early reign of the King, who did not remove his Court to Amarna until Year 5 at the earliest.

Plate 117

It might seem wilfully obtuse for anyone in the face of such well-founded testimony to suggest that even so a co-regency between Amenophis III and Akhenaten is the only explanation for a number of curious facts and anomalies among the heterogeneous records that have survived from this remote era. Nevertheless, the theory has been advanced, and is still maintained by a small body of opinion among which, the reader must be warned, the present writer ranges himself without much hesitation. Let us review some of the main arguments in turn to show the extent of this particular problem which lies at the heart of Amarna studies.

Two dockets inscribed with the Years 28 and 30 have been found on jar fragments uncovered at Amarna, and it is very likely that these high numbers refer to the regnal years of Amenophis III. The dockets show no signs of having been expunged or written over, and as it is improbable that empty jars would have been brought to Amarna and not used again (if they had, the texts would have been in palimpsest), it looks as though they reached the city full of wine and properly sealed. If there were no co-regency, one must conclude that the wine was at least fourteen years old by the time it reached Amarna. As it is presumed that the wine would not keep long in permeable pottery jars in a warm climate, it is more likely that Years 28 and 30 of Amenophis III were near Year 6 of Akhenaten when Amarna began to be occupied by the official classes. Unfortunately, no-one has tried the experiment of seeing for how long wine will remain drinkable in sealed pottery jars in Egypt. The wine in question may have been used for libations where its potability was not important. In any case, these jars may have held not wine but dried fruits or incense or some other imperishable commodity.

Plate 80

A stela from the ruins of the house of Pinhasy at Amarna, and now in the British Museum, shows Amenophis III as a corpulent old man slumped on his throne beside his wife Tiye under the rays of the Aten in its later form. It is clear that the royal pair are represented as living persons, the King in the last years of his life when his health appears to have been poor, and not as dead and deified, in which case the figure of the King would have been idealized in a more heroic form and would not have been accompanied by that of his still living wife around whose neck he affection-ately puts his arm. This stela shows that Amenophis III lived and was venerated at Amarna after Year 9 of his son at least. That he resided at Amarna is to be inferred from the references which have been found to his estate and mansion there, besides other texts which may indicate that he owned several other habitations in the city. To these conclusions, however, it has been objected that the stela merely commemorates a posthumous cult of Amenophis III and his Chief Queen. Similarly, whenever a juxtaposition of the names of Amenophis III and Akhenaten occur with the late form of the Aten, as it does for instance on a lintel

Plates 52, 53

and door-jambs in the tomb of the Steward Huya at Amarna, it is due to filial piety. The fact that several buildings at Amarna were associated with Amenophis III only serves to emphasize the importance there of the cult of dead ancestors, since the houses of Tuthmosis I, Amenophis II and Tuthmosis IV are also referred to at Amarna, and no one would claim that these kings ever lived there.

A limestone offering-table broken from a kneeling statue is inscribed with the later Aten titulary followed by the *prenomina* of Amenophis III and Akhenaten, the former king receiving greater prominence than his son. It is difficult to know what the name of the senior king, described in such a way as to infer that he was still living, is doing in association with that of his son during the later years of his reign. Similar juxtapositions of king's names have been used in other cases, as evidence of co-regencies. Moreover, it is not sufficient to dismiss this association of names on the same monument as resulting from filial piety. It is exceedingly curious, to use no stronger term, that the young king should wait until his later years before making memorials of his father. It might also well be asked, why only of his father? If houses connected with the cult of such dead kings as Tuthmosis I, Amenophis II and Tuthmosis IV existed at Amarna, why have no fragments come to light in which their names are associated with those of Akhenaten?

More positive evidence of a co-regency between Akhenaten and Amenophis III is provided by a block of stone from the ruins of Athribis, the natal town of Amenophis-son-of-Hapu who speaks of his King erecting a large temple to the god of that city. This fragment is inscribed with parts of three cartouches which Professor Fairman has plausibly shown must be restored to give the name of Akhenaten in its early Amenophis form side by side with that of his father but preceding it. The dimensions and character of this block tend to show that it came from a stout and imposing wall on which were probably represented in relief figures of Akhenaten and Amenophis III making offerings to a god. The position of the cartouches makes it certain that the two kings were standing one behind the other, the younger to the fore, and this rules out any possibility that Akhenaten is making an offering to his dead and deified father, in which case he would be facing him. The Athribis block in fact gives such unequivocal testimony that the two kings were ruling together, the younger taking precedence of the elder at some time before Year 6 of Amenophis IV (when he changed his name to Akhenaten), that opponents of the co-regency theory have been obliged to accept grudgingly the possibility of a co-regency between the two kings which however they reduce to a few months only.

For further testimony as to the length of this joint-rule we must go elsewhere. In the Theban tomb of Kheruef, who was the Steward of Queen Tiye during the last decade of her husband's life, there are reliefs showing events in the First and Third jubilees that Amenophis III celebrated in his thirtieth and thirty-seventh regnal years. These appear on the rear wall of an inner court which admits to the hypostyle halls of the tomb. The lintel over the entrance has been carved with a double scene showing

Plate 20

Plate 41

Plate 40

Akhenaten followed by his mother Tiye making an offering to Atum and Hat-Hor on the right, and to Re-Herakhty and Maet on the left. On the side-walls of the entrance Akhenaten offers an oblation to Re-Herakhty left and to a pair of mysterious figures right to whom we shall refer later. At the back of the inner court is a portico leading to two more columned halls, and the outer lintel of this is carved with a scene of Akhenaten and Tiye worshipping divinities. The appearance of Akhenaten in the traditional art-style of his father's reign, with his name in its early Amenophis form, and the presence of divinities from the old Egyptian pantheon have induced most Egyptologists to regard this tomb as one of the earliest monuments of Akhenaten's reign, when he was still under the tutelage of his mother. It must therefore have been begun, so they argue, under Amenophis III and continued in the first years of his successor. Work on this magnificent tomb-chapel stopped when Kheruef suffered the fate of so many royal stewards in being disgraced and his monuments desecrated.

Such an interpretation of the date of the construction of this tomb, however, disregards certain features of its decoration. The reliefs which show Akhenaten with his mother Tiye are precisely in those positions which, as we know from the half-completed tombs at Amarna, the Egyptian sculptors finished first, as soon as the wall space became available, in fact, and often well in advance of the release by the stone-masons of the pillared halls from their matrix of rock. Opponents of the co-regency theory, therefore, can only explain these features in the tomb by postulating that it must have been started very early in the reign of Akhenaten to which it would belong entirely; and the scenes of the First and Third Jubilees of Amenophis III, carved on walls that only became available later must be retrospective. If this is so, however, it is odd that the tomb, which would then have been given to Kheruef by the bounty of Akhenaten, shows nothing of the development of the Aten religion, particularly as we know that it was of very rapid growth. Re-Herakhty, for instance, is referred to without any of those epithets that were so soon expanded into his didactic name. It is remarkable that the king commemorated most prominently in the tomb-scenes is not Akhenaten, the putative donor, but Amenophis III whom Kheruef did not directly serve.

An alternative explanation, therefore, that better accounts for the peculiar decoration of this chapel would be that Kheruef was given the tomb by Amenophis III, whose Chief Wife he served, some time about the King's First Jubilee; and in selecting subjects for the sculptors to carve, he naturally associated the son of his patroness with her husband, particularly as he had recently been made co-regent. Further than this Kheruef did not choose to go and apart from an unexceptional reference to the sun-god as Aten, he ignored the ideas of the younger Pharaoh and the new art-style in which they were being expressed.

That Akhenaten appears in one relief at least with his father is revealed on the right-hand wall of the entrance vestibule which though heavily damaged has been skilfully repaired by the University of Chicago Oriental Institute who have succeeded in replacing some of the fallen pieces of carved stone. The scene shows the young king making an offering to a pair who have been recognized as Amenophis III and his wife Tiye and the identification has been confirmed during recent restorations. The crown worn by the king has been likened to the Atef crown invariably worn by Osiris. The figure of the king has therefore been regarded as Amenophis III dead and deified to whom Akhenaten, the living king, makes an offering.

Plate 40

Plate XVII

This interpretation is open to some serious criticism. In the first place it must be emphasised that the Atef crown is one of the varieties of headgear worn by the king at his coronation and particularly at his jubilees. To say that a Pharaoh is wearing the crown of Osiris is to inverse the proper order of things. Osiris wears the crown of a king in jubilee, *i.e.* in resurrection; and the presumption is strong that in this relief Amenophis III is shown living and in jubilee garb. There is supporting evidence. He is said to be 'beloved of Sokar', an epithet applied to the living and not the dead king when the esteem of a fellow deity would be an irrelevancy. He wears the costume of a living king with sandals and a panther skin, showing himself as the chief priest of Sokar, a Memphite god who is particularly associated with resurrection and therefore with jubilee ceremonies. The cult of this god of death and resurrection was especially appropriate for a ceremony of the renewal of life in nature and man; and his rites were observed not only at the First but also at the Third Jubilee of Amenophis III. Lastly, if Amenophis III is shown dead and deified, his wife who grasps his arm in such a close embrace must be dead and deified also, yet she is shown in other scenes in the tomb with her son Akhenaten making offerings to the gods. The writer has little doubt that the scene in question represents Akhenaten makings offering to his living parents during the First Jubilee ceremonies of Amenophis III. The fact that he should worship his living father in this way is not exceptional. Amenophis III makes an offering to himself on a relief in his temple at Sulb where Akhenaten is also shown worshipping Amenophis III in company with him.

Plate 10

Plate 40

Plate 41

If this is so, however, it postulates that there was a long co-regency between these two kings of eight years or more; and this is what most historians find impossible to accept. The late John Pendlebury however, who excavated for the Egypt Exploration Society at Amarna between the two world wars, came to the conclusion that the co-regency lasted eleven years and the writer is a firm upholder of this view for reasons which will now be adduced.

A group of four papyri found near Ghurab deal with transactions conducted by a certain herdsman, Mose, with various slave-owners at different times between regnal years 27 of Amenophis III and 4 of Akhenaten.[20] If there was a co-regency of eleven to twelve years, these documents would cover a span of six years (since two of the papyri are dated to Year 33). Without this proviso, the period must be increased to fifteen years. In Year 27, Mose gave commodities to the herdsman Neb-mehy in exchange for the services of his slaves; and he completed a similar sort of deal with him again in Year 2; that is, at an interval of either two or thirteen years, depending upon whether a co-regency of eleven years is accepted or not. Now taking into account the generally short expectation of life in the ancient world, it is quite possible that Mose could have carried on his business dealings over a period of fifteen years, but it is stretching coincidence a little far to expect that one of his associates would also still be in the position of a borrower after an interval of thirteen years. Moreover, the two transactions are entered on the same document (Pap. Berlin 9784) by the scribe Tutu one after the other, as though there were little interval between them, and are immediately followed by particulars of another deal with a different client in the following year, suggesting that this papyrus lists Mose's business transactions as they fell over a period of time and is not a register of his exclusive dealings with Neb-mehy. It will be noted then that the interval between the first and second deal is ostensibly thirteen years while that between the second and third is but one year or even less, if the change in regnal year fell between the two dates. The woman Henut whose services were hired in Year 27 is called upon again in Year 3, a record of fourteen years as a slave, which is possible but unlikely in the Late Bronze Age when the average expectation of life was low.

No less significant is the fact that some of the witnesses to the first document in Year 27 were also witnesses in Years 2 and 3, a remarkable case of general longevity, if there were no co-regency, even if allowance is made for a profusion of one or two common names. The names of the

herdsmen Aper and Nanu occur several times in these papyri, and it is to
be suspected that they were closely related to the herdsman Mose. That
they would also still be with him after thirteen or fifteen years is again
possible but rather too coincidental to be probable.

It should be noted, too, that none of Mose's transactions was a simple
barter of goods such as a bronze bowl for a web of linen or several pots
of oil. A *present* commodity belonging to Mose was exchanged for a
future service or yield promised by his debtors and these contracts were
drawn up to safeguard his interests. That they were necessary is shown by
the *procès-verbal* (Pap. Berlin 9785) where the accused was found guilty of
failing to carry out his part of the bargain made with Mose. But once
the service had been rendered, the reason for keeping records of these
transactions must have vanished, and that they should need to be written
retrospectively and not as each contract was made seems incredible. The three
scribes who drew up these documents use different but consistent systems
of dating. Tutu of Ghurab (?) changes from the regnal years of Akhenaten
after Year 27 of Amenophis III; Wen-nefer of Abusir el-Melek dates both
his papyri to regnal year 33 of Amenophis III; and To of Ghurab dates his
procès-verbal to Year 4 of Akhenaten. The evidence of these papyri, as the
writer sees it, is strongly in favour of the appointment of a co-regent soon
after regnal year 27 of Amenophis III.

Further evidence that the co-regency was established around regnal
year 30 of Amenophis III comes from the tomb (No. 55) at Qurna of the
Southern Vizier Ramose. This man is represented on reliefs carved on the
rocks at Konosso and again at the Island of Biga worshipping the names of
Amenophis III; and the concensus of opinion has therefore been that he
was appointed the successor of the Vizier Amun-hotpe late in the reign of
Amenophis III and continued in office under Akhenaten. On the left-hand
side of the rear wall of the great columned hall of his tomb, No. 55,
Ramose is shown in delicate low relief presenting the traditional bouquet to
the young King at his advent. On the opposite half of the same wall
is a scene of the Investitute of Ramose by Akhenaten and Nefert-iti
from a Window of Appearances—the first version of a theme that was
to become so popular during the new reign and is a feature of the tombs
at Amarna. In contrast to the reliefs in the rest of the hall which are in
the purest traditional style of the reign of Amenophis III, this scene
of the investiture is in the bizarre and distorted manner of the extreme
Atenist style, and the dramatic impact of the old and the new, the orthodox
and the revolutionary in juxtaposition can still be felt even at this distance of

Plate 42

Fig. 2
Plate 43

Plate 119

Fig. 2

time. The scene of the investiture has been sketched on the wall in ink and has been partly cut, but before it could be fully carved in relief, all work on the tomb ceased. Most authorities are of the opinion that this cessation was due to a decision by the King to abandon Thebes for Amarna, whither Ramose is supposed to have removed himself.

This view, however, has been greatly undermined in recent years when dockets were published from the Malkata Palace showing that Ramose donated at least four jars of ale for the First Jubilee of Amenophis III in his regnal year 30. So far from succeeding to office on the death of the (Northern) Vizier Amun-hotpe in Year 35, he must have run in double harness with him. The reliefs at Sulb also show the two Viziers officiating at the jubilee celebrations of Amenophis III in Year 30. No more is heard of Ramose. He contributed nothing to the jubilee festivals of Years 34 and 37 held at Thebes, although he was Mayor of that city. He was also conspicuously absent on another important occasion in Year 31 when his close relative Amenophis-son-of Hapu was endowed with a mortuary temple at Thebes by royal decree. There were present at this ceremony the Governor of the City and Vizier Amun-hotpe and the overseer of the Treasury Mery-Ptah besides the army scribes. The most extraordinary member of this body is Amun-hotpe who was poaching on the preserves of his Southern colleague by officiating as Vizier at a Theban function. As the edict speaks of the King actually being in the mortuary temple where he summoned the high officials to him, there is no doubt that the function took place on Theban soil. The inference to be drawn from these notable silences is that Ramose had died soon after Year 30; otherwise we have to postulate that he was appointed Vizier before the First Jubilee of Amenophis III and thereupon faded completely from the scene only to reappear nine years later to be reappointed to the same high office by the new king Akhenaten whom he served until the move from Thebes to Amarna took

Plate 115

place. It should be added that there is absolutely no trace of Ramose at Amarna, where Nakht officiated as Vizier.

Strong proof that Ramose died about Year 30 of Amenophis III is afforded by tomb No. 55 which was surely granted to him on his appointment as Vizier and which was largely incomplete and still in process of

Plate 75

being decorated at the time of his disappearance when work on the relief of the Investiture stopped. The tomb was then hastily prepared to receive its owner and a wall of the main hall which had been started in relief was

Plate 76

finished in colour. Among the mourners shown in the procession are the four Prophets of Amun. All are designated by their titles only, with one

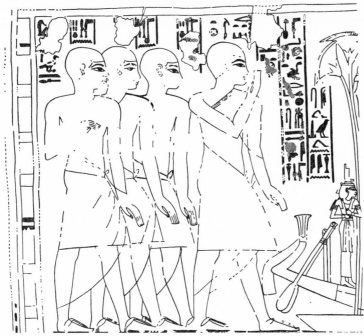

5 *Copy in line of a painting on the south wall of the tomb of Ramose, showing the Four Prophets of Amun, the last of whom is named as Si–Mut, though the names of Mut and Amun have been erased*

exception—the Fourth Prophet of Amun whose name can be read with certainty as Si-Mut though it has been damaged. This official is well known, and why his name alone of all the others should have been included in the tomb will remain an enigma. He may have been related to Ramose, though he is more likely to have been a member of the widespread Yuya family.[21] On the other hand, he was responible *ex officio* for all kinds of building activities in Thebes; and it is probable that having been commissioned by either of the kings to finish off the tomb of Ramose, he took the opportunity of securing a little immortality on his own account by adding his name to his figure in the funerary scene, much as Anen had done when preparing his mother's burial furniture (see p. 80). It is known from his other memorials that Si-Mut advanced to the position of Second Prophet under Amenophis III before he died, and this promotion came about the time of the King's Second Jubilee or a little after it.

It will hardly escape the reader's attention that this posthumous completion of the tomb of Ramose must have been made while Si-Mut was still in a position in the hierarchy of Amun which he relinquished later in the reign of Amenophis III. Akhenaten, therefore, who is shown in this tomb

Fig. 5

as a young king appointing Ramose to office at his advent, must have come to the throne while his father was still reigning; and if the arguments *ex silentio* have any force, this was before Year 31 when Ramose was presumably dead. Two years must perhaps be allowed for such a large tomb as No. 55 to be hewn out of the hill of the Sheikh Abd el-Qurna even in its incomplete state, and it looks therefore as though Akhenaten was appointed co-regent about Year 28 of his father's reign and entered upon sole rule in his twelfth regnal year.

This event is what appears to be recorded in two tombs, probably among the last to be cut, in the northern cliffs at Amarna, one belonging to Huya who had replaced Kheruef as the Steward of Queen Tiye, and the other belonging to Mery-Re, the Steward of Queen Nefert-iti. These two men rose to importance later in the reign of Akhenaten, and as the late form of the name of the Aten only appears in these tombs, they must date to after Year 9. In both tombs there is a scene which is represented nowhere else at Amarna and Thebes and shows the Royal Family attending the great *durbar* at Akhet-Aten. Each of the two different versions of the scene is accompanied by a similar text which is the only one in the Amarna tombs to bear a precise date—Year 12, second month of Winter, Day 8. It goes on to speak of the King making a state appearance on the Great Throne in order to receive gifts from Syria and Kush, the East and the West, collected at the same time and from the islands in the Mediterranean, in order that 'he should grant them the breath of life.' The nature of this tribute from all the nations of the contemporary world shows that this was no parade of plunder from some successful raid; and if it were annual tribute or the products of foreign trade represented with typical one-sidedness as tribute, why should the impost of the Year 12 be singled out for representation in this way? Why also does such a theme not appear in the earlier tombs at Akhet-Aten, when it is obvious from similar scenes in Theban tombs throughout the Dynasty that such a subject was a favourite choice of the tomb-owner, doubtless because he is invariably shown at the acme of his career presenting the tribute to the king?

The writer has sought to show that such scenes are entirely concerned with the great *durbar* that occurred after the Pharaoh had taken his place upon the throne and received homage and gifts not only from his own people but from foreign nations as well. He in turn gave them his divine blessing, granting them that breath by which they lived (see p. 25). The occasion was one of great joy and jubilation and release from anxiety. We see these feelings expressed in the two scenes in question where youths

Plate 44

Plate 77

engage in boxing, singlestick fencing, wrestling, running, dancing and hand-clapping; such games are represented elsewhere as taking place during similar functions such as the jubilee of a Pharaoh.

The writer has little doubt that the scenes carved in the tombs of Mery-Re and Huya, and so precisely dated, commemorate the accession to sole rule of Akhenaten on the death of his father, when foreign potentates recognized him as their new correspondent and sent him appropriate gifts according to time-honoured custom.

That this event took place in his regnal year 12 appears to be supported by other evidence. In one of the Amarna Letters (Kn. No. 27) Tushratta writes to the Pharaoh in such terms as to infer that the latter has just ascended the throne and mentions the celebration of mourning which the Mitannian messengers were to attend in order to bring their condolences to the king of Egypt. This latter is one of the very few in the archive which is dated by a docket written in ink on the edge of the tablet by the Egyptian filing clerk. Unhappily, the hieratic text is broken at the beginning just where the year number occurs and only a 2 can be recognized for certain. Now Professor Erman, the great German philologist, read this text in 1889 soon after the tablet entered the Berlin Museum and in advance of any careful decipherment of the cuneiform message that it bore. Without any prompting he stated that the number was $X + 2$, since 'before the 2 a 10 may stand.'[22] When the letter was translated more fully and carefully it was clear from the context that it dated from Akhenaten's accession to the throne on the death of his father; and since the docket spoke of it as being a copy of the letter which the Mitannian messengers brought while the King was residing in a palace at Thebes, it appeared to belong to his earliest years before he had moved to Amarna. Year 2 was therefore considered the correct date, since no one at that time envisaged that a long co-regency between Akhenaten and his father was possible. In the published facsimile of the docket the lacuna has been foreshortened, and Gardiner, who worked entirely from this copy, had no doubt that Year 2 was the only translation because there was not space enough to write a 10 in front of it. Erman, however, was a most careful scholar, who seldom fell into error except when he listened to others; and if he saw that the year was possibly 12 when it superficially was more obviously 2, then there is warrant for taking his reading very seriously. Professor Richard A. Parker has examined the docket with great care, from recent photographs of the side and top of the tablet, and is satisfied, as he told the writer, that before it was broken there was space enough to write a 10 in front of

Plate 117

the 2. Erman, in fact, had good reason for seeing a 10 in front of the 2, since the bottom of the left-hand stroke of the 10-sign appears to be visible and takes a slight hook to the right as it should do in the hieratic script of this period[23]. The date of this docket shows that Akhenaten was staying temporarily in Thebes some few days before the *durbar* at Akhet-Aten and this accords well with the belief that he was in Thebes to attend the burial ceremonies of his father in the Biban el-Moluk.

To argue that the letter belongs to Year 2 because the new king was residing at Thebes in the first years of his reign is to accuse the Egyptian scribe of stating the obvious. All such documents, even copies, in that early period of the reign would be known by every scribe to belong to the time when the king was living at Thebes, and such information would have been particularly otiose. If a special note was taken of the fact that when letter No. Kn. 27 was received, the King was in a palace at Thebes, that can only denote that it was not his normal place of residence (see also Chapter XI).

Plate 37

While the evidence therefore suggests that Akhenaten did not enter upon sole rule until his regnal year 12, it is less clear when the co-regency started. The highest date yet found for the reign of Amenophis III is Year 38, inscribed on sixteen potsherds from the Malkata Palace, and as three types of label are dated to the last three months of that year, the presumption is strong that the old king lasted into his thirty-ninth regnal year. If this were the year of his death and also that of the accession to sole rule of Akhenaten, then Year 28 must have been the date of the co-regent's accession. It may be, however, that Amenophis III lived some time after his thirty-ninth regnal year and did not visit the Malkata Palace again in his lifetime after Year 38. Such a conclusion would be more satisfactory to some students since it would explain the significance of a somewhat cryptic graffito, scribbled on a wall of the chapel of the pyramid at Meydum and dated to Year 30 of Amenophis III, which speaks of the placing of the male offspring upon his father's throne and establishing his inheritance in the land. This has been taken by some scholars to refer to the appointment of a co-regent in Year 30. It would also account for a reign of thirty years and ten months accorded by Manetho, as reported by Josephus, to an Amenophis usually taken to be Amenophis III.[24]

31 Part of the wall paintings in the Theban tomb of Menna, earlier reign of Amenophis III, showing in the upper register scribes with standard-length cords measuring the standing crops. Below they record the yield for tax levies, as workers measure out the winnowed grain, either barley or emmer wheat, with standard tubs

32 Part of the wall paintings in the greatly wrecked and usurped tomb of Anen (*see* Plate 18) at Thebes, showing the owner's sister, Queen Tiye, seated beside her husband on their thrones beneath a baldachin. On the podium are represented the traditional native and foreign subjects of Pharaoh. Beneath the Queen's throne, her pet monkey, goose and cat disport themselves

33–35 South of Medinet Habu in Western Thebes lie ruins which are popularly known as the 'Malkata'—'the place where things are picked up'. Excavation has shown that it was a vast complex built by Amenophis III containing several palaces. Part of the painted ceiling from the King's robing-room, *left*, echoes the Aegean world with the bucrania between interlocking spirals although the motif is as old as prehistoric Egypt. Other ceilings had a design of birds and butterflies on sky-coloured grounds. *Below*, view across the harim quarters adjoining a columned hall, with plastered brick shelf-supports to the store-rooms. Note the bull emerging from a papyrus thicket, perhaps a recollection of the King's wild cattle hunt in Year 2. On another support a bull-calf dashes through a clump of papyrus in a Helladic flying gallop. Similar calves decorate a palace pot of Malkata type, *opposite*, made in buff pottery painted with designs in pale blue mostly based upon wreaths of leaves and petals (*see also* Plate X)

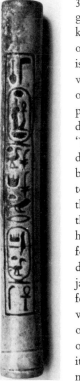

36, 37 *Left*, kohl-tube in bright blue glazed faience probably from the Malkata site. It is inscribed with the names of Amenophis III and Sit-Amun who is described on it as his Chief Wife as well as his daughter. *Right*, fragment of a jar found in a house adjoining a palace at Malkata, with a hieratic docket written on the shoulder reading, 'Year 38 . . . birthday of Osiris (361st day of the Civil year). Dripping from breast-meat of the cattle stable. A gift to His Majesty from the stockyards of the Royal Scribe Ahmose. Prepared by the fat-renderer Yu-Amun.' Many hundreds of such potsherds have been found at Malkata and Amarna carrying dockets giving the date when the jars were sealed, a reference to the festival for which the food or drink was prepared and the names of the officials who gave the commodity, or who were responsible for delivering it, together with the name of the vintner, butcher or other supplier

38–41 Scenes from the Theban tomb of Kheruef, the High Steward of Queen Tiye. *Above*, a drawing of a relief showing Amenophis III with officiating priests pulling cords to raise the *Djed*-fetish to an upright position, a rite which was performed at the dawn preceding the beginning of winter. Left, he makes an offering to the *Djed* within a shrine. The *Djed*-pillar was an ancient fetish symbolizing the resurrection of the new vegetation from the dead herbage. At Memphis it was associated with the city god Ptah and the local death-god Sokar, though its later identification with Osiris produced a triune god of resurrection, Ptah-Sokar-Osiris. The texts accompanying this relief speak of Osiris as well as Sokar as the recipient of the offerings. The entire rite symbolizes the resurrection not only of the old king during his jubilee, but of the dead to a new life

39 Four of the sixteen daughters of Amenophis III in gala robes, pouring libations at ceremonies connected with his Third Jubilee. These can be only a token representation of his numerous progeny

40, 41 *Right*, lower part of a damaged relief on the right-hand wall of the entrance showing a standing man wearing a long gown, bull's tail and sandals and a panther-skin over his jewelled apron. His hanging arm is clasped by the woman who stands beside him. The upper part has been largely replaced by the Oriental Institute, Chicago, to show the man wearing a White Crown flanked by plumes. Two cartouches of Akhenaten facing those of his father were found in the debris fallen from this part of the wall, together with epithets describing Amenophis III as 'beloved of Sokar'. The pair thus prove to be Amenophis III and Tiye in the costume of the living gods to whom their son makes an offering. *Below*, Lintel over the entrance showing half of a double scene with Amenophis IV, right, and his mother Queen Tiye burning incense before Atum of Heliopolis, enthroned with Hat-Hor of Thebes standing beside him. Behind the deities is the *prenomen* of the King described as 'the image of Horus of Edfu'

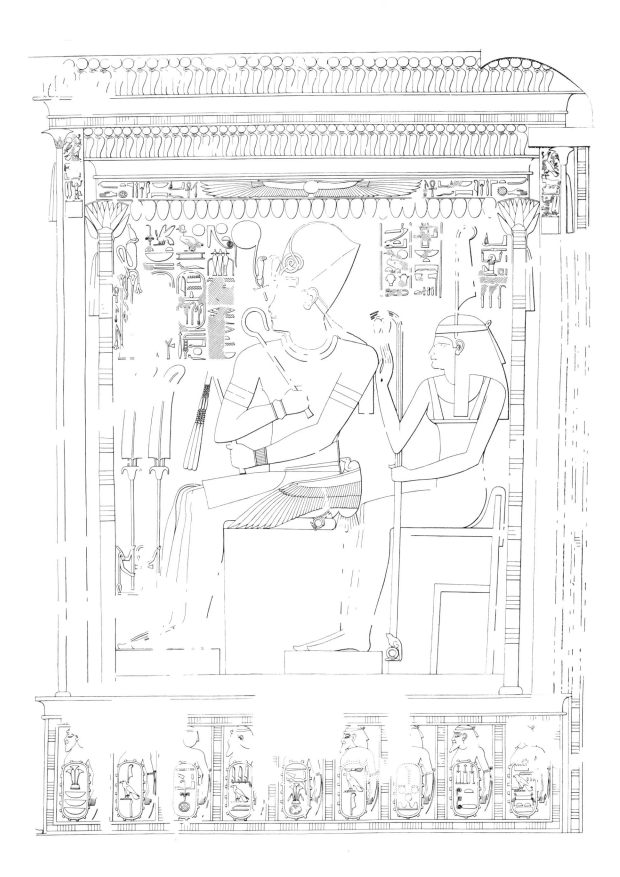

42, 43 Drawings by Norman Davies of reliefs on opposite sides of a doorway in the west wall
of the great hall in the tomb of Ramose (*cf*. Plates 75, 76). *Opposite*, Amenophis IV appears on his
throne under the state baldachin (*cf*. Plate 32) accompanied by the goddess Maet who grants him an
'eternity of rule'. A continuation of the scene shows Ramose presenting a 'bouquet of Herakhty',
evidently on his appointment as Vizier, at the King's advent. This relief, in the pure classical style
of the reign of Amenophis III (*cf*. Plates 39, 75) is completely carved. *Above*, the Palace Window
of Appearances with Amenophis IV and Nefert-iti leaning out while Ramose prostrates himself
(*see Fig.* 2). This relief, in the revolutionary new style that appears with the rayed disk of the Aten
(*cf*. Plate 47), is sketched in line and only partly carved

44   Drawing by Norman Davies of a relief in the tomb of Mery-Re at Amarna showing the great
durbar of Year 12. Akhenaten and Nefert-iti sit on their thrones holding hands under a baldachin
while their six daughters stand behind. Meryt-Aten and Meket-Aten are old enough to wear
their hair long showing that they have reached puberty (*cf*. Plate 93). The latter turns to Ankhes-
en-pa-Aten to smell the mandrake fruit (now lost) held to her nose (*cf*. Plate 9), Nefer-neferu-Aten-

ta-sherit holds up a baby gazelle, while her sister Nefer-neferu-Re has a similar pet in her arms
which Sotpe-en-Re tickles with her fore-finger. Before them, high officials present the delegates of
Nubia and Kush who bring products including slaves and captives, which were often included in
the gifts sent by foreign rulers to Pharaoh, while games are held in celebration. A continuation
of this relief shows the northern tribute-bearers from Asia and the Aegean

45, 46　Two fragments of sandstone relief found built into the Xth Pylon at Karnak. *Above,* Re-Herakhty appearing on the left, as a falcon-headed man wearing the sundisk encircled by a uraeus. His name is in its early didactic form but not enclosed within two cartouches. On the right Amenophis IV makes an invocation below a symbol of the sun-god with *ankhs* (life-signs) radiating from its disk and having *uraei* with *ankhs* hanging from their necks. The relief must come from the sanctuary of the great temple of the Aten, the building of which began almost immediately with the King's advent (*see* p. 66). The drawing is in the traditional style of the reign of Amenophis III. The Aten symbol *(below),* now appears as a radiating sundisk encircled by a uraeus having an *ankh* around its neck and accompanied by a titulary and its name in two large cartouches (*see* Plate 105). In a double scene Amenophis IV censes his god. His *nomen* has been altered from its early Amenophis form to Akhenaten. Although the relief is not in the style that appears with the advent of the Aten sundisk, there is surely an attempt in the over-grown jaw, pot-belly and prominent buttocks to render the curious anatomy of the King, albeit in a very discreet manner

47 Fragment of a hard crystalline limestone balustrade from the Broad Hall of the Great Palace excavated by Petrie at Amarna in 1891, showing the features of the revolutionary art-style at its most extreme. Akhenaten and Nefertiti offer libations to the Aten, whose rays terminate in hands, two of which hold the breath of life to their nostrils (*cf.* the *ankhs* in Plate 45). The eldest princess shakes her sistrum behind them. The King appears with a lined face, receding forehead, hanging jaw, thick lips, arched scrawny neck, pronounced breasts and buttocks, bulbous hips, inflated thighs and thin, spindle-shanks. This pathological anatomy is shared by his entourage to a lesser extent (*cf.* Plates 84, 88)

48 Fragment of sandstone relief from the Aten temple at Karnak with the figure of a queen holding a fly-flapper. The drawing is in the revolutionary style of the great mass of this dismantled temple and the carving is summary, as befits the granular nature of the rather coarse stone and the haste in which it was evidently worked. The queen represented, however, has none of the exaggerated angular features of Nefert-iti found on other fragments from this same temple, and has been most plausibly identified as Tiye, her slight double chin and down-turned mouth being unmistakable

49 Limestone slab, probably from the Aten temple at Karnak showing Amenophis IV taking part in jubilee celebrations as an officiating priest. He wears the short archaic cloak of the Heir or 'Great One of the God' and, like other officials, a fillet, the ends of which hang down behind. Left, he offers to the rayed Aten above an altar within a roofless shrine (cf. Plate 105). On the right carrying sceptres he walks in procession preceded by priests, the second of whom is a chief lector, and followed by a third carrying his staff and sandals and a box to contain them. This last officiant is described as the First Prophet of the King, who must therefore have had a personal cult as a god. The name of the King has been altered from its Amenophis form, showing that the relief belongs to his early reign, doubtless to the period of the First Jubilee of the Aten (and probably also of Amenophis III). The ill-cut inscription within the shrine indicating that the Aten now resided at Akhet-Aten must also have been added later

50 Relief in the Theban tomb of Kha-em-het, Overseer of the Granaries of Egypt, showing him being rewarded before Amenophis III on the occasion of the First Jubilee. At the right, other recipients await their turn while one chamberlain puts a perfumed ointment cone on Kha-em-het's hair and another loads him with bracelets and ties a collar around his neck from the stock upon the table. In the lower register, participants in the Investiture raise their hands in adoration before the King on his throne. The slight inclination of the head and the pose should be compared with the abject prostration of Ramose at a similar ceremony (*cf. Fig.* 2)

51 Portions of two adjacent blocks from Hermopolis showing a relief of the Queen's state-barge. Aft of the steering oars is a cabin decorated with an unprecedented scene of Nefert-iti in the pose of a Pharaoh smiting a northern foe. A continuation of the lower block shows the forecastle of another barge moored alongside with the design of the King clubbing a helpless foe. A third block from a lower course of the same wall has a cabin decorated with a relief of Akhenaten accompanied by his wife and daughter slaughtering a foreigner. This war-like stance of the Royal Family tends to subvert a pacifist view of Akhenaten's policies

52, 53 Drawing by Norman Davies of a relief on the lintel of an inner doorway in the tomb of Huya at Amarna. *Above left*, Akhenaten and Nefert-iti seated on thrones while four of their daughters wave fans before them. *Above right*, Amenophis III seated left greeting his wife, Tiye, and his daughter Beket-Aten who raise their hands in his praise. Behind are three ladies-in-waiting who balance the procession of princesses on the left. Some scholars interpret this equipoise of the two Courts as indicating a co-regency. Others have argued that the inclusion of Amenophis III in the scene is posthumous. The writer was inclined to agree with the latter opinion but has now changed his views. Huya was an official of Queen Tiye and, in order to give her the prominence that was her due, has shown her apart from her husband in this relief. Her importance is further enhanced by the inscription which is largely concerned with her titles and epithets. The lintel was probably carved therefore during the co-regency

< 54 Limestone stela from Amarna showing the Royal Family within a light kiosk. Nefert-iti sits on a cushioned chair of state with the plants symbolic of the union of Egypt worked *à jour* between the rails. By contrast, Akhenaten sits upon a plain stool. Their feet rest upon foot-stools. Akhenaten kisses Meryt-Aten, while Nefert-iti holds Meket-Aten on her lap. The infant Ankhes-en-pa-Aten climbs on her mother's arm to play with her fillet. Four pairs of wine-jars on stands add a festive touch to this scene of domestic bliss. The relief is carved in the bizarre style of the earlier years of the reign

55 Restoration by Norman Davies of a damaged ink sketch on the wall of the tomb of Ahmose at Amarna, showing Akhenaten driving with assurance in the state chariot while Nefert-iti embraces him and Meryt-Aten leans over the bow-case to urge on the horses. The representation is of a peaceful event and may therefore have borne some resemblance to actuality. Although the Pharaoh is shown alone in his chariot in warlike or athletic scenes (*cf.* Plate 13), in reality he was driven by a skilled groom

56 Grey granite statue of the Army Commander, Har-em-hab, from the site of the temple of Ptah at Memphis. In his role of King's Scribe he is writing a hymn to Thoth, the god of learning, on the papyrus roll he holds on his lap. Some scholars identify him with the general Pa-Aten-em-hab, whose modest tomb had only been started at Amarna, and assume that he changed his name on the removal of the Court from Akhet-Aten. Though this is possible, the rise of Har-em-hab to a position of major importance in the State dates from the reign of Tut-ankh-Amun when, like other high officials of the day, he was granted a tomb at Sakkara near the Residence at Memphis. This tomb was decorated with magnificent reliefs in which he appeared in his capacity as a great officer of State, but when he became King a uraeus was added to his figure, even though the tomb was abandoned for one at Thebes (*see* Plate 77)

57 Grey granite statue of Har-em-hab as King with his Queen, Mut-nodjme. On her side of the throne is a recumbent winged female sphinx receiving her name, perhaps a Helladic importation or a representation of Tefnut (*see* Plate 89). The relief on the King's side of the throne, showing traditional foreign subjects bound beneath him, is summarily carved, probably because the statue was so sited that it was impossible for the sculptor to finish this relief in detail. The inscription on the back of the throne hints that Har-em-hab was inducted into the Kingship as 'eldest son of Horus', an unusual phrase implying that he was adopted as co-regent by the reigning Pharaoh

VIII

The Pathology of Akhenaten

THE EARLY TRAVELLERS who found their way to Amarna and visited its rock tombs may well be pardoned for thinking that the figure of Akhenaten was that of a woman; and two queens were depicted together in the reliefs. He is represented with the same elegant swan-like neck, broad hips, swelling breasts and plump thighs as Nefert-iti. Since he frequently wears a long gown similar to a woman's, figures of the King have often been confused with those of the Queen, especially when his characteristic headgear has been destroyed, or he wears the same kind of short wig as is frequently sported by his womenfolk. The feminine nature of Akhenaten's physique is well illustrated in the torsos from the broken statues which the young Howard Carter found in the ruins of the Great Temple at Amarna. It is quite impossible to decide on anatomical grounds alone whether they represent the King or Nefert-iti.

Plates 5, 6, 54

Plate 88

Between the wars, excavations at Thebes uncovered parts of the huge temple to the Aten which Akhenaten erected at Karnak in the earliest years of his reign, and these include several remarkable colossal statues of the King which are unparalleled in Egyptian art for their grotesque distortion of the human form. Most Egyptologists have eyed them askance and while obliged to note their peculiarities, have failed to comment on their full significance apart from dismissing them as 'frankly hideous.' John Pendlebury, however, quite properly described them as 'a wonderful pathological study', though it is a pity that he had no chance to expand his views.

Plates 2–4

The most remarkable of these colossi shows the King entirely naked without any signs of genitalia, a deficiency that cannot be due to reasons of prudery. Though the Egyptians were extremely reticent in showing their kings without a covering for the loins, certain examples have survived in which the Pharaoh is represented naked with his sexual organs faithfully delineated. Indeed, as he was in essence a fertility king, whose seminal powers were implicit in one of his titles, 'The Strong Bull,' a Pharaoh without a phallus is almost a contradiction in terms. There have been various attempts to explain away this colossus. It has been postulated, for instance, that metal clothing was to be fitted (for which no attachments are traceable), though

Plate 2

why that should induce the sculptor to omit the sexual member is not explained. Another theory has been advanced that Akhenaten wished in this statue to translate a theological concept, often expressed in the Amarna texts, that the King, the Son of the Aten, is an image of his divine father. The Aten could not be represented except by the symbol of the rayed disk, but the royal statues could in some way replace the image of the god. As the latter is often called the mother and father of men, this colossus expresses the idea of the bi-sexuality attributed to the Creator. Ingenious as this suggestion may be, it will not withstand close examination. Tuthmosis III is called the 'father and mother of mankind', but he is never represented as anything else than a virile conquering king. It is doubtful in fact whether the Aten concept of bi-sexuality means anything more than that he was self-engendered, a quality that had long been attributed to the sun-god Atum who had impregnated himself in order to create the Universe. Moreover, in choosing to have himself portrayed in such an effeminate and bizarre form, Akhenaten stipulated that certain peculiar traits should be emphasized which are not without their significance.

It was not simply that Akhenaten had himself represented as effeminate or as a hermaphrodite; he specified certain distortions that belong neither to normal women nor men. In an exaggerated form these are the abnormalities that have enabled a number of pathologists independently to diagnose that the subject represented in this way may have suffered from a disorder of the endocrine system; more specifically from a malfunctioning of the pituitary gland.

All the indications are that such peculiar physical characteristics were the result of a complaint known to physicians and pathologists as Fröhlich's syndrome. Male patients with this disorder frequently exhibit a corpulence similar to Akhenaten's. The genitalia remain infantile and may be so embedded in fat as not to be visible. Adiposity may vary in degree but there is a typical feminine distribution of fat in the region of the breasts, abdomen, pubis, thighs and buttocks. The lower limbs, however, are slender and the legs, for instance, resemble 'plus-fours.'

Fröhlich's syndrome may arise from a number of causes, but among the commoner is a tumour of the pituitary gland which controls the gonadal characteristics of animals, including human beings. Lesions in the area of the pituitary often interfere with the adjacent hypothalamus, and *vice versa*, and this may affect the adiposity of the patient. At an early stage of the complaint there may be a fugitive over-activity of the pituitary which can lead to such distortions in the skull as an excessive growth of the jaw, but

Plate 12

Plate 3
Plates 6, 47

Plates 4, I

this is followed by a sub-normal functioning of the gland and by hypogonad-ism. The diagnosis of Fröhlich's syndrome may only be made when the patient, having reached the age of puberty, fails to develop normally, his voice stays shrill, body hair does not appear and his sexual organs remain infantile. Moreover, as tumours in this gland are rare before puberty, the onset of the disorder may occur at the same time as adolescence. A later stage of the complaint is the plumping out of breasts, abdomen, buttocks and thighs. An occasional concomitant is hydrocephalus which because it has arisen when the bones of the skull have hardened and closed does not distort the cranium to the usual globular shape, but results in a bulging of the thinner parietal areas.

Plate 85

The pathological condition in which Akhenaten chose to have himself represented is shared to a lesser extent by all his family and entourage. Unfortunately no portrait of Akhenaten with his head bare has come to light—it is invariably concealed under a wig or crown. But it is to be suspected that it, like the rest of the peculiar Amarna anatomy, was the ideal shape which his artists were bidden to portray. It is probable that Akhenaten had an unusual platycephalic skull, like those of Tut-ankh-Amun and Smenkh-ka-Re, a trait which they doubtless inherited through their ancestor Yuya. But if the representation of the princesses' shaven skulls, as revealed in statues and reliefs are but a reflection of the ideal which Akhenaten sanctioned in portrayal of the royal head, they go far beyond the unusual. The exaggerated shape of the skulls of these princesses is such that it is legitimate to wonder whether they, or the pattern after which they were modelled, did not suffer from a form of hydrocephalus.

Fig. 2

Plate 79

Plates 84, 85

Such a violent departure from the whole idealistic nature of Egyptian portraiture could have been made only at the Pharaoh's insistence, since no artist would have dared to produce such an unflattering portrait of his king even if it had occurred to him to flout all the traditions of his hereditary craft. Bek, the Chief Sculptor of Akhenaten, makes this clear in a relief on the rocks at Aswan where he described himself as having been taught by the King. Attempts have been made to explain the peculiar art-style of the reign as a kind of 'expressionism,' embodying the same revolutionary ideas which the king promoted in the spheres of religion and society. It needs to be emphasised, therefore, that Akhenaten did not alter a single convention of traditional Egyptian drawing. The human figure continued to be rendered by the artist in precisely the same visual terms as had persisted from archaic times when Egyptian art crystallized out at a conceptual stage of its development in the service of the divine king, and adhered to the same conventions for as long as kingship lasted. Akhenaten's innovations were mostly in the choice of subject-matter: style remained unchanged in its fundamentals and consisted in the faithful acceptance of all the old conventions with the wilful distorting of some of them. These distortions are limited to representations of the human figure and then only to those of the Royal Family. His followers also hastened to have themselves depicted in the same fashionable mode as their 'god who had made them,' though mostly to a lesser extent. Soldiers, servants, the common folk and foreigners are shown without these stigmata of the elect, albeit their proportions and often careless drawing are in the manner of the art of the period.

Plate 79

Fig. 2

Fig. 1

It is strange that the 'expressionism' that Akhenaten introduced into Egyptian art should take the form only of showing the human figure as though it were exhibiting in an exaggerated degree the abnormalities of an endocrine disorder. As it is the figure of the King that shows these traits to the most marked extent, there is warrant for thinking that he suffered from Fröhlich's syndrome and wished to have himself represented with all those deformities that distinguished his appearance from the rest of humanity.

Plates 42, 45

The earliest reliefs from his reign, show him in the pure and orthodox style of Amenophis III. These representations, therefore, are usually taken to indicate that in his first years on the throne he did not depart from the artistic and religious traditions of his father, which promoted the Pharaoh as the ideal king, normal, nay, perfect. On the other hand, they may indicate that at his advent as a young co-regent, probably at the age of manhood, he did not exhibit to a gross extent those outwards signs of the disorder that became so conspicuous after a year or two of rule. A relief

Plate 46

in the Louvre, which from its style belongs to the early pre-revolutionary phase though it shows the Aten as a rayed sun-disk, represents Akhenaten with a heavy jaw and pronounced paunch and buttocks. These are clear, if somewhat moderated, signs of those physical peculiarities which very shortly were to be emphasised in a blatant manner, if indeed they were not already being exhibited on contemporary monuments in the new style.

There is, however, a serious obstacle in the way of attributing to Akhenaten a disorder such as Fröhlich's syndrome, which has deterred pathologists from being more categorical in their diagnoses. Akhenaten is unique among the Pharaohs in having himself represented as the family man. He seldom appears except in the company of his wife and some or all of her six daughters. How can so uxorious a husband and so philoprogenitive a parent have suffered from Fröhlich's syndrome which of necessity would have rendered him impotent and passive?

To one or two students of the period, it has appeared that in such an ostentatious parade of his family life Akhenaten was protesting too much; and they have had their private reservations about his fatherhood. In the first place, despite Akhenaten's extraordinary display of affection for the daughters of Nefert-iti, he never explicitly claims to be their father. Each bears the title of the King's Daughter, and it has gone without question that the King is Akhenaten, but that is merely an inference. In only one place is Akhenaten said to be the father of one of them, but this is in a text which originally concerned Nefert-iti as the wife of Akhenaten and has been changed to refer to Meryt-Aten, the expunged titles of the Queen being replaced by stereotyped phrases referring to the princess. The affiliation which has resulted is highly suspect and should be disregarded.

There is the same ambiguity about Akhenaten's being the father of the child of Ankhes-en-pa-Aten. This infant has been referred to above (see p. 95) and the proximity of Akhenaten's name in the same incomplete text has resulted in his being credited with the paternity of the little princess, though the father is not explicitly stated. Similarly the paternity of Meryt-Aten's daughter has been imputed to him, though as she was the wife of Smenkh-ka-Re, it is possible that the latter was the child's father[25].

If Akhenaten was the virile progenitor of all these princesses, both daughters and grand-daughters, it is curious that although the palace harim is shown in a relief in the tomb of Ay at Amarna and the occupations of its inmates are exposed in some detail, whether in dancing, playing musical instruments, eating a meal or attending to their toilet, there is not a single child or baby in evidence. The fact that Nefert-iti's daughters are described as king's daughters, means only that their father was a king without specifying who he was. In view of the strong probability that Amenophis III was still living at least two years after the youngest had been born, he may with greater likelihood have been their father.

If it should seem preposterous that Amenophis III should have under-taken the marital duties of a sterile co-regent, there are other indications that point in the same direction. Amenophis III departed from age-old custom in espousing his heiress daughter, Sit-Amun, who should by tradition have married the heir-apparent. He also spent his last years, as we know from the Amarna letters, negotiating for princesses from Mitanni, Babylon, Arzawa and elsewhere to enter his harim. He never asked for a spouse in respect of his son or co-regent. After his death, the maintenance of his harim became the responsibility of his successor according to the usual practice but no evidence has survived from the Letters that Akhenaten

Plate 36

asked for the hand of a foreign princess or attempted to employ this instrument of statecraft so commonly used by the Pharaohs of the New Kingdom (see p. 240).

(see p. 240)

Plates 44, 105

Plates 52, 53

While it was normal for princesses to be described as the daughters of a king, whose identity was to be inferred, it is rare for the titles of the mother to be given, and during Dynasty XVIII almost unknown for the mother to be named. Yet whenever the six Amarna princesses are represented on the monuments they are invariably distinguished by full hieroglyphic labels which give not only their titles and names, but those of Nefert-iti also as though to dispel any ambiguity about who their mother was. The exceptional nature of these inflated pedigrees is shown in the Tomb of Huya at Amarna where in the equipoise of the two households, the Princess Beket-Aten, seen in the close company of Tiye, is described merely as 'the King's Daughter, of his loins, Beket-Aten.' It is inferred that her father was Amenophis III, and her mother, Tiye. In contrast, each of her contemporaries in the other royal family depicted in the same reliefs carries the distinctive label, 'the King's Daughter, of his loins, N. born of the King's Chief Wife Nefert-iti,' etc. One is left with the impression that while the father remains the same, the identity of the mother has to be defined in the case of Nefert-iti since she was the junior queen. The close connection of Amenophis III with one at least of the daughters of Nefert-iti is suggested by the fragment of sarcophagus, found in the burial chamber of Meket-Aten in the Royal Tomb at Amarna, and inscribed with the names of Amenophis III and Akhenaten as well as her own. In this connection it needs to be stressed that Amenophis III had died before Meket-Aten.

If Akhenaten was the father of Nefert-iti's six daughters, and in addition kept the usual extensive harims of a Pharaoh, it is surprising that he was unable to beget one son at least who could have been nominated his successor. Instead, he accepted as his co-regent a prince who appears to have been his brother, and this at a time during his reign when he could still be expected to father sons. Was Smenkh-ka-Re appointed as his co-regent because it was obvious that he could never procreate a successor?

Lastly, the copyists of Manetho have perhaps given more than a hint of the peculiar situation in their confused end to the king-list for Dynasty XVIII. Here Amenophis, 'reputed to be Memnon and a speaking statue,' is followed by Orus and then by 'his daughter Acencheres,' who is given a reign of twelve years, one month. The Amenophis in question is generally identified as Amenophis III, and Orus is taken to be either an interpolation, or Amenophis III repeated and misplaced. The daughter Acencheres is much more of a problem but in this greatly corrupted entry it is tempting to see, as Lefébure did many years ago, Akhenaten masquerading as a woman. The reign of twelve years one month should be very near the total span of his rule before Smenkh-ka-Re was inducted as his co-regent. According to the Armenian version of Eusebius, 'Acencheres' ruled for sixteen years, perhaps representing a chronology in which the reign of Smenkh-ka-Re was ignored as being contained within that of his co-regent.

It must be confessed that none of the evidence marshalled above is conclusive. There is, moreover, testimony that tends to subvert the theory that Akhenaten was impotent. During the excavations at Amarna in 1931, a trial-piece was unearthed with what must surely be a portrait of Akhenaten on one side showing him with several days' growth of beard. This seems to confirm that Akhenaten had all the secondary sexual characteristics that have been denied him, though these could, of course, have been provided artificially for an occasion of state mourning.

Plate 83

Again, an unfinished stela from Amarna which has been the subject of some discussion shows two kings seated side by side, the foremost being identified as Akhenaten and the other as his co-regent Smenkh-ka-Re. The homosexual relations between the elder and the younger monarch revealed by this monument have been likened to those subsisting between the Emperor Hadrian and the youth Antinous, and gives significance to the epithet 'beloved of Akhenaten', which Smenkh-ka-Re incorporated into both his cartouches. He also assumed the name of Akhenaten's chief queen Nefert-iti, presumably on her death; and this, and the intimacy so frankly exhibited on the stela by the elder Pharaoh who chucks the younger under the chin, suggest that Akhenaten was the active partner in the relationship. This does not look like the behaviour of a eunuchoid pathic, though it would probably be dangerous to draw far-reaching conclusions from such slender evidence.

Plate 81

The whole problem is not likely to be solved to everyone's satisfaction until the body of Akhenaten comes to light, a most improbable occurrence, or inscriptions turn up which dispel all ambiguities as to his fatherhood, a contingency almost as remote. In all the circumstances, whatever reservations one may have, it seems preferable to accept as a working hypothesis that Akhenaten, despite the exaggerations with which he encouraged his artists to represent his person, did not suffer from an abnormality which was chronic enough to interfere seriously with his sexual activity. He is therefore probably the father of Nefert-iti's daughters and possibly of her grand-daughters as well.

IX

The Occupants of Valley Tomb No. 55

EARLY IN HIS SEASON OF 1907, Theodore M. Davis, an American lawyer and amateur of Egyptology (see p. 17 above) succeeded in uncovering a tomb a few yards west of the tomb of Ramesses IX in the Biban el-Moluk. Now catalogued as Tomb No. 55, it lies on the other side of the path and almost opposite the spot where fifteen years later, when Davis's concession had passed to the Earl of Carnarvon, the tomb of Tut-ankh-Amun was discovered. Davis had some friends with him in 1907, including an American painter, Joseph Lindon Smith, and his wife Corinna, Edward Ayrton as his archaeologist and Arthur Weigall representing the Antiquities Service. They were later joined by an artist Harold Jones.

After clearing a considerable mass of limestone chips thrown out by the ancient masons engaged in cutting Ramesside tombs in the vicinity, the excavators reached an earlier level and were eventually rewarded by striking a flight of twenty-one well-cut stone steps leading to a sealed entrance. This doorway was completely closed by a 'loosely-built wall of limestone fragments, resting not on the rock beneath, but on the loose rubbish which had filled the doorway.' This was unusual and should have made the party pause and reflect. Unfortunately, the evidence is all too clear that instead of proceeding with caution and finesse, these men, two of them at least with specialized training and experience, somehow managed to conduct one of the worst pieces of excavation on record in the Valley. The word 'record' is used only loosely. The official publication is perfunctory in the extreme, no plans nor dimensions are given, the descriptions are slip-shod and in-complete, and the various accounts that the eye-witnesses subsequently gave, sometimes long after the event when their recollections were at fault, are often conflicting where they are not so vague as to be worthless. Where they do correspond, it is to be suspected that the writers have merely cribbed from each other's reports[26].

Behind the dry-stone wall that formed the door to this tomb lay another sealing of rough blocks of limestone set in mortar and coated on the outside with very hard cement bearing impressions of an oval seal, the jackal couchant over nine captives. This device, which often appears on similar tomb-sealings in the Theban necropolis, was found also on the walled-up doorway to the tomb of Tut-ankh-Amun. There it was used only on those areas of the blocking which had been replastered by the necropolis officials when they made good the damage caused by thieves who had tunnelled through the entrance to gain access to the interior of the tomb. The intact portion of the original doorway bore seals giving the name of the royal occupant. In the case of Tomb No. 55, the excavators report only the presence of the seal with the jackal over nine captives, so it would appear that either they failed to notice other seals, or the deposit had been moved thither from its original resting-place and re-sealed. They also omitted to search for foundation deposits, which might have shown for whom the tomb was designed in the first place.

The second walled-up doorway was found to be partly demolished, suggesting that the tomb had been closed after a previous opening, but whether by plunderers or officials on legitimate business could only have been decided by proper excavation and a meticulous study of any clues that lay to hand. If such an investigation was made, it was never reported. The excavators demolished the second doorway and then found themselves in a corridor about six feet wide and filled with clean limestone chips to within some three or four feet of the ceiling at the proximal end and to within six feet at the distal end about thirty feet away. Reposing on this filling a few feet from the entrance was the side of a gilded wooden shrine and on it lay a door, also part of the same shrine, with its copper pivots still in place.

Plate 94

At the other end of the sloping approach corridor was a large oblong room, twenty-one feet long, sixteen feet wide, thirteen feet high, and sunk three feet below the level of its ingress from the sill of which a long broad ramp of stone debris extended into the room. On this second slope of chippings lay a counterpart to the door in the corridor, and a large alabaster vase-stand. Against the opposite wall of the tomb were leaning other parts of the shrine and a second long side lay on the floor with its posts and beams scattered about it. All the woodwork in the tomb was in a very fragile condition and of the large dismantled shrine strewn over the chamber and its corridor, only two fragmentary planks are all that is now exhibited in the Cairo Museum.

Plate 96

Plate 102

The walls of the room had been plastered but not decorated. At its southern end, a start had been made on hewing a second chamber but this had not progressed beyond the stage of forming a deep recess, six feet high, four and a half feet wide and about five feet deep. In it had been placed four

Plate 96

141

Akhenaten

Plate 67 — Canopic jars of polished calcite with exquisitely wrought stoppers in the form of human heads.

Plates 97, 98, XIV — Just outside the recess lay a handsome coffin of a kind which had not been found up to that time; but which we can now see bore a distinct resemblance to the second inner coffin of Tut-ankh-Amun, except that the wig which was of the same type as that represented on the Canopic jars was quite different from the usual funerary royal head-dress. It had been placed on a lion-headed bier, also similar to one which supported the nest of coffins within the stone sarcophagus of Tut-ankh-Amun, but this had collapsed through decay and brought the coffin crashing to the ground, jerking off the split lid and exposing its occupant.

Plates 100, 101 — When the excavators came to clear the tomb of its contents they found a number of small objects strewn among the chippings and rubbish in the corridor and main-chamber, including four 'magic bricks' of a kind which were sealed at the four cardinal points in the walls of royal tombs of this period. Three of them, from the excavators' vague accounts, appear to have been more or less correctly orientated against appropriate walls except for one brick which was found under the bier. In addition, a number of faience vessels, boxes and amulets were found, also the base of a wooden statue, statuettes and model boomerangs in faience and the remains of ritual implements used in burial ceremonies. One stone toilet vase was inscribed with the name of Amenophis III; another with the names of Queen Tiye and Amenophis III whose *nomen* had been erased; and a fragment of wood from a piece of furniture bore the names of the same king and his queen. A stone *pesesh-kef* amulet bore the name of Queen Tiye alone. In the rubbish under the bier and behind the wooden panels leaning against the east wall were found numerous fragments of small clay seals, some of which were impressed with the cartouche of Tut-ankh-Amun.

Plate 94 — It was clear to the excavators that the tomb and its furnishings had suffered damage from two sources. A long crack in the ceiling of the corridor, ineffectually stopped with cement, had allowed rainwater, scouring down the valley floor in the occasional torrents that sweep the area, to seep into the tomb and wreak havoc with most of its contents, chiefly the woodwork and the mummy in the coffin. But in addition, there were evident signs of deliberate destruction wrought by the hand of man. The names on the coffin had been cut out and the gold portrait mask ripped off the lid and removed. Inscribed gold bands which encircled the decayed mummy-wrappings also had had the cartouches excised; and certain figures and names had been hacked out of the reliefs on what was left of the gold-

Plate 98

Plates 95, 102

covered shrine. The uraei on the Canopic jars had been snapped off and
were missing. The amulets on the magic bricks had also been removed.
At the same time it was apparent that this selective destruction was hardly
the work of thieves who would not have left any gold-work behind them
nor bothered to close up the tomb with a new dry-stone blocking. The
tomb, in fact, bore all the signs of having been opened since its original
sealing and its contents deliberately desecrated by removing all traces of
the name and features of the owner, though there were one or two
oversights. Thereafter it had been sealed with a new blocking, care being
taken to leave no stamp nor inscription on it that would serve to identify
the owner.

The burial posed a number of questions to which the excavators offered
radically different answers. Davis had little doubt that although he had
found an incomplete or secondary burial, it was that of Queen Tiye, since
the smaller inscribed pieces bore her name sometimes accompanied by
those of her husband. He insisted that the heads of the Canopic jars were
portraits of Queen Tiye: and a vulture made of sheet gold, which was
found bent around the head of the mummy, was a queen's crown, the same
vulture head-dress shown so frequently in portraits of the royal consorts.
Above all, the undamaged parts of the dismembered shrine were decorated
in relief with figures of the Queen and with her name, and an inscription
on it declared that it had been made for her by Akhenaten, whose name,
however, was erased, though it was clear from the context that it could
only be his.

Weigall, on the other hand, took the view that the bones could not be
those of Tiye, but must be of Akhenaten, and that his burial must have been
hastily removed from Amarna, when that city was abandoned, brought to
Thebes for re-interment and subsequently desecrated. In support of his
theory, he could point to the fact that everywhere in the tomb Tiye's figure
and name remained intact, whereas Akhenaten's had been hacked out except
for some careless omissions. Every name on the coffin and the gold
mummy bands, however, had been excised and the portrait mask removed
from the lid. Moreover, the magic bricks which were designed to protect
the tomb-owner from hostile intruders were inscribed with the cartouche
of Akhenaten on those two specimens which were substantially intact. The
other pair were of a flimsier construction and were greatly decayed and
damaged and their ink inscriptions were illegible. The gold-sheet vulture
amulet over the face was not a crown but the 'vulture collar' of Pharaonic
burials.

Plate 67

Plate IX
Plate 95

Plate 102

Plate 98

Plates 100, 101

The argument became somewhat heated and to settle the matter Davis invited the local European physician at Luxor, and a prominent American obstetrician who was visiting Thebes at the time, to examine the body while it was still *in situ* in its coffin and pronounce upon its sex. The mummy-wrappings had decayed through damp and could be lifted off in great pads exposing the bones from end to end. The pelvis was admitted to be the criterion of sex. It is reported that both surgeons instantly agreed that it was the pelvis of a woman. This opinion seemed to vindicate Davis' beliefs and he published his account of the excavations of 1907 under the title of *The Tomb of Queen Tiyi*.

The bones, together with the decayed mummy-wrappings and gold bands,[27] were sent to Elliot Smith, then Professor of Anatomy in the Cairo School of Medicine; but when Smith came to examine them in July 1907, he found to his intense surprise that instead of the body of an old woman that he had been led to expect, he had been sent the remains of a young man who had apparently died at the age of twenty-three or twenty-five since among other features, certain epiphyses had not united with their bones. Elliot Smith soon found himself engaged in controversy not only with Davis and his supporters for denying that the bones were those of Tiye, but also with several Egyptologists for asserting that they were those of Akhenaten, since they found it impossible to crowd all the momentous events of the 'Heretic's' reign into so short a life-span. A way out of the difficulty was suggested by Norman de Garis Davies who identified the bones as those of Smenkh-ka-Re whose memory was persecuted in the same way as Akhenaten's. Elliot Smith considered this, but was obviously much influenced by tendentious reports that the coffin and gold bands had borne the names and titles of Akhenaten.

In after years, he attempted to reconcile the anatomical evidence of the bones with the demand for an age at death for them of at least thirty years if they were to be considered as the remains of Akhenaten. Nearly twenty years after his first examination he wrote:

> In considering this difficult problem I naturally turned to consider those pathological conditions which might cause delay in the union of the epiphyses. Of these, the most likely seemed to be the syndrome described by Fröhlich in 1900,... In patients presenting this condition cases have been recorded in which the bones at 36 years of age revealed the condition which in the normal individual they show at 22 or 23, so this suggested the possibility of bringing the anatomical evidence into harmony with the historical data. In support of this solution there are the very peculiar

anatomical features of Akhenaten when alive, which have been made familiar to us by a large series of contemporary portraits,... In the light of our present knowledge, however, they seem to be quite distinctive of Fröhlich's syndrome and afford valuable support to the suggestion that this was the real cause for the delay in the fusion of the epiphyses. In addition to this, the skull—both the brain-case and the face—reveals certain important peculiarities. There is a slight degree of hydrocephalus such as is often associated with Fröhlich's syndrome and also an overgrowth of the mandible, such as may result from interference with the pituitary.

He admitted, however, the difficulty of reconciling his diagnosis with Akhenaten's putative fatherhood.[28]

In 1931, the uneasy acceptance of Elliot Smith's opinions was subverted by a new study of the coffin and its contents. Rex Engelbach of the Cairo Museum had the greatly damaged coffin-lid repaired and restored, during which time he was able to devote close attention to its texts and alterations that had been made to them. Previously, in 1916, the French scholar Georges Daressy had argued that the inscriptions showed that the coffin had first been made for a woman, whom he took to be Queen Tiye, and subsequently adapted for a king. Engelbach now tried to show that the coffin had been made for Smenkh-ka-Re as a private person and modified for him when he became a king. There were thus strong reasons for regarding the bones found in the coffin as those of the young co-regent. At the same time, Professor D. E. Derry, Elliot Smith's successor at Cairo, who had examined the mummy of Tut-ankh-Amun and written the official report on it, published a re-examination of the skeletal remains from Tomb No. 55. He denied that the skull showed signs of hydrocephalus, and claimed that while undoubtedly of unusual shape, it was not abnormal but closely resembled the platycephalic skull of Tut-ankh-Amun. His study of epiphyseal closure in modern Egyptians convinced him that the bones were those of a young man of not more than twenty-three years of age at death, and he accepted that the occupant of the coffin found in Tomb No. 55 must be Smenkh-ka-Re.

Plates 98, XIV

This solution of the problem was accepted generally by Egyptologists with relief. Views which had been advanced almost from the first by Norman Davies and Kurt Sethe could now prevail. The bones were undoubtedly those of Smenkh-ka-Re, and the body of Akhenaten was still to seek with the strong probability that it would never come to light, having been destroyed by his persecutors.

In 1957, the late Sir Alan Gardiner opened the whole case again by publishing a new study of the texts on the restored coffin, and reached the conclusion that there was no reason to believe that the coffin had ever belonged, or was ever intended to belong, to anyone other than Akhenaten. According to him, whatever the anatomical examinations may have disclosed, the archaeological evidence suggested that the people who buried the mummy in Tomb No. 55 believed it was that of the 'Heretic King' himself.

This thesis provoked rejoinders from Professor H. W. Fairman and the writer who, arguing from different standpoints, independently reached the conclusion that the coffin had undoubtedly been designed for a woman of the Royal Family, most probably Meryt-Aten, and subsequently adapted for the person who was found buried in it. On the identity of the occupant, however, their views diverged, Professor Fairman believing it was Smenkh-ka-Re, and the writer, Akhenaten. For the latter opinion there was the archaeological testimony of the magic bricks. Moreover, the several reports, both published and unpublished on the human remains gave grounds for believing that they showed abnormalities which could be reconciled with the peculiar anatomy of Akhenaten as revealed on his monuments. The pathologist Dr A. T. Sandison, and the writer subsequently reviewed the evidence at greater length and offered the conclusion that the monuments suggest that Akhenaten suffered from an endocrine disorder with hypogonadism and the bones found in Tomb No. 55 support a diagnosis of hypogonadism and pituitary cranial dysplasia. They expressed the hope, however, that the skeletal remains should be re-examined with all the resources of up-to-date techniques and knowledge. Their motive in issuing this study was largely to interest the medical profession in the importance of a properly conducted and published investigation in view of the perfunctory, ambiguous and contradictory reports which then prevailed.

Such an examination followed with a rapidity and thoroughness that exceeded all their expectations when in 1963 the anatomists, Professor H. G. Harrison of Liverpool and Professor A. Batrawi of Cairo with the assistance of M. S. Mahmoud, Professor of Radiology in the Qasr el-Aini Hospital, Cairo, subjected the remains to a minute and fully documented investigation which sets entirely new standards in the medical examination of the royal mummies. Evidence in certain parts of the skeleton of a trend towards feminity, consistent with a minimal effect of hypogonadism, was found but it was not sufficiently marked to correspond with the features of eunuchoidism and the sort of physique displayed by Akhenaten on his monuments. The subject was undoubtedly male, and it is possible to be definite that he died in his twentieth year. The form of the facial skeleton and mandible is inconsistent with the appearance of the face and chin represented on the Akhenaten monuments, but closely resembles those of Tut-ankh-Amun.

These findings, which have been accepted by Dr Sandison and the writer, leave no room for doubt that the human remains from Tomb No. 55 are those of Smenkh-ka-Re who died in his twentieth year and was evidently buried in a coffin which originally had been made for his wife but which was adapted to accommodate his fully embalmed corpse. It would also appear that the Canopic jars had been made *en suite* with the coffin for Meryt-Aten's burial and were altered for Smenkh-ka-Re.

Plate 67

It has been suggested that the corpse of Meryt-Aten was removed from this coffin in order that the mummy of her husband should be placed in it. Presumably a similar transposition would have been made of the embalmed viscera in the Canopic jars. To the writer it appears exceedingly improbable that such sacrilegious measures would have been permitted by the Royal Family at this particular period towards their near relatives. We know from the Boundary Stelae that Akhenaten had promised his eldest daughter burial in the Royal Tomb at Amarna, and her funerary equipment would therefore have been prepared from her very first years. The inscriptions on the coffin in fact have features which point to its having been made early in the reign of Akhenaten. When, however, Meryt-Aten did not die as a princess but became the queen of Smenkh-ka-Re, her burial arrangements would have become her husband's responsibility; and he doubtless provided her with new funerary equipment commensurate with her enhanced status. Her old coffins must have been kept in store and it was one of them and the accompanying Canopic equipment that were brought out and re-furbished for the burial of Smenkh-ka-Re.

The rest of the contents of Tomb No. 55 have not received the same attention from Egyptologists as the mummy and coffin and in general have been summarily dismissed. Maspero attempted to explain the presence of the shrine of Tiye in a tomb with the body of a king as the result of confusion on the part of the officials in charge of the removal of the royal burials from Amarna to Thebes. They had put the son where the mother ought to have been. Gardiner thought that at the end of Akhenaten's life the tomb he had prepared for himself at Amarna was mercilessly ravaged and the funerary equipment damaged. Some loyalists, however, hastened to repair the coffin, placed in it the mummy that they believed to be his and took it to Thebes together with the shrine of Tiye which they had also found in the debris of the wrecked tomb and which was to serve the king as a shelter in his final resting-place. In the Biban el-Moluk they were lucky enough to find available an empty tomb, such as in earlier days might have been granted to some non-royal personage, and here they bestowed all the equipment found by the modern explorers. We shall deal with some of these hypotheses later: here we shall limit ourselves to the observation that if the tomb had been 'mercilessly ravaged' the coffins and shrine would have been more extensively damaged and robbed. Since the mummy was encircled by gold bands bearing the titles and name of the owner, and the burial party would have consisted of officials well able to read, the possibility of confusion in the disposal of the bodies can be discounted.

Professor Fairman has produced another explanation. According to him, most of Smenkh-ka-Re's funerary furniture was taken over for the burial of Tut-ankh-Amun since on the latter's death a substantial proportion of his equipment had not yet been prepared, and the deficiency was made up by commandeering material from the tomb of Smenkh-ka-Re which presumably was at Thebes where his funerary temple had certainly been built. A semblance of a decent burial for Smenkh-ka-Re was made by removing him to a convenient but small tomb, putting him in a coffin made for Meryt-Aten, his wife, after the necessary changes had been made, and equipping him with a small and makeshift collection of miscellaneous objects of various royal persons that happened to lie more or less conveniently to hand.

The weakness of this argument, among other things, is that it postulates that Smenkh-ka-Re, an ephemeral co-regent, in his brief reign of about three years was able to acquire a more complete burial equipment than Tut-ankh-Amun in his eight or nine years of rule as sole Pharaoh. It also asks us to believe that the rulers of this period, all closely related to each other, instead of acting as the dutiful son towards their immediate pre-decessors, indulged in an orgy of impiety, desecrating their burials in order to usurp their furnishings. While the royalty of this time may not always have been buried in the trappings they had prepared for themselves, when once they had been interred with due rites, it is difficult to see their descendants provoking what they believed were great malefic powers by such sacrilegious appropriation.

The coffin and Canopic jars of Meryt-Aten had been adapted at some trouble for the burial of Smenkh-ka-Re and there is no warrant, therefore, for thinking that miscellaneous objects would have been put in his tomb without undergoing similar alterations in his favour, unless they had no relevance to his burial. If the magic bricks, for instance, had been intended for Smenkh-ka-Re's burial, they would have been inscribed with his name, not Akhenaten's. Otherwise, they would have been ineffectual to protect him, and the officials in charge of the burial would not have bothered to include them. As they were modest objects, modelled out of mud, and two of them bore rapid inscriptions in hieratic, it is to be presumed that it would have been the work of a few minutes to manufacture a set of bricks for Smenkh-ka-Re and to inscribe them for him. Similarly, if the shrine made for Queen Tiye by Akhenaten in the late years of his reign and bearing his figure and names, were intended for the burial of Smenkh-ka-Re, it would have been re-inscribed for him.

Another explanation which has been offered for the presence of this shrine in the tomb is that it was stored there as surplus equipment no longer wanted, since Queen Tiye was probably buried in furniture prepared for her by Amenophis III. This, however, is equally improbable. A large shrine, made of imported fine woods, and lavishly covered with gold leaf, was an exceedingly costly item and would not have been consigned to oblivion in another's tomb when its metal could have been stripped off and melted down, and the carcase overlaid with fresh gesso and re-gilded for someone else.

Nearly all the experts who have studied the contents of Tomb No. 55 write as though what the excavators found was the entire deposit, whereas it is clear that it represented only a minimal proportion of the equipment originally installed there. For this there is ample proof. The clay seals found scattered over the floor were of a kind that were used to seal boxes and caskets and had evidently been broken off when the lids were prised open to examine the contents. One such box was found in a greatly damaged state in the south-eastern corner, the knob on its lid torn off and missing. It was empty, but a hieratic docket written in ink listed the contents as 'gold vases of the household.' A comparable casket was found in the tomb of Tut-ankh-Amun bearing a similar docket. There were also gold-covered roundels among the rubbish and chippings in the tomb which had fallen from funerary objects which in the tomb of Tut-ankh-Amun were found intact and to these we shall refer shortly.

At this point we shall revert to the shrine, which has been treated by nearly all commentators as though it had been in process of being moved into the tomb when the operation came to a halt. Only Weigall has seen that it was in fact being moved out. The erection of such shrines, as we know from those around the sarcophagus of Tut-ankh-Amun, demanded a prescribed drill with the various marked parts disposed along the tomb walls in a methodical fashion so that they could come together around the sarcophagus or coffins in a properly orientated position with a minimum of handling and effort. It cannot be claimed that the disorderly strewing of parts of the shrine in the main chamber and corridor of Tomb No. 55 supports the view that it was in process of being erected.

Plates 94, 96

There is also another reason why it was not being brought into the tomb at the time of its abandonment. Although the excavators give no details, the construction and proportions of the shrine must have followed closely those of the similar tabernacles enclosing the sarcophagus of Tut-ankh-Amun. From the two planks now exhibited in the Cairo Museum, each six feet long, it can be calculated that the shrine was seven feet three inches wide and six feet two inches high without the cavetto cornice and roof. In other words, it was slightly smaller than the second shrine of Tut-ankh-Amun; and on the same proportions it would be nearly ten feet long at the base. A long side would therefore consist of a panel ten feet long by over six feet high; and it would have been impossible to bring this into the tomb, bearing in mind the slope of the approach staircase, without removing more than four feet of blocking at the entrance, even if the heavy, gold-covered panel were canted as much as thirty degrees to the perpendicular. It was in fact the impossibility of getting a long side out of the tomb without demolishing more of the blocking at the entrance that induced the removers to leave it jammed in the corridor. They had evidently brought out a door without much difficulty but when they decided to leave the shrine in the tomb, they heaved it back on top of the long side.

Plate 92
Plate 102

Plate 94

If, however, the shrine of Queen Tiye was being moved from the tomb at the time of its second closure, we must postulate that the burial of the queen was also housed there originally, as Weigall maintained from the start; and there is other evidence to support this view. A number of small objects inscribed with her name were found among the debris, evidently overlooked during the removal of her goods and chattels, an operation that would have been conducted in an uncertain light since much of the doorway was blocked. Among these was the *pesesh-kef* amulet in schist used in the burial ceremonies and surely, therefore, part of her personal funerary equipment. There were also two large gilded copper marguerites of a kind which have been found in other royal tombs and which in the tomb of Tut-ankh-Amun were sewn on a linen pall covering the second shrine. In Tomb No. 55 these stray roundels must have been torn or lost from a similar pall[29] during the dismantling operations, and this can only have been provided for an important member of royalty.

Nevertheless, while it is probable that a pall was fixed over the coffin of Tiye, there was yet another occupant who may have been resting under a similar canopy. The magic bricks were inscribed with the name of Akhenaten, in so far as the name could be read on two of them: and the only logical conclusion is that they must have been placed there for the protection of that king who was therefore resting in that particular tomb. In fact, it is almost certain that the first action taken by the desecrators on gaining entry to the tomb chamber was to search for the magic bricks and neutralize them by removing their amulets before they felt safe to proceed with the spoliation of the burial. The same motive may account for the removal of the uraei from the Canopic jar lids, though why the heavy bronze uraeus should then have been left on the coffin lid is a mystery. Tiye and her husband never incurred the odium that fell on their sons in after years; and the kings of the next dynasty fully recognized them as legitimate rulers. If Tiye's burial had been reposing alone in the tomb it would probably have been left in peace. The fact that it was moved elsewhere, as we have argued, suggests that there were circumstances which made someone think it proper to house it in another place. Those circumstances, in the writer's view, were the proximity of the burial of the hated 'Criminal of Akhet-Aten' and the Queen's entombment in furniture and among surroundings that were redolent of his heresy.

We may now be in a position to do what the excavators never seriously attempted and that is to piece together the history of this deposit in Tomb No. 55. Queen Tiye must have died some time between Akhenaten's twelfth regnal year and his seventeenth, probably nearer the latter. Amenophis III had almost certainly provided his spouse with a full set of burial equipment in the orthodox fashion of the early years of his reign and if, as some scholars believe, he intended that she should eventually repose in a chamber of his own tomb, the bulk of it was already in position there. Akhenaten probably had other plans for his mother and had provided her with a golden shrine decorated with scenes inspired by the ritual of Aten worship and not with the traditional funerary texts. Whether he provided her with matching equipment is unknown but probable. He apparently intended that she should be buried in the Royal Tomb at Amarna, for according to Engelbach one set of sarcophagus fragments have been recovered from there, bearing the names of Akhenaten and Tiye. She may in fact have been interred in the Royal Tomb before the end of her son's reign.

Plates 100, 101

151

Smenkh-ka-Re almost certainly died before Akhenaten who would then have had to assume responsibility for the burial of his young co-regent. It would appear that Smenkh-ka-Re had already begun to prepare his tomb furniture at Thebes in the traditional style in conformity with the more orthodox views that he seemed to cherish; but this may not have been to the taste of Akhenaten who must have arranged for Smenkh-ka-Re to be buried, perhaps at Amarna, in equipment that expressed the Atenist view of immortality. A coffin made earlier in the reign for his daughter, Meryt-Aten was removed from store and adapted for Smenkh-ka-Re. When the mummy was prepared, the King's arms instead of being flexed over the chest as though to grasp sceptres were arranged in a posture more appropriate to the burial of a woman with the left hand clenched on the breast and the right arm stretched along the side. Whether this was done by order of Akhenaten for one who had borne the name of Nefert-iti (Nefer-Neferu-Aten) during his co-regency can only be conjectured. What seems more certain is that soon after Smenkh-ka-Re had been buried, Akhenaten died too, and his successor was faced with the responsibility of making the funerary arrangements.

As the new Pharaoh, Tut-ankh-Amun, was a mere boy of little more than nine years, it is to be presumed that many of the suggestions if not the decisions in the matter emanated from his advisers. Akhenaten would have had a complete set of funerary furniture prepared for himself from his earliest years and some of it was doubtless already in position in the Royal Tomb at Amarna including such heavy items as his sarcophagus and Canopic chest, but it seems clear that there was never any intention of burying Akhenaten in the tomb he had made for his family at Akhet-Aten. In the writer's view this was not because the equipment had been smashed, as Gardiner suggests, but because the decision had already been taken to abandon Amarna as an ill-omened Residence in favour of a return to Memphis. The idea that there was an execration of Akhenaten and all his works as soon as he had died, or even a little in advance of his death, in the writer's view has nothing to support it. A vicious persecution only began half a century later when the Ramessides were firmly in the saddle and with the characteristic hostility of new dynasts *vis à vis* their immediate predecessors anathematized all the successors of Amenophis III up to Har-em-hab. Certainly the names of Akhenaten and Smenkh-ka-Re were not erased under Tut-ankh-Amun and Ay, who were both closely related to them, and this will have to be taken into account when we weigh the evidence of the obliterated cartouches on the coffin.

Plate 110

While, therefore, Tut-ankh-Amun and his advisers decided to return to the necropolis of their dynasty in the Biban el-Moluk for the burials of members of the royal house, it is doubtful how much of the furniture which Akhenaten had prepared for himself early in his reign was used for his interment. While Akhenaten had accepted a great many traditional funerary customs, he had discarded much that referred to the Osirification of the deceased. He provided himself and Nefert-iti, for instance, with the magic shawabti figures that were to perform menial tasks in the Osirian hereafter, but he excluded from them the appropriate texts. It is in fact doubtful whether his successors believed that Akhenaten, either by his opinions or his personality, could ever be assimilated to Osiris after death, and whether the elaborate burial of a Pharaoh was therefore necessary in his case. Akhenaten, himself, probably had modified his own funerary equipment to exclude the old Osirian beliefs. What is certain is that his heavy Canopic chest and presumably his massive sarcophagus were left behind in the Royal Tomb at Amarna. His mummy was probably encased in a coffin or coffins with a minimum of auxiliary equipment.

Plates 106–108

His was not the only burial for which provision had to be made. The decision to abandon Amarna must have imposed upon Tut-ankh-Amun's officials the task of having to find at short notice a number of tombs at Thebes in which to house the royal burials including those of Nefert-iti, Meket-Aten, Meryt-Aten, Tiye, Smenkh-ka-Re and Akhenaten himself. It is probable that two or three small tombs were hastily prepared in the Theban hills in which to re-inter several members of the family together, since to hew individual tombs of a proper type and decoration in so short a time would have been beyond the State's resources. Tomb No. 55 was put into requisition before the cutting of a second chamber had proceeded very far, but despite the improvised nature of this burial, it was in the writer's opinion a proper interment and not a mere makeshift arrangement. It is probable that although Akhenaten's was considered the main burial, Tut-Ankh-Amun was concerned to make more lavish provision for his mother Tiye and it was her furniture that occupied the bulk of the sepulchral chamber, her nest of coffins being covered by a linen pall sewn with gilded copper roundels and supported on struts within her shrine. Despite the size of her furniture there was still ample room for the coffins of Akhenaten and Smenkh-ka-Re, though it is clear that if they were protected by enclosing tabernacles, they must have been of modest size, no bigger than the fourth shrine of Tut-ankh-Amun, the largest panel of which was seven feet long by four and a half feet high, otherwise they could not subsequently have been removed from the half-opened tomb. There would also have been gilded chests for containing the Canopic jars and presumably other equipment including stone vessels for holding the sacramental oils. Ritual objects used in the burial ceremonies were also provided and a whole range of model furniture in faience. Chests containing gold vessels, clothing and similar possessions were evidently supplied and sealed with the cartouche of the reigning sovereign. It is probable that the burial chamber was stuffed as full of treasure as the 'antechamber' of the tomb of Tut-ankh-Amun was later to be. The protective magic bricks were not forgotten but only two specimens seem to have survived from Akhenaten's original quartet, and they had to be supplemented with thinner east and west bricks hastily moulded out of a different mud and inscribed in ink with texts written in hieratic. When all was in position and the final rites had been concluded with a funerary repast, the sepulchral chamber was blocked off by a dry-stone wall and the passage filled with much of the spoil removed during the process of cutting the tomb. The entrance was sealed with a wall of stones set in mortar, the outer face being smeared with cement and stamped with the 'necropolis' seal.

Some sixty years later, in early Ramesside times, the final act in this drama must have been played. Someone, who can only have been a Pharaoh, evidently decided that Tiye's burial ought to be removed from the polluting presence of Akhenaten, perhaps to the tomb of her husband, and all record of the King and his co-regent destroyed. Howard Carter, who made clearances in the tomb of Amenophis III, claimed to have discovered that Tiye had been buried there, and his unpublished notes speak of his finding objects bearing her name in the tomb itself and an alabaster shawabti inscribed with her cartouche below the tomb entrance, and the lower half of another in the 'protective' well. He also recovered a faience ring-bezel of Ramesses II and other fragments which led him to suggest that the tomb had been opened in Ramesside times.

The officials charged with these duties were no desperate tomb-robbers with nothing to lose. We may not unreasonably suppose them to have been devout and superstitious men, sincerely believing that they would risk divine vengeance by desecrating the Pharaohs' burials without some dispensation. They appear to have carried out their orders in a somewhat hurried and slip-shod manner. It is probable that the tomb and its contents were already suffering from damp when they re-entered it; and falls of rock which often occur when such walled-up sepulchres are opened may have encouraged them to get their unpleasant duty over as quickly as possible. Their first task was to break down the tomb-sealing, but only half-way, and to remove the filling so as to form a slope down the corridor until the blocking at the other end could be reached and mostly removed. The lighter articles, vessels, chests, shawabtis and the like, could then be easily manhandled from the burial chamber to the higher level of the corridor, but as soon as space around the ingress had been cleared, more filling had to be thrown down to form a ramp extending from the very heart of the burial chamber to the entrance some forty feet away. Up this slope the heavier equipment must have been carried. Before the coffins of Tiye could be removed, her shrine had to be dismantled and stacked out of the way against the east wall, hiding some of the seals that had fallen from the boxes previously stored at its foot. The pall was then taken off, losing some of its gilded roundels in the process. The coffins of Tiye, like those of Akhenaten, could be carried out of the tomb and easily passed through the orifice at the door jambs which measured some three or four feet high by five and a quarter feet wide. Such a size of opening would permit all but the largest items to be removed without any trouble.

What happened to the burial of Akhenaten is unlikely ever to be known. There was no intention merely of desecrating it and destroying its identity, otherwise it would have been left nameless in the tomb. The most dire fate that could overtake the mummy of the deceased was that it should be consumed by fire; and this was the threat against Osiris, the mummified god, that magicians of a later age used in order to gain his support for their ends. To suggest that the corpse of Akhenaten was stripped of its trappings and burnt, is to speculate beyond the possibility of proof, but it is as good a guess as any.

Before tackling the last big operation, the removal of the shrine, the officials turned their attention to the burial of Smenkh-ka-Re which they decided to leave in the tomb deprived of all traces of its identity. They therefore cut out his names from the gold bands that encircled his mummy, chiselled away the signs in his cartouches on the coffin, and ripped off the gold portrait mask over the face on the lid. His Canopic jars were presumably removed from their chest and stored in the recess, after the uraei had been snapped off. All his other equipment was removed, together with that of the other occupants with the exception of the lion-headed bier on which his coffin rested. The officials had, however, overlooked a number of smaller items that had got mixed up with the filling that they had thrown into the sepulchral chamber from the corridor. They also ignored a decayed box that contained faience objects and a larger casket from which they

Plate 98

VIII   Painted limestone bust of Queen Nefert-iti from the ruins of sculptors' studios at Amarna (ht. 58.5 cm.). This bust, which does not appear to have been made for any of the ritualistic uses of Egyptian sculpture, was doubtless the master-portrait from which lesser sculptors derived their representations of the Queen. The so-called 'un-Egyptian' features of Nefert-iti in this bust owe much to the fact that the face is not framed in the heavy mass of the women's conventional wigs *(cf.* Plate 64). The tall blue cap is peculiar to representations of this queen though it is also found on certain female sphinxes of the period *(cf.* Plate 89) and may have been assumed in order to match the Blue Crown so often worn by her husband *(cf.* Plate 105)

IX   Upper part of a fragmentary double statuette of Queen Tiye and her husband Amenophis III in green glazed steatite (ht. 29 cm.), perhaps originally from Edfu. The Queen wears a dress embroidered with a bird's-wing design suggesting the vulture mother-goddess Mut, who is also represented on her head-dress. The features of the Queen are here shown in the official mode of the day and resemble closely those of her husband who was most probably her cousin *(see* p. 89). A different tradition of portraiture is seen in the more realistic head from Sinai which probably belongs to the later years of the reign *(see* Plate 22)

X   Pottery jar (ht. 30 cm.), decorated with a design of lotus petals and marshscapes in blue, of 'Malkata' type *(see* Plate 34). A girl punting a papyrus skiff among the weed-grown water-ways is represented in this view. For a continuation of the scene see Plate 35

XI   Fragment of limestone relief (ht. 22 cm.), showing one of the princesses, perhaps Meryt-Aten, caressing a younger sister or daughter. The relief, excavated in the foundations of a building of Ramesses II at Hermopolis, originally came from a temple at Amarna across the river. The colours have been enhanced or added recently. The elder girl in this scene has reached puberty judging from her coiffure and developed bosom. She wears a diaphanous garment on the upper part of her body beneath which both breasts are shown in a frontal aspect, an unusual feature in Egyptian drawing but not unknown from earlier paintings of the Dynasty *(cf.* Plate VI). The younger girl has her head shaven except for the sidelock of childhood

XII   Group of gold jewellery found in 1882 in the vicinity of the Royal Tomb at Amarna. Top left is an ear-plug consisting of a hollow fusiform shank soldered to a roundel with a boss imitating a marguerite. A similar roundel severed from its shank is shown below. In the top right-hand corner is a heavy signet-ring bearing the name of Nefert-iti. In the opposite lower corner is a massive finger-ring with swivelling bezel in the form of a frog upon a scaraboid, the underside of which is inscribed with hieroglyphs reading 'Mut, Lady of Heaven' *(see also* Plate 109)

VIII

IX

X

XI

XII

XIII

XVI

XVII

XIII Gold statuette of Amenophis III (ht. 5 cm.), found sealed in a nest of miniature coffins in the tomb of Tut-ankh-Amun. The King wearing the Blue Crown and carrying sceptres squats in the pose of the newly-born sun-god arising from the waters of chaos on a lotus flower. The statuette was evidently worn on a chain by Tut-ankh-Amun and may be compared to the badges of the Family Orders of British royalty

XIV Lid of the coffin of Smenkh-ka-Re found in Valley Tomb No. 55. It is of wood, gilded and inlaid with coloured opaque glass similar to the second coffin of Tut-ankh-Amun. The gold mask has been ripped off below the eyes leaving the summarily modelled wooden core exposed. The imbricated shawl swathing the upper body is a feature of women's coffins, while the military coiffure may be worn by both men and women at this period. The beard, uraeus and sceptres were later added and the texts altered to make this coffin apply to a king *(see also* Plate 98)

XV Detail of the lid of a painted box (width 61 cm.), from the tomb of Tut-ankh-Amun showing the Pharaoh, accompanied by his hound and retinue, hunting a pride of lions from his chariot in the sporting tradition of his dynasty. The reins are tied around his waist to leave his arms free to use the composite bow—a piece of artistic licence. The text speaks of the King in his might as like the 'son of Nut' *i.e.* Seth, the Egyptian Baal *(see p. 24)*

XVI Reconstructed red quartzite statues of Amun and his female principle Amunet at Karnak, erected by Tut-ankh-Amun in the vestibule of the sanctuary of Amun-Re, as part of his rehabilitation of the temples after the Amarna iconoclasm. The face of the god is carved in the likeness of the King, and the features of Amunet would have resembled those of Queen Ankhes-en-Amun, but are badly mutilated. Both statues were later cut with the name of Har-em-hab

XVII Part of the wall paintings in the tomb of Tut-ankh-Amun showing King Ay officiating like the pious son at the last rites of his predecessor. Ay, right, in the costume of a living king and wearing the leopard skin of the ritualist priest, lifts an adze from the table before him in order to 'open the mouth' of the dead king and restore his senses to him. Tut-ankh-Amun in the guise of the mummified Osiris, with whom he has become assimilated on death, wears the long beard of a divinity and a pectoral that symbolizes his new Transfiguration had removed gold vases. Neither of these objects was, however, inscribed with a royal name. Their last move was never completed. They had begun to take the shrine out of the tomb, and had got a door into the open, when they found that a long side would not go through the gap at the entrance. Rather than widen the opening, they decided, for some reason, perhaps because it was already in bad condition, to leave the shrine in the tomb, and word was passed down to the workmen waiting with the larger elements on the ramp and in the chamber. These let the heavy members fall where they had been supporting them and contented themselves with adzing out the figure and names of Akhenaten before scrambling up the corridor and through the opening into the daylight. In their haste, however, they omitted to obliterate a cartouche on one of the long sides and forgot that though they had neutralized the magic bricks, two at least still bore the name of their original owner. Since their object was to consign to complete oblivion all memory of the two kings who had rested in this tomb, it is of some satisfaction to the moralist that, like most miscreants, they left behind them enough clues to enable their crime to be reconstructed and the victims identified. The decayed coffin of Smenkh-ka-Re was inscribed with a prayer that he should be called by his name and it should not falter on the lips of the deity; and in a long-delayed and roundabout way his plea has been answered.

Plate 95

X

The Heresy

OST MODERN INVESTIGATORS who attempt the study of Ancient
Egyptian religion, find themselves baffled by a plethora of gods who
change names and shape with great versatility, who may appear in human,
animal, vegetable or composite form and whose identity often cannot be
recognized for certain without an accompanying inscriptional label. The
modern taxonomic method of cataloguing these deities and their attributes
only adds to the confusion.

We learn, for instance, that Amun, the city god of Thebes, bore the
titles, 'King of the Gods,' and 'Lord of Heaven,' and is generally represented Plates 11, VII
as a man of heroic appearance. But he may sometimes be manifest in a goose
or a ram. Assimilated to the sun-god Re, he represents that invisible (the
name 'Amun' means 'hidden') force in the sun which causes Nature to
germinate. He may also have sovereignty over the air, and is 'Lord of the
(Cool) Sweet Breeze,' which revives the wretched man stricken with heat.
He may come at the call of the poor and under-privileged to succour them
as a good vizier listens to the complaints of his petitioners. He may also
exchange his shape for that of an old prehistoric ithyphallic god, Min, of
the Eastern Desert, the sky and storm god who sometimes thunders and
promotes fertility in crops, beasts and man. Amun-Re could also be the
father figure in a trinity of gods, so sympathetic to Egyptian ideas about
the sanctity of family life, with a wife, Mut, and a son, Khons. His fetish
may be a meteorite fallen from the holy sky-realms of which he is master.

The mere enumeration of these forms and attributes of Amun, imposes
upon the ancient beliefs an order which the Egyptian never felt. All these
aspects existed together in the same dimension and were equally true at
the very same moment. But in this bewildering polytheism four main
spheres of activity can be distinguished, though it is impossible to isolate
them without doing them violence.

There are firstly the cattle cults of a remote prehistoric origin. The
pastoral milieu in which these flourished is still of great economic and cultural
significance to the Hamitic herdsmen of East Africa. The cow whose milk
could sustain human life was the natural mother of mankind. The bull and

ram were the dark powers of virility incarnate. Without an immanent fertility promoted by such deities, crops withered and beasts and mankind perished. Such animal cults are of importance in a primitive peasant society and though in Egypt they became overlaid with more sophisticated ideas, they still had meaning in an environment which was predominantly agricultural, and they lasted as long as paganism, and even beyond it. Akhenaten, for all his complex religious ideas, did not interdict the worship of the Mnevis bull of Heliopolis.

Another series of beliefs centred around the peculiar natural conditions of Ancient Egypt, where the Nile rose in flood every year and reduced the entire cultivated area to a watery chaos from which the new world was in due course reborn. This annual miracle of the emergence of the new land, at first as a spit of sand or a mound of earth from the waste of waters, deeply impressed the Egyptian imagination. It was on the primeval mound that the demiurge found a firm place upon which to perform his act of creation whereby the world and all that was in it came into being out of chaos. It was also on such a mound that the god first alighted as a huge bird, a falcon in one place, a phoenix in another, an ibis elsewhere, as the god incarnate. From this primeval mound sprang the new vegetation and the animal life that fed upon it and each other. Year after year the waters that are under the earth rose to engulf the dead parched land, and after their fertilizing flood had impregnated it, to renew life in it. This idea of resurrection from the earth by means of the life-giving waters entered profoundly into Egyptian beliefs about this world and the next and inspired a whole cosmogony.

A third cycle of dogma belongs to the concept of the divine king, the god incarnate. Originating in prehistoric ages with the idea of a chief or rain-maker whose power over the elements and whose authority kept his people together in health and prosperity, by dynastic times the Pharaoh had become the supreme god, Horus, incarnate. His powers had extended from a local tribe to the whole nation. Horus, made manifest as a falcon, was the universal sky-god whose imagery still permeated Egyptian thought in Dynasty XVIII when the Pharaohs at their inception are regarded as falcons in the nest and who fly to the horizon at death.

A fourth sphere in which divine power manifested itself was in sun-worship. This was a later and more intellectual development, and its teaching and its persistence must have owed much to the learning and mental qualities of the priesthood of Re of Heliopolis whose strong theological traditions constantly refurbished its dogma, and whose close connection with the kingship gave it an unchallenged authority. The sun-

Plate VII

Plate 41

god, Re-Atum, was conceived as the creator of the Universe and its first ruler. The Pharaoh was his successor: he was not, however, the sun-god incarnate but his son, begotten of the Chief Queen by the god who had taken the appearance of the Pharaoh in order to perform the creative act.

These various cycles of religious thought did not exist as separate entities but interpenetrated each other inextricably. Because Horus the sky-god bore on his wings the disk of the sun across the heavens, he was assimilated into the sun-religion; and Horus, incarnate in the Pharaoh, was the son of the sun-god. A primeval divine king, Osiris, who had suffered death and dismemberment when his powers began to wane and was buried for the greater fertility of his domain and its inhabitants, connected the cycle of earth and resurrection with the cult of the divine king and that of the solar religion. Pharaoh, the living Horus, became Osiris at his death

Plate XVII

and was buried in the primeval mound for the benefit of all Egypt, while his son, the new Horus, stood in his place. Thus Osiris merges into the sun-cult and is there regarded as belonging to that third generation of gods who were created from the self-fertilization of the demiurge. The Ancient Egyptian world of gods and man was a vast cosmic creation, existing at several levels at the very same moment and enshrining many mutually contradictory beliefs, but 'alive from end to end.' It defies modern dissection more than most religions, having a tendency to dissolve into some other Protean shape as soon as one concept is firmly grasped.

The polytheistic nature of Egyptian religion, perhaps the result of three or four cosmogonic ideas finding a habitation and a name in some *genius loci*, did not entirely fail to confuse the ancient theologians themselves and there is little doubt that the priesthood of Re, for instance, attempted to syncretise several cults, not only in Dynasties IV and V, when sun-worship acquired a preponderating influence in the state, but also during the Second Intermediate Period when foreign invasion and alien ideas in a divided and impoverished land encouraged its devotees to probe more deeply into its dogmas. Some of the results of this re-thinking are evident in the sacred books which first appear in the royal tombs at Thebes during the early New Kingdom under the titles of *The Book of What is in the*

Plate II

Nether World, *The Litany of the Sun*, and *The Book of Caverns*. As the late Alexandre Piankoff has so cogently pointed out,[30] these texts reveal a new preoccupation with a monotheistic syncretism of ancient beliefs. In them, Re is more than the sun-god, he is the universe, the 'sole god who has made himself for eternity.' He is invoked in *The Litany* under his seventy-five names which are his bodies, and these bodies are the gods. Thus Re is the bodies of Atum, Shu, Tefnut, Geb and Nut, the entire first and second generation of solar deities. He is invoked as 'Re of the Disk,' 'supreme power whose forms are his transformations when he takes the form of Aten the Great (or his Great Disk).' In other words his activity is his perpetual transformation when he makes successively his appearance in the form of the Aten or solar disk. This dogma is already very close to that proclaimed by the didactic name of Akhenaten's sole god, the Aten, if not identical with it (see p. 168). The idea of the perpetual return of Re under the form of the Disk is precisely stated in the second version of the dogmatic name of the Aten (see p. 187). We shall also see that the belief inherent in *The Litany* that Re, the supreme power, not only illumines and brings to life, the world of the living (at his rising) but also gives light to those in the West (*i.e.* the Dead), is an important tenet in Amarna ideas about life after death. If it is a question of a unique god it is, however, undoubtedly Re, and not Aten, who is only the visible manifestation of the solar deity.

The predominant influence of the solar cult on Egyptian beliefs in the New Kingdom can be traced as a constant progress. Rekh-mi-re, the Vizier of Tuthmosis III refers to the closeness of his relations with his lord as 'I saw his person in his true form—Re, the Lord of Heaven, the King of Upper and Lower Egypt when he rises, the Aten when he reveals himself.' Here 'Aten' is a name for the sun's disk which had long been in use, and a number of kings had been spoken of as departing to the sky at death and becoming united with the Aten. In the reign of Amenophis II, the symbol of the sun-disk appears with a pair of enveloping arms, though it is probable that these represent the Egyptian *Ka* or manifestation of spiritual sustenance rather than an idea imported from some Indo-European source, Mitanni, for instance, where the Aryan sun-god Savriti is regarded as raising long arms of gold in the morning. Under Tuthmosis IV, the Aten is referred to on a scarab as a god of battles who makes the Pharaoh mighty in his domains and brings all his subjects under the sway of the sun-disk. It would appear by this that the aspect of the sun-god symbolized by the Aten-disk was now thought of as a separate deity. In the reign of Amenophis III, references to the Aten become more numerous. The name, 'Radiance-of-the-Aten' is applied to his state barge on the scarabs of Year 11, and to the Malkata palace before his first jubilee. There are also grounds for thinking that 'Radiance-of-the-Aten' was an epithet of Amenophis III himself. Two, at least, of his children bore names compounded with Aten[31].

Plate 25

While there appears, therefore, a steady development in the influence of the Aten during Dynasty XVIII, it has to be remembered that by far the greater part of our information comes from Thebes, the city of Amun-Re, who would be expected to take to himself any references to the solar religion. The centre of sun-worship was, of course, at Heliopolis, and that site is far too ruined to testify whether references to the Aten there show a similar growth-rate. What does seem clear is that the increase in the mention of the Aten coincides with a rise to predominance in the State of officials who were not Theban in origin but came from the Delta towns, Plates 19, 20, 79 Athribis and Memphis in particular, where the royal princes spent so much of their formative years and where the cult of Re of Helipolis was widespread. The sun-god of Heliopolis most to the fore in this Dynasty was Re-Herakhty, Horus of the Horizon, a conflation of the sun-god Re Plate 45 with the sky-god Horus, represented usually as a falcon-headed man, but also as a sphinx in his aspect of the sun in its redness at dawn and sunset. The special favour shown by certain kings of the dynasty towards this god is revealed in the stelae which were set up at the temple of the Great Sphinx at Giza, particularly that of Tuthmosis IV who, as we have Plate 14 recounted above (p. 40), had been promised the throne by Herakhty in return for clearing the sands from his great image. Many of the funerary prayers of the Dynasty are addressed to Herakhty, particularly at his rising and setting and most of the Theban tombs in their complete state had a scene at the entrance showing the owner 'coming forth into the day-light' to praise Herakhty at dawn. A complementary prayer was addressed to the same god at sunset. Herakhty also enters into the Osirian cycle of myths and is frequently represented leading the deceased by the hand in the presence of Osiris, the Divine Judge of the Dead.

The rapid evolution of the Atenist doctrines can be traced during the early years of Akhenaten's reign, but its development was a continuous process throughout the period, suggesting the maturing of one mind behind the manifestation of thought, which can only belong to Akhenaten himself. Herakhty emerges at Thebes as a prominent deity. Thus in the tomb of Ramose, the Vizier presents a bouquet of Re-Herakhty, instead of Amun, to the new king; and in this case the name of the god is expanded to the didactic form which prevails for about the first nine years of the reign and is a statement of faith that Re, the supreme divine power, is manifest from dawn to sunset in the light that comes from the Disk. Such a dogma had been implicit for over a century in the texts of the sacred books that had to do with the eternal life after death (see p. 165). The god

Plate 110

at this stage is still represented as a falcon-headed man wearing a sun's-disk encircled by a uraeus and may even appear as a falcon wearing the disk as on the Canopic chest of Akhenaten. The next step in his evolution occurs when his didactic name is incorporated in two cartouches, like those of a Pharaoh, and the idea of a heavenly king, the Aten, emerges. This development bursts into full glory with the appearance of a new abstract image of

Plate 46

the deity—the rayed sun-disk, which replaces the former anthropomorphic and therianthropic forms. This symbol is no more than an elaborated hieroglyph in which the old sign for 'sunshine,' a disk with three short emergent rays, has become a disk having the encircling uraeus of kingship with an *ankh* around its neck and a dozen or more long rays each ending

Plate 47

in a hand. The hands may hold the *ankh*-sign of life to the nostrils of the king and queen, but to no-one else. The meaning is clearly stated in an inscription on the ceiling of the Third Shrine of Tut-ankh-Amun, where we read; 'The rays of the Aten are as a protection over thee, their hands possessing health and life. They are to thee as prosperity for thy members.'

The kingly status of the Aten is also emphasised by his acquisition of a titulary as well as names within cartouches. At the same time as the symbol of the rayed disk appears, a full designation accompanies it, which in its expanded form reads:

> May the Good God live, who takes pleasure in Truth, Lord of all that the Sun-disk encompasses, Lord of Heaven, Lord of Earth, the Great Living Aten who illumines the Two Lands! May the Father Live, Divine and Royal (Re-Herakhty, the Living, who rejoices on the horizon) (in his manifestation of Light which is in the Aten), giving life for ever and to all eternity, the Great Living Aten who is in Jubilee!

Aten is regarded as a Heavenly Pharaoh whose rule has begun with that of Akhenaten. Indeed the *durbar* of Year 12 is dated in the one place in the reign of the Aten; and in the other to the reign of Akhenaten. The Aten, like his earthly counterpart, could hold a jubilee; and in fact during his career appears to have celebrated three, which the writer has tried to show coincide with those of the senior co-regent Amenophis III[32]. Akhenaten is spoken of as the beloved son of the Aten, but the correspondence of his regnal years with those of the Aten shows that he was also regarded as its co-regent. That his divinity is greatly enhanced with the appearance of the fully developed symbol of the Aten is seen in all representations subsequent to that epiphany, where court officials and bystanders bend compliant backs low in his presence.

Plate 49, 104
Fig. 2

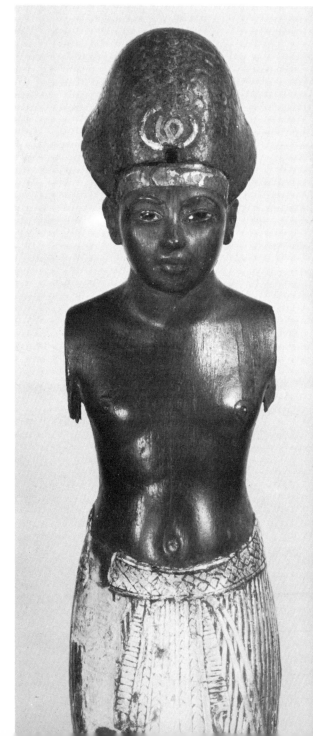

59   Upper part of an armless wooden statuette of Amenophis III made for his Second or Third Jubilee, and showing him in his later obesity but with a more flattering appearance. The portrait, with its inlaid eyes, is more realistic than usual and resembles that of his wife (*cf.* Plate 22)

58   Headless serpentine statuette of Amenophis III as a corpulent man wearing a fringed garment, his hands clasped in a pose more characteristic of Asia than Egypt. The back-pillar is carved as a *Djed*-column suggesting that the statue was made for one of his later jubilees (*cf.* Plate 38). The name of Amun has been erased in both places. The realistic features of this statuette, which also appear in broken torsos from Medinet Habu, must owe much to the contemporary Amarna style

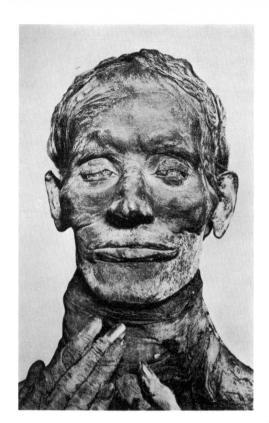

60, 61 Front and profile views of the head of Yuya from his well-preserved mummy. The fleshy lips, wide cheek bones, prominent nose, deep jaw and receding forehead should be noted as characteristic of a physiognomy which the anatomist Elliot Smith has described as by no means common in the pure Egyptian

62 Part of the relief illustrated in Plate 119, originally from the wall of the tomb of Ay at Amarna and now in Cairo. The large thick lips, deep jaw and receding forehead characteristic of Yuya are also shared by Ay in this representation, which appears to be a fairly careful portrait

63 Upper part of a hard crystalline limestone seated colossus of Ay as King from his usurped mortuary temple at Medinet Habu. The large nose has been restored. The features are distinctive: the bossy cheekbones, thick lips and a jaw, the depth of which has been disguised by the massive false beard, recall the anatomical pecularities of Yuya and suggest that there was some close family resemblance between these two men

64, 65 Parts of a magnificent life-sized crystalline limestone statue of the General Nakht-Min and his wife, perhaps from the Memphis area. Nakht-Min carries the flabellum of a Fan-Bearer on the Right of the King. His wife, in the traditional large gala wig that hides a head cast in the Amarna mould (*cf.* Plate 8), wears a close-fitting pleated gown and holds the necklace with counterpoise of a devotee of the goddess Hat-Hor. This statue must be dated on stylistic grounds to the immediate post-Amarna period, and in fact Nakht-Min presented some of the funeral furnishings to the burial of Tut-ankh-Amun (*see* Plate 73)

66 Block statue in hard crystalline limestone of the > Second Prophet of Amun, the Chief Prophet of Mut, King's Scribe and Steward of the House of Queen Tiye in the Estate of Amun, Ay, born of Mut-em-nub, the sister of the King's Chief Wife (Tey), and begotten of the worthy Nakht-Min. This statue, which was found at Er-Rezeikat, about seventeen miles south-west of Thebes, is dated by intact cartouches of King Ay inscribed on the upper right shoulder. The Prophet Ay was a nephew of the Pharaoh Ay by marriage, and evidently steward of the estate of another relative, the late wife of King Amenophis III

67 Calcite stopper from one of the four Canopic jars, seen in the recess in Plate 96, in the form of a human head wearing a short military wig and broad collar. The eyes and brows are inlaid with glass. These heads have been identified as representing Queen Tiye, Akhenaten and Smenkh-ka-Re, but there is little doubt that they are of one of the princesses, probably Meryt-Aten, and made for her early in life before she became a queen. They were later adapted by fixing a multi-coloured glass uraeus to a hole drilled in each brow, and cutting a snake's body among the striations on top of each wig. At a still later period each uraeus was snapped off, leaving a stump of lilac-coloured glass in this particular example

68 Sculptor's model in limestone, found at Amarna, carved with the heads of two kings, which has been explained as a student's exercise with Akhenaten represented twice. The head on the left being judged wrong a better attempt was made on the right. This interpretation implies that the sculptor began at the extreme left because he expected to get his portrait wrong from the start. But it is certain that the master-sculptor would have corrected the drawing of his pupil before any carving was done. The same degree of finish in both heads and the distinctly different portraits leave little doubt that these are official portraits of Akhenaten and Smenkh-ka-Re

69, 70 A profile of the gold mask of Tut-ankh-Amun is here shown with a similar view of a wooden head believed to be of Queen Tiye. The strong family resemblance between them suggests a mother-son relationship. The wooden head however may rather represent Sit-Amun, the daughter of Amenophis III and Tiye, in which case the relationship would be that of a sister and brother having the same parents. A likeness has also been traced between certain portraits of Amenophis III and Tut-ankh-Amun (cf. Plates 59, 73)

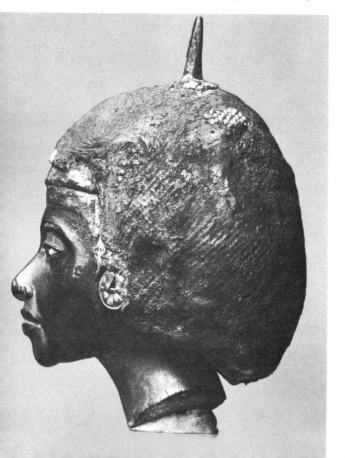

71 If Tut-ankh-Amun was the son of Sit-Amun it is strange that no heirlooms of his mother were included in his funeral furniture, whereas several articles originally belonging to Tiye and Amenophis III were buried with him. Most notable of these is the gold statuette of Amenophis III which in life had been worn by Tut-ankh-Amun (*see also* Plate XIII) and a lock of Queen Tiye's hair wrapped, anointed and sealed in a miniature coffin. Both heirlooms were enclosed together in other coffins. If Akhenaten had been the father of Tut-ankh-Amun, no such intimate mementoes of him were included in the burial equipment, though a casket and state-fan bearing the intact names of Akhenaten show that there was no interdict against putting objects of the 'Heretic' in his successor's tomb

72 Ivory palette of Meryt-Aten as Princess, found in the tomb of Tut-ankh-Amun, and revealing evidence of use in the six colour-pans. The used writing palettes of Meket-Aten, as well as those of Amenophis III and Tut-ankh-Amun, also exist to show that all the Royal Family, women as well as men, at this period were trained to read and write

73, 74 *Below*, upper part of a wooden shawabti-figure dedicated to the dead Tut-ankh-Amun by the General Nakht-Min (*see* Plate 65). When called upon, such figures were supposed to perform all the heavy labour in the fields of the Osirian underworld. Even the dead Pharaoh, who was assimilated to Osiris, did not seem to be exempt from this agricultural corvée. *Right*, gold statuette surmounting one of Tut-ankh-Amun's ceremonial sticks found stacked between his first and second outermost shrines (*see* Plate 93). It serves to show the extreme youth of the King at his advent, when as a child of eight or nine he succeeded to the throne of a troubled realm and was married to Ankhesen-pa-Aten who was then nearly twice his age. He wears a short kilt with apron and the Blue Crown

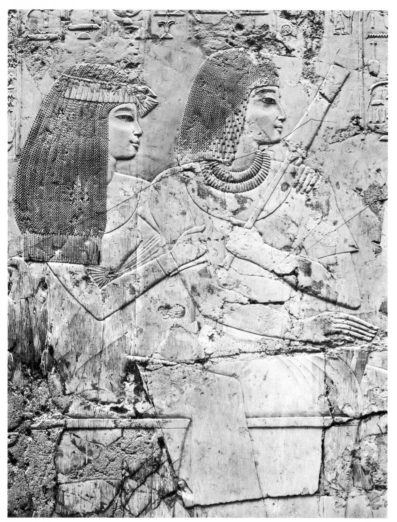

75   On the east wall of the great hall of his tomb chapel at Thebes, Ramose is shown partaking of the funeral repast with his parents and relatives. All are designated as 'deceased' though they were not necessarily so at the time the wall was carved. The pair illustrated are his half-brother, Amun-hotpe (*see* Plate 19) and the latter's wife, May. These exquisite reliefs have been faultlessly cut in rock that is full of blemishes

76   The south wall of the same hall was begun in relief but finished in colour with this scene of the funeral cortège. In the upper register, right, is the catafalque followed by relatives who haul the Canopic chest. At the rear walk the four Chief Prophets of Amun, the last of whom is named as Si-Mut. In the lower register, Ramose's servants bring his funerary furniture followed by the high officers of State (*cf.* Plate 78)

77 Relief which originally formed part of a wall of the tomb of Har-em-hab at Sakkara, showing the reception of nine delegates from Libya and Asia by Tut-ankh-Amun and his Queen at their Window of Appearances (*cf.* Plate 119). Two of the ambassadors prostrate themselves 'on breast and back' according to the form of abasement known from the Amarna Letters. Here Har-em-hab, newly installed as the King's Deputy, loaded with gold collars and carrying his fan and insignia of office transmits through an interpreter the gracious reply of his King to the traditional prayer for 'the breath of life'. Other scenes from the tomb showing foreign captives and slaves (presented as tribute) have been interpreted as indicating that a campaign was fought in Asia during the early years of Tut-ankh-Amun, but for this there is no real evidence

78 Detail of a relief from the tomb of a High Priest of Memphis showing the procession to the tomb. At the head walking apart is a figure who is described as 'the King's Scribe, Crown-Prince designate and General'. This person has been identified as Har-em-hab in his capacity of 'regent' before he ascended the throne. He is followed by the two Viziers neither of whom resembles the distinctive Ay who may therefore have been King at the time this relief was carved.

79 Naos stela in quartzite of Bek, the Chief Sculptor and Master of Works under Akhenaten, standing within the shrine embraced by his wife, Ta-heret. The inscribed prayers are addressed to Herakhty, 'the Living Aten', suggesting that the stela dates to the earlier years of Akhenaten. Bek refers to himself as 'the apprentice' of His Majesty, just as in a graffito at Aswan he claims to have been taught by the King. Bek, the son of Men, a Chief Sculptor of Amenophis III, belonged to a family originating in Heliopolis. He represents himself with the same heavy breasts and prominent paunch of his King, although the latter was still young at the time this was carved

80 Painted limestone stela from the house of Pinhasy at Amarna, showing Amenophis III and
Queen Tiye seated on thrones before altars piled with offerings under the rays of the Aten, whose
name appears in its late form, suggesting that the stela was carved after Year 9 of Akhenaten. The
old King's *prenomen*, Neb-maet-Re, is repeated in place of his *nomen*, thus avoiding the use of
the name Amun in the City of the Aten. Although the royal pair are shown as living persons,
some scholars have insisted that this is a posthumous representation used in a cult of the dead King
even though his wife may have been still living at the time. The garments worn by the King, whose
corpulence is obvious, are similar to those shown in the New York statuette (Plate 58)

81–83 Limestone stelae from Amarna. *Above left*, dedicated by Pasi, the captain of the state-barge(?) 'Kha-em-maet'. Two kings are seated side by side before an altar beneath the rayed Aten who brings life to their nostrils. The king on the left wearing the Blue Crown, puts his left arm around the neck of the other who wears the Double Crown and a pectoral. The latter king turns to stroke his companion's chin. Despite the unfinished cartouches which lack names and the mutilated faces of the monarchs, the pair must be the co-regents Smenkh-ka-Re and Akhenaten, the hanging jaw of the latter being unmistakable (*cf.* Plate 68). *Below left*, another unfinished limestone stela showing a king, right, wearing the Blue Crown and pouring wine into the cup of another king seated left. The design is known from a relief in the tomb of Mery-Re at Amarna, where Nefert-iti pours wine through a strainer into her husband's cup. The co-regents represented in this stela are doubtless Akhenaten and Smenkh-ka-Re. *Above right*, a sketch found at Amarna upon the back of a fragment of destroyed relief of earlier date. The head is of a king, evidently Akhenaten, represented with a few days' growth of beard. Despite the grotesque nature of the sketch, this is not a caricature, as its excavator at first believed, but appears to show the king in mourning when he went unshaven

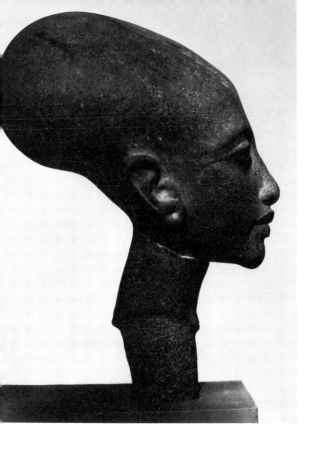

84, 85 Life-sized heads in quartzite of two of the daughters of the royal house, from workshops at Amarna. The head on the right lacks its glass inlays (*cf*. Plate 59). The extraordinary distortion of these statue heads has prompted the suggestion that the princesses' skulls were artificially deformed, a practice for which there is no evidence in ancient Egypt. The princesses are the only members of the Royal Family who are shown with their heads shaven and bare, and we are to suppose, therefore, that their shape approximated to that of their father's which set the fashion in anatomical representation. If so, there is reason for suspecting that his skull was deformed by disease

86 Life-sized plaster mask of a man from studios at Amarna. This has been identified as a death-mask of Amenophis III, but the tension of the muscles around eyes and mouth has none of the complete relaxation of death. Also it is clear that Amenophis III was very obese in his last years and this mask is not the face of a fat man. It is more likely a cast taken from a portrait modelled in clay. Such rapid studies from life must have been practised for subsequent working-over to the approved idealization

87 Drawing of a scene in one of the chambers of the Royal Tomb at Amarna reserved for the burial of Meket-Aten. In the upper register, Akhenaten leads Nefert-iti by the arm into the bed-room of the dead Princess, while outside mourners make gestures of grief. The nurse or princess carrying a child in her arms and accompanied by a fan-bearer should be noted. In the lower register, the King and Queen mourn over Meket-Aten on her death-bed. The private persons on the extreme left may be Ay and Tey

88 Torsos in hard crystalline limestone recovered from a dump near the Great Temple at Amarna. The one on the left is presumed to be of Nefert-iti though the identification is not absolutely certain. There is less doubt that the other is of Akhenaten

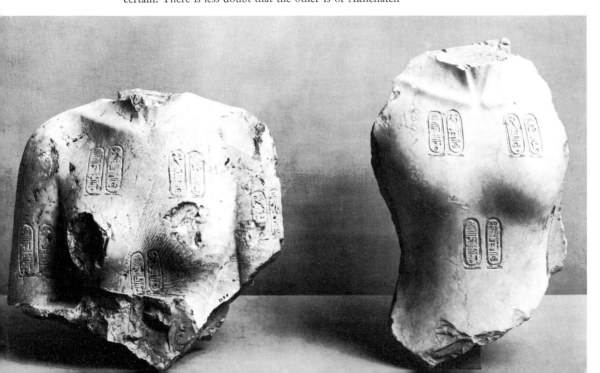

Revolutionary though this manifestation may now appear to us its most novel feature is the bizarre appearance of the Pharaoh and his family. The doctrine implicit in the name and titles of the god had nothing in it that would not be readily comprehended by a contemporary well versed in the dogmas of the sun religion; and the divinity manifest in the Pharaoh was something that had existed from earliest times, and although overlaid by other ideas, had enjoyed a steady revival in Dynasty XVIII until under Amenophis III the King worships his own divine self.

There may have been more than a touch of antiquarianism in this return to an earlier and more exalted status for the Pharaoh. During the reign of Amenophis III the records had been diligently studied, not only in an endeavour to find the tomb of Osiris reputed to be at Abydos, but also to reconstitute the correct primal rites for the King's First Jubilee. It is in these researches that we can perhaps detect the influence of the sage Amenophis-son-of-Hapu, whose learning was to become proverbial. Akhenaten and the other Amarna kings make a great claim to *Ankh em Maet*, usually translated as 'Living in Truth', and more has been read into this phrase than the words warrant. By *Maet* was meant the established order of things as they had existed at the creation of the world, and not some abstract principle of verity. It is more likely that Akhenaten revived a concept of kingship that went back to the earliest dynasties when the Pharaoh bore names signifying that he was more than the son of the sun-god, he was the sun-god himself. Gardiner and other scholars have gained the impression that Akhenaten's share in the divinity of the Aten approached complete identity, and this appears to be particularly evident in the name that the King chose for himself on the occasion of the Second Jubilee of the Aten when he changed his *nomen* from Amenophis to Akhenaten. This is usually translated as 'serviceable to the Aten,' a weak and meaningless rendering; and the writer would prefer, 'The Effective Spirit (= incarnation)[33] of the Aten,' thus indicating that the same power that was manifest in the Disk was flesh in the person of the King.

If the Aten were a Sole God, as is so often proclaimed, it is clear that his son, Akhenaten, can only be an incarnation of himself. The courtiers pray to the Aten only through the intermediary of the King. Thus in place of figures of the deceased worshipping Re-Herakhty at the entrance to the tomb, one finds in the case of Kheruef that it is Akhenaten who makes the offering to the god. At Amarna, the equivalent scene is always of the Royal Family adoring the Aten. Even the funerary prayers on the coffin of Meryt-Aten/Smenkh-ka-Re are addressed exclusively to Akhenaten.

Plate 20

Plate 105

Plate 98

During the Second Intermediate Period figures of gods had first appeared on stelae and other monuments of private persons; and this tendency operates with increasing frequency during the New Kingdom when commoners are shown in the presence of gods, lifting their arms to them in worship or making offerings to them. All this disappears during the Amarna Period when a reversion takes place to the former custom whereby the king was the only mortal who was entitled to have direct contact with divinities: in the case of Akhenaten, with the sole god, the Aten.

Another feature of religious development which had come to the fore during the New Kingdom had been the worship of a group of gods consisting of a Father and Mother figure and a Son, a trinity which appealed strongly to the feeling for family among the Egyptians. The Aten was the sole god, and though he is referred to as the Father, and the King as his Son, the female principal is lacking. Nevertheless, one is left with the impression that in publicizing his private life as the family man, Akhenaten may have been satisfying this need for a focal point in the worship of a divine family. At the same time as he changed his name to Akhenaten, his queen added to her name the epithet Nefer-neferu-Aten ('Fair is the Goodness of the Aten') and appears wearing a curious conoidal cap which is her distinguishing feature of dress and which may equate her

Plate 89

with a solar divinity who sometimes takes the form of a female sphinx wearing a crown of similar pattern. This elevation of Nefert-iti to quasi-

Plate 51

Pharaonic status is seen nowhere more vividly than in a representation of the royal barge which is decorated with an unprecedented scene of the Queen wearing her tall cap, seizing a foe by the hair and smiting him with upraised mace. Such an icon had hitherto been reserved entirely for kings. While Akhenaten and Nefert-iti form a well-matched pair of divine sovereigns, they evidently had no son to represent the third member of a trinity; and it is the eldest daughter, Meryt-Aten, who receives special attention, being promised burial in the Eastern mountain-range at Amarna and taking her mother's place after her death. The other children are later associated with their parents in scenes at which the Royal Family assists,

Plate 44

though it is very rare to find all six represented. Even in reliefs dated to the later years of the reign, Meryt-Aten alone frequently has to serve for the entire generation of daughters.

Before the end of the reign, the Aten underwent another change, an epithet being altered to read 'Lord of Jubilees' a title usually bestowed upon a king who has celebrated more than one such festival. At the same time the didactic name of the god within its cartouches was changed to a form which has been translated in various ways but which to the writer seems to have the meaning, (Re, the Living, the Ruler of the Horizon, who rejoices on the horizon) (in his manifestation of Re-the-Father who returns as the Aten). This modification is in step with an increasing emphasis upon the abstract nature of the deity whose equation with the old falcon god Horus is now evaded. It also expresses an idea, which is repeated again and again in the Amarna hymns to the Aten, that the daily return of the sun-disk at dawn and his journey across the heavens brings life to mankind and is the assurance of the presence and loving-kindness of Re, the supreme deity who is the invisible force that animates the Disk. There is nothing novel in this concept which, as emphasised above, was already embedded in the religious compositions of the Dynasty found in the tombs of the kings where the sun-god, the great universal deity, dies at sunset and traverses the body of the goddess Nut, the night sky, in a journey which, at the same time, is the gestation of the new sun which will be reborn the next dawn. The eternal transfiguration and return of the Creator in the form of the sun-disk is the central feature of both doctrines.

Our knowledge of the 'new' teaching of Akhenaten has to be gleaned from the great hymn to the Aten which is inscribed in the tombs of some of his courtiers at Amarna, particularly in that of Ay who, as the King's private secretary, is most likely to have given the full authorized version. It runs as follows:

Plate 120

> Thou arisest fair in the horizon of Heaven, O Living Aten, Beginner of Life. When thou dawnest in the East, thou fillest every land with thy beauty. Thou art indeed comely, great, radiant and high over every land. Thy rays embrace the lands to the full extent of all that thou hast made, for thou art Re and thou attainest their limits and subdueth them for thy beloved son (Akhenaten). Thou art remote yet thy rays are upon the earth. Thou art in the sight of men, yet thy ways are not known.
>
> When thou settest in the Western horizon, the earth is in darkness after the manner of death. Men spend the night indoors with the head covered, the eye not seeing its fellow. Their possessions might be stolen, even when under their heads, and they would be unaware of it. Every lion comes forth from its lair and all snakes bite. Darkness is the only light, and the earth is silent when their Creator rests in his habitation.
>
> The earth brightens when thou arisest in the Eastern horizon and shinest forth as Aten in the day-time. Thou drivest away the night when thou givest forth thy beams. The Two Lands are in festival. They awake

and stand upon their feet for thou hast raised them up. They wash their limbs, they put on raiment and raise their arms in adoration at thy appearance. The entire earth performs its labours. All cattle are at peace in their pastures. The trees and herbage grow green. The birds fly from their nests, their wings (raised) in praise of thy spirit. All animals gambol on their feet, all the winged creation live when thou hast risen for them. The boats sail upstream, and likewise downstream. All ways open at thy dawning. The fish in the river leap in thy presence. Thy rays are in the midst of the sea.

Thou it is who causest women to conceive and maketh seed into man, who giveth life to the child in the womb of its mother, who comforteth him so that he cries not therein, nurse that thou art, even in the womb, who giveth breath to quicken all that he hath made. When the child comes forth from the body on the day of his birth, then thou openest his mouth completely and thou furnisheth his sustenance. When the chick in the egg chirps within the shell, thou givest him the breath within it to sustain him. Thou createst for him his proper term within the egg, so that he shall break it and come forth from it to testify to his completion as he runs about on his two feet when he emerges.

How manifold are thy works! They are hidden from the sight of men, O Sole God, like unto whom there is no other! Thou didst fashion the earth according to thy desire when thou wast alone—all men, all cattle great and small, all that are upon the earth that run upon their feet or rise up on high flying with their wings. And the lands of Syria and Kush and Egypt—thou appointest every man to his place and satisfieth his needs. Everyone receives his sustenance and his days are numbered. Their tongues are diverse in speech and their qualities likewise, and their colour is differentiated for thou hast distinguished the nations.

Thou makest the waters under the earth and thou bringest them forth (as the Nile) at thy pleasure to sustain the people of Egypt even as thou hast made them live for thee, O Divine Lord of them all, toiling for them, the Lord of every land, shining forth for them, the Aten Disk of the day time, great in majesty!

All distant foreign lands also, thou createst their life. Thou hast placed a Nile in heaven to come forth for them and make a flood upon the mountains like the sea in order to water the fields of their villages. How excellent are thy plans, O Lord of Eternity!—a Nile in the sky is thy gift to the foreigners and to the beasts of their lands; but the true Nile flows from under the earth for Egypt.

Thy beams nourish every field and when thou shinest they live and grow for thee. Thou makest the seasons in order to sustain all that thou hast made, the winter to cool them, the summer heat that they may taste (of thy quality). Thou hast made heaven afar off that thou mayest behold all that thou hast made when thou wast alone, appearing in thy aspect of the Living Aten, rising and shining forth. Thou makest millions of forms out of thyself, towns, villages, fields, roads, the river. All eyes behold thee before them, for thou art the Aten of the day-time, above all that thou hast created.

Thou art in my heart, but there is none other who knows thee save thy son Akhenaten. Thou hast made him wise in thy plans and thy power.

All the sentiments expressed in the above hymn, which has many times been compared to Psalm 104, both in its sequence, content and forms of expression, have nothing revolutionary about them. The sun-god is regarded as the demiurge who created the Universe by his hand 'when he was alone' (in Chaos), a concept which is of great antiquity. Many of the other ideas expressed in this hymn had appeared in similar compositions to other gods during the Dynasty. A hymn to Amun, which dates to the reign of Amenophis II, for instance, but which has elements of greater antiquity, reveals the same joy in nature and speaks of the god almost exclusively in his solar aspect which had resulted from his fusion with Re-Atum. He is referred to as:

father of the gods who fashioned mankind and made the beasts . . . and the herbage which sustains cattle . . . Lord of the sunbeams who creates light . . .

Thou art the Sole One who made all that there is; the Unique One who made what exists . . . He it is who has made pasturage for cattle, and the fruit-tree for mankind. He it is who has made that whereon the fish live in the river and the birds in the heavens. It is he who gives breath to him in the egg, and sustains the son of the worm . . .[34]

He is also identified with Atum, 'who fashioned men of different natures, and created their life. He made them differ in colour each from the other.'

This sentiment, that all the nations, barbarians as well as Egyptians, are God's creatures, is expressed with greater force in the Hymn to the Aten; nevertheless, epithets of Thoth, the god of writing and wisdom, refer to him as he 'who made different the tongue of one land from another,' an idea that appears to be of some antiquity.[35]

Another hymn, this time to Osiris, which antedates the Amarna Period, speaks of the god in the following terms:

> He hath made this land with his hand, its water and its air, its vegetation and all its cattle, all that flieth and fluttereth, its creeping things and the beasts of the desert[36].

It is thus clear, even from the haphazard body of texts that have survived from an earlier time, that the Great Hymn to the Aten enshrines ideas and phrases which had long persisted in the religious literature. Its novelty lies not in what it expresses, but in what it leaves unsaid. Nowhere in it is the slightest mention of other gods. The great hymn to Amun which echoes many of its sentiments, also speaks of Amun as a Sole God, yet equates him with Ptah, Min, Re, Khepre-Re and Atum. It apostrophizes him as the One and Only Creator from whose tears men originated and from whose mouth the gods came into existence, thus identifying him with Atum and Ptah in the same breath. There is no such pantheism evident in the hymn to the Aten, but on the contrary an austere monotheism which is quite unique in the world of the Late Bronze Age.

That this is deliberate and not fortuitous is shown from the careful suppression of the plural form of 'god' wherever it appears in earlier texts. There was but one god and Akhenaten was his prophet, for the character of this innovation must be attributed to the King's own religious experience, fostered perhaps by the thinkers of the age who were only too ready to create God in the image of Pharaoh. The temper of the time had encouraged the emergence of such a supreme and divine ruler. The religious books of the Dynasty, closely concerned with the apotheosis of the Pharaoh, who on death mingled with the sun-god who had begat him, express a distinct monotheism. In the words of Piankoff:

> In this religious literature of the New Kingdom, Re is the motor which operates the *perpetuum mobile*—Creation. Night is the coupling of the male and female principle, earth with heaven, the god Geb with the goddess Nut. It is equally the nocturnal voyage of the dead sun through the body of Nut, from the West to the East. The solar machine is the boat which during the night carries the god Flesh with a staff of divinities who are his attributes. The disk which the god carries on his head is the visible sun. It is this visible image of the god that the adepts of the Amarna reform wished to adopt for their cult without denying that the activating and active force is Re, as is clearly expressed in the name of Akhenaten's god (particularly in its later redaction).[37]

This elevation of the sun-god Re to a position of primacy, if not uniqueness, had its reflection in the sphere of politics and *vice versa*. It is indeed difficult to separate the worlds of religion and politics in the Late Bronze Age, and the one interacted with the other on a reciprocal basis. The elevation of Amenophis III to the divine kingship of the wealthiest and most powerful state of the ancient world was the epiphany of a ruler who, even as a child, was worshipped by his subjects and whose utterances were oracular. A situation had thus arisen which was ripe for exploitation by the mono-maniac and the megalomaniac. The peculiar physical features of Akhenaten no doubt helped to convince his entourage of his uniqueness and super-human substance, an incarnation in fact of the unique and divine Creator.

It is not that other gods are reviled by the Atenists, they are totally ignored. It has long been accepted that a kind of duel was fought between Amun of Thebes and the Aten for supremacy as state gods, an interpre-tation which we shall examine shortly. What has been less emphasised is the total eclipse of Osiris, the god of the Dead whose cult, rising rapidly to prominence from the end of the Old Kingdom, had since grown enormously in importance and popularity. The adherents of Aten rejected completely the Osirian conception of life after death—the journey of the wandering soul to the West, the Last Judgement before Osiris in the Hall of the Two Truths, the agricultural life of the blessed in the Elysian Fields where the corn grew to a height of nine cubits in a sort of eternal spring-time. The very title, 'Osiris' which is attached to the name of the dead person with little more significance than 'deceased,' is carefully excluded from tomb-inscriptions at Amarna, and from coffins and other funerary equipment; and although the shawabti figure, intimately bound up with agricultural duties in the Elysian Fields, is still retained with typical Egyptian conservatism, its texts are changed to remove all reference to Osiris.

Plates 106–108

The Atenist eschatology, in fact, is not easy to discover, but it appears to lay emphasis on an earlier concept which had been overlaid by the agricultural life of the Osiris cult. This enshrined the belief that the souls of the dead came forth by day at sun-rise, sometimes in the form of twittering birds, and enjoyed a full life in an invisible twin to the material universe, returning to the tomb at nightfall. The significance of the re-creation of the universe with the rebirth of the Aten at each daybreak, so insistently affirmed in the hymns, is that it brought life not only to the tangible world, but to the world of the Dead also.

Akhenaten declared that after death he was to be buried at Akhet-Aten where the tombs of his courtiers were also to be prepared. He was to practise in death the same control over them and the same intervention as he had exercised in life. His officials prayed that they might rest eternally near him and behold him daily. In this they were reverting to beliefs current in the Old Kingdom when the mastaba tombs of the dead were erected in rows around the pyramids of the sun-kings whom they had served in life. As Norman Davies put it over half a century ago:

> The gods of burial . . . were supposed to be no more and their priesthood had no place in Akhet-Aten . . . The prayers for burial favours, therefore, which would have been addressed to other powers are naturally directed to the King as patron of the dead, in whose control all privilege and means of happiness for both worlds lay.

The evolution of the Atenist doctrines is reflected in the progress of external events. The King had been given the name of Amenophis at birth and continued to use that form for his *nomen* up to his sixth regnal year. Soon after his accession, he opened a sandstone quarry at Gebel Silsila for new buildings to Aten throughout Egypt and particularly for the sanctuary of the *Ben-Ben* in Karnak. In a large damaged stela commemorating the event, he is shown making an offering to Amun in whose territory the temple was to be built; but the king is described as merely the Chief Prophet of the Aten. The Pharaoh was, *ex officio*, the Chief Prophet of every god in Egypt, though his duties were discharged by a surrogate in all the local cult-centres. The emphasis upon his sacerdotal role in the case of the Aten shows that he proposed to celebrate the daily ritual in person at Thebes. As far as Amun was concerned, he had already appointed a deputy and it is known that a certain Maya was functioning as his First Prophet of Amun as late as his regnal year 4. Up to then, at least, there was thus no conflict between Akhenaten and the god of Thebes.

The founding of Akhet-Aten at modern Amarna, however, has been interpreted as a deliberate act of state policy on the part of the King to challenge or curb the secular power of Amun and his priesthood and to diminish the importance of the Southern Residence, Thebes. This assumption, so generally admitted, requires careful examination. In the first place, the founding of Akhet-Aten was no more than the creation of a local habitation for the Aten. All the great gods of Egypt had their seats, Ptah in Memphis, Re-Atum in Heliopolis, Amun in Thebes and so on, where they were believed to have first manifested themselves, and from which they could hardly be evicted without the destruction of the cities themselves. Aten at Thebes was no more than a visitor, and his increasing importance demanded that he should have a 'horizon' or seat as his 'place of origin.'

Plate 6

The King on the earlier Boundary Stelae at Amarna speaks of how he was directed to the site by the Aten, his father, and found that it was in no-one's possession: 'It belonged not to a god, goddess, prince, princess, . . . and no man had any right to act as its owner.' The early planning of the move appears from the recognition that there were other gods and goddesses who might be in possession of local cult-centres. Unfortunately the date on the early stelae is damaged and the year 4 has been read with reservations. It is probable that the search for a suitable site had begun even earlier, and the carving of the two great stelae at its northern and southern extremities would not have begun until after the township had been demarcated and formally dedicated by the King and some buildings perhaps already erected. A greatly damaged passage in these two stelae has often been quoted to mean that Akhenaten met opposition from the priesthood of Amun; but this is certainly incorrect and the passage appears to be no more than a florid statement of the evil thing it would be if the tombs of the King's courtiers were not made in the foothills of the eastern mountain range at Amarna. Perhaps this was an attempt on the part of the King to allay the dismay that may have been created when he decided to abandon the old family burial places at Thebes in favour of these new ones at Amarna.[38] His officials had to have their tombs near to that of their king at Amarna so that according to Atenist eschatology they could share in the life and worship at Amarna after death.

The traditional interpretation of this damaged passage in the early stelae has bequeathed a persistent idea that Akhenaten quarrelled violently with the hierarchy of Amun, as a result of which he left Thebes in a mood of bitter resentment to found Akhet-Aten and thereafter to persecute Amun, whose priesthood carried on an open or covert policy of antagonism to the Pharaoh. The idea of a priestly *imperium in imperio* that could effectively challenge the central authority in Bronze Age Egypt is an invention of nineteenth-century historians, obsessed by contemporary struggles between Church and State in Europe. It suggests that there was some separation of function in Ancient Egypt, whereas the two were indissolubly linked, in so far as it is possible to speak of an Ancient Egyptian 'Church' or priestly party. The power of Amun, its wealth, and the bureaucracy that administered it, had been the creation of grateful sovereigns of the Dynasty who had accredited so much of their good fortune to the favour of their city god. But as they had given, so they could take away. All the endowments were in their hands. The appointment of priests of Amun, even to minor posts, had to be sanctioned by the Pharaoh. Many of the King's closest relatives held important positions in the hierarchy of which he was himself the leader. Since the King was the nominal owner of all the land of Egypt, the power of any priesthood could be reduced almost overnight by diverting its income to the coffers of other temple treasuries or the State. There can be little doubt that the resources of the great gods of Egypt were re-allocated to the sanctuaries of the Aten up and down the country and particularly to the great cult-centre at Amarna. It was the wealthy Amun of Thebes, whose worship appears to have spread to other towns in the land during Dynasty XVIII, who must have suffered most. His powers were whittled away by increasing poverty, reducing the need for so large a staff both secular and sacerdotal. His prelates doubtless received appointments in new religious centres, probably of the Aten itself at Thebes, since its enormous temple at Karnak would have required an expert staff to administer it, and it continued to function even when Amarna had been built and occupied.

Plate 49

Plate 113

One of the features of the Aten cult was the presentation of lavish offerings at the Great Temple at Amarna, where after Year 9 a positive forest of mud-brick altars was built to be heaped each day with fresh offerings, doubtless on behalf of the dead as well as the living; and such lavish provision could only have been made at the expense of other cults. The proof that the priesthood of Amun was eliminated as an effective body during the reign of Akhenaten is found in the failure of Tut-ankh-Amun, as he reports in his Restoration Stela, to find any cadre of priests who could resume office in the re-established shrines and his induction of well-known persons in each town to fill the ranks of the priesthood. Indeed, one at least of the highest appointments in the hierarchy of Amun, that of Second Prophet, was filled by a member of the Royal Family in the reign of Ay, as had been the case under Amenophis III. There is nothing to show that the appointment had not been made earlier in the preceding reign. Any suggestion, therefore, that an official or unofficial opposition to Akhenaten existed can be discounted. When a god governed the land, his wishes and decrees were taken as inspired; and whether they were wise, criminal, beneficent or stupid could only be seen in retrospect when the god had ceased to rule. Recent developments in modern totalitarian states ruled by similar semi-divine 'personalities' provide a useful parallel. The only focal points from which a legitimate challenge could have been issued to Akhenaten were the oracles of a god or a pretender to the

Plate 66
Plate 18

throne. The only god with sufficient power and influence to have an oracle worth attention was Akhenaten's own deity the Aten. The only pretender to the throne was a younger brother, who seems to have been on terms of affectionate intimacy with Akhenaten.

The blind acceptance of Akhenaten's divine guidance can be seen in the thoroughness with which the name of the gods of Thebes, particularly those of Mut and Amun were hammered out in a later phase of the Aten heresy. This iconoclasm has been dated by those who deny a co-regency between Amenophis III and his son, from the moment of the move to Amarna, about Year 6, when the king changed his name to Akhenaten. Those, on the other hand, who believe in a co-regency, find it difficult to accept that any such fury was unleashed until the old king, Amenophis III, was safely in his grave. Both schools of thought then have to explain how later, during the co-regency of Smenkh-ka-Re, two ordinary priests of Amun in the funerary temple of that king could have scribbled their graffito in the tomb of Pere which gives us our only date in his reign. The account that has received general favour is that towards the end of his reign it was brought home to Akhenaten that his policy was causing disaster to Egypt. He was prevailed upon to send the young co-regent Smenkh-ka-Re to Thebes to patch up the quarrel with the priesthood of Amun and to attempt some compromise with the old religion. In the present writer's view this interpretation is open to objections. There was no opposition at Thebes to placate; and the evidence that Smenkh-ka-Re lived there permanently is scanty, though he certainly was building his mortuary temple, and therefore, presumably, his tomb at Thebes. Rather more of his monuments have been found in the Memphis area where, as the heir-apparent, he was doubtless reared.[39] It seems highly improbable, moreover, that Akhenaten would have compromised his religious faith by recognizing other gods, particularly Amun, when the progress of his thought, in so far as it can be mapped, is all in the direction of a greater abstraction and monotheism.

In the writer's view it is more likely that the iconoclasm against the gods, and particularly against Amun, falls towards the very end of Akhenaten's reign, probably after the death of Smenkh-ka-Re and was perhaps the last great act of his reign. For this there is some meagre evidence. The shrine which Akhenaten made for his mother and which was found in Valley Tomb No. 55, had the *nomen* of Amenophis III inscribed upon it, according to Daressy, but the Amun element had been cut out. This suggests that though it was made as late as Year 9, at the earliest, and probably after

Fig. 5

Plate 9

Plate 102

Plate 80

Plate 109

Plate XII

Year 12, yet the god Amun was not at that time proscribed in the royal names, though it was usually avoided by duplicating the *prenomen*. Again, in 1883 the local Arabs found a cache of gold objects in the vicinity of the Royal Tomb at Amarna probably hidden during the removal of the burials to Thebes in the reign of Tut-ankh-Amun. Among the objects retrieved were two massive gold rings, one inscribed with the name of Nefert-iti, the other having a bezel in the form of a frog. The underside of this latter specimen is delicately engraved with an inscription reading, 'Mut, Lady of Heaven,' suggesting that by the time the tomb was used for the burials of Nefert-iti and Meket-Aten, the name of Mut, the consort of Amun at Thebes, was not proscribed.[40] The incompletely excavated tomb-chapels near the workmen's village at Amarna produced evidence for an occupation late in the reign of Akhenaten, yet the names of other gods such as Shed, Isis and Amun himself were found. The information yielded up by these remains is, however, very indeterminate. They may date to the period immediately following the death of Akhenaten and before the city was completely abandoned. They may indicate that what the toiling masses in Egypt thought or worshipped was of no consequence to Akhenaten. On the other hand, they may show that to the last years of his reign, the worship of other gods, including Amun, was tolerated, if not encouraged.

It must be confessed that all this evidence is tenuous and far from conclusive and the problem of Akhenaten's proscription of Amun and Smenkh-ka-Re's cult of him is at present somewhat intractable. The enigma is bound up with another mystery—why the colossal statues of Akhenaten from the Broad Hall of the Aten temple at Thebes still bear his name in its Amenophis form. The presumption has been that they must have been taken down and buried before the king changed his name to Akhenaten and the suggestion has been made that it was the senior co-regent, Amenophis III, who had these 'deplorable' monuments dismantled and decently covered up, since they bear no marks of mutulation or desecration. With the very meagre information at our disposal it would be wrong to dismiss such speculation out of hand, but to the present writer it seems more likely that they were demolished by Akhenaten himself as a result of a change of plan in the construction of the Aten temple.

Plate 3

The Amarna Letters

DESPITE THE MAGIC CASEMENTS that they throw open on the world of the fourteenth century BC, the Amarna Letters show only interrupted glimpses of the shifting historical scene and the characters who played their parts in it. Scholars have from time to time attempted to fit bits of the puzzle together so as to produce a coherent picture; but no one solution has been generally accepted, and the suspicion remains that most of the important pieces are missing. The shadows these letters cast are unfortunately as numerous as the vistas they reveal. We have already referred to the finding of this part of the State archives; and we have given brief samples of their contents (see pp. 46–49). In this chapter we shall touch upon some of the problems they raise for the historians of Ancient Egypt.

The Amarna Letters consist of nearly three hundred and fifty pillow-shaped slabs of sun-dried clay impressed with cuneiform signs in a language which for the most part is Akkadian or Babylonian, the diplomatic *lingua franca* of the day, in use among the great kings and princelings of the Near East. The majority of these documents are despatches sent from the local prince or governor to the Egyptian Court; but there are also one or two copies or drafts of the letters which the Pharaoh sent to his correspondents.

Plates 116, 117

The translation of these letters has proved very difficult, and is far from settled since the scribes who wrote them were using a language which was not their own but derived from an earlier form of Old Babylonian, modified however by Canaanite innovations in its vocabulary, morphology and grammar, and fossilized by inaccurate teaching from one generation to the next into a kind of Volapuk, a diplomatic jargon, unintelligible except to its adepts. A leading expert in this field has recently summed up the difficulties of translation in these words: 'it is not enough for the would-be interpreter to know Akkadian, he must also be a specialist in Hebrew and Ugaritic, and above all he must be so familiar with all the letters that he knows what to expect from their writers.'[41] This is important because it reveals that very few specialists in the ancient world could have been capable of translating these texts; and the existence of school exercises, vocabularies and literary works show that they had to employ some of their time teaching pupils to carry on their esoteric learning, doubtless perfecting their own knowledge in the process.

The difficulties of interpretation are just as great as the problems of translation; and the sorting of this archive into its proper sequence has not achieved universal agreement, though several solutions have been proposed. The obstacles in the way are formidable. In the first place, the tablets have survived in a generally poor condition, their edges in particular having crumbled away and taken with them many of the superscriptions containing the names of the sender and recipient. Moreover, the cuneiform scribes did not date their documents, probably because an international calendrical system did not exist; and not a single Amarna Letter has any indication to show in what order it should be read. It may be that at the time of their abandonment, a number of them, the majority perhaps, did bear dates written in ink on the margins in hieratic by the methodical Egyptian filing-clerks, for some of them still carry dockets showing when and where they were received, but they are now in so fragmentary a condition that only one (Kn. No. 23) can be read for certain as 'Year 36, fourth month of Winter...' and even that has its day omitted. Another (Kn. No. 27), as we have seen, was inscribed with the controversial date 'Year (1)2.'

A third obstacle is the fact that with one or two exceptions, only the Kings of Mitanni, Babylon and Assyria name the Pharaoh with whom they are corresponding by employing his *prenomen*, Nibmuaria (Neb-maet-Re) and other variants in the case of Amenophis III, or Naphuria (Nefer-kheperu-Re) among other versions for Akhenaten. The King of Alashia addresses his letters to 'The King of Egypt' without specifying which particular Pharaoh he is writing to. Except in two instances, the vassals address their correspondent as 'The King of Egypt', or by some such circumlocution as 'My God,' 'The Sun,' 'My Father,' 'The Great King', 'My Lord,' and so forth. Similarly, in the few copies that exist of despatches sent by the Pharaoh to his vassals, the sender refers to himself by his title of 'The King,' and not by name. In general, therefore, with little more than two dozen exceptions, there is no indication of the Pharaoh who sent or received the letter. When it is remembered that besides Amenophis III and Akhenaten, Smenkh-ka-Re and Tut-ankh-Amun have left evidence of their sojourn at Amarna, opportunities for confusion are increased several-fold.

Another difficulty in the way of putting these letters in their chrono-logical order is doubt about the exact circumstances in which they were found. The original report was that they were discovered by a peasant

Plate 116

Plate 117

woman searching for *sebakh* among the ancient ruins at Amarna, and the area was then rummaged by other villagers who got wind of the find. It has been alleged that many of the tablets were broken during this illicit grubbing; but since they were small and readily portable, it is unlikely that much damage was done to them during their recovery, especially as it is most probable that they were found deposited together in one particular spot. It has also been surmised that the finders deliberately broke up many of the tablets, 'either for the purpose of easy carriage on their persons ... or so that the number of men who were to share in the sale of the tablets might be increased.' It may be doubted, however, whether any were broken up for the purpose of easy carriage, since they were neither large nor heavy and were already in an eminently portable form. It is equally improbable that any were broken to increase the number of shareholders in the proceeds of a prospective sale. This was not a single papyrus, for instance, that had to be cut up into as many portions as there were shareholders and sold piecemeal. Over three hundred tablets had been found, and the number of diggers, one may be certain, was limited probably numbering not more than the members of the family of the original finder, and each would get a fair number of complete specimens, assuming that they were all in sound condition when found. Moreover, it should be remembered that the vendors could have had no idea of what these lumps of clay covered with strange indentations really were, since nothing like them had been unearthed in Egypt before. With true peasant caution, it is more likely that the owners would have tried to find out the value of a single intact specimen before flooding the market with the entire mass of tablets, or resorting to division and the other tricks of their trade. In the event, they must have been disappointed by the responses they received, because no-one in Egypt would at first accept them as genuine.

It is then that the tablets may have suffered some damage in being hawked from one dealer to the next. A story is related, for instance, of their being taken to Luxor in sacks thrown across the backs of asses and camels. This would have been an unusual, slow and costly method of transport when the river was at hand, and its truth may be doubted. The Rev. A. H. Sayce, who travelled extensively in the Near East throughout most of the eighty-eight years of his life, reported in 1917 that he had heard from those who made the find in 1887 that in the process of recovery nearly two hundred tablets had been totally destroyed and fully as many broken and otherwise seriously damaged. It would, however, have required considerable skill and experience of interrogating Orientals on the part of

Plate 113

Plate 118

Plate 118

Sayce to have elicited the true answer from his informants and not the one that they thought he wanted to hear, assuming that they could divine his motives for questioning them. It is probable that here, too, the amount of destruction has been exaggerated. It is indeed remarkable, in the light of all these horrific tales, that of the three-hundred and forty tablets that are despatches, only some thirty-five are not substantially complete. Since the original find was made, other tablets have been unearthed at different times as a result of careful excavation on the site of the Records Office at Amarna by Petrie, Borchardt and Pendlebury, and it is curious that of the thirty-five tablets so recovered, only two are intact; the rest are mere fragments, none of which fits on to incomplete letters found earlier. This suggests that the original finders may not have bothered to collect mere fragments and reduces still further the probability that they deliberately broke up tablets in order to divide the spoils.

It might be justly claimed, therefore, that a substantial part of the original archive has survived, and if it is now damaged that is mainly because it was in such a dilapidated condition when it was abandoned. This conclusion, however, is not accepted by the majority of scholars for the following reason. There are too few letters, they argue, in the hoard, if one assumes that the records extend over the seventeen years of Akhenaten's reign, as well as a probable three years of Tut-ankh-Amun, and in addition include a number of despatches dating from the reign of Amenophis III and brought to Akhet-Aten for reference purposes. Thus some students have set a minimum of about thirty years for the scope of the correspondence, and a total of three hundred and forty despatches for this period is remarkably small. Some of the correspondents are represented by one letter only, whereas Ribaddi, the Prince of Byblos, is represented by nearly seventy. On the other hand, there is not a single draft letter to any of the Egyptian officials resident in Palestine and Syria at such centres as Gaza, Jaffa, Simyra, Beth-Shan and elsewhere.

The incompleteness of this dossier has not deterred scholars from attempting to put the tablets into some kind of order. The pioneer work was done by the Norwegian Knudtzon and his successors during the years 1907–14, and in their publication the letters have been grouped according to their place of origin from north to south; and within each group the arrangement is chronological in so far as the editors could estimate the provenances and sequences from internal evidence. It is obvious, however, in the present state of our knowledge, and in the postulated incomplete state of the archive, that any arrangement can only be arbitrary and subjective. The many letters of Ribaddi, for instance, have been used to tell a story of the progressive decline of Egyptian power in Asia, whereas the course of events, by a re-arrangement of the sequence, could be shown to have been an ebb and flow rather than a constant retreat.

In recent years, valiant attempts have been made by scholars in America, Britain and Germany, taking advantage of improvements in the translation of the documents, to seek out internal clues that would help to put the group of letters from each correspondent into a chronological sequence and to relate the groups to each other. It is possible, for instance, by taking note of the mention of neighbouring rulers with whom the correspondent had dealings to decide which princelings were near-contemporaries. Where letters have been received from these neighbouring states, it is possible to arrange groups to form 'clusters.' Thus Abimilki, the ruler of Tyre, wrote ten letters to Pharaoh, during the course of which he named Zimridi of Sidon, Etakkama of Kadesh, Aziru of Amurru, the King of Hazor and others. Since letters also exist from these rulers, it is possible to bring them into some kind of relationship, and the events which they recount, especially as the letters from Abimilki must from their context be spread over the short space of about four to five years. Similar 'clusters' can be built around other nuclei, but it is not possible to bring the whole archive into order in this way owing to lack of contacts between some of the groups and complete ignorance of the length of reign of a particular prince. Moreover, it has proved very difficult to find data that would show during what particular period in a Pharaoh's reign a contemporary princeling exercised power, and whether his tenure of office was spread over several reigns.

A useful peg, however, on which one group of letters can be hung has been the demonstration by Professor Albright that a certain Mayati, whose name appears in the Abimilki correspondence and in other letters, is a pet-name for Akhenaten's eldest daughter Meryt-Aten who played an important role in his later years and as the wife of his co-regent Smenkh-ka-Re. This has resulted in the firm placing of a number of letters to the last four years or so of the reign of Akhenaten. Unfortunately, it has not been possible to find similar pegs for other batches of letters. In this impasse, Albright and his pupil E. F. Campbell, have fastened upon the mention of a certain Maia, the deputy or high official of Pharaoh, in a few letters from Palestinian rulers, and have equated him with the official May, who was granted a tomb at Amarna which was never completed. They have pointed out that the name of the Aten occurs in its early form in this tomb, where the depiction of three princesses only shows that it could not have been inscribed earlier than Year 7 of Akhenaten. Soon after this date, so they claim, May was disgraced and his name and figure erased from his tomb-reliefs, apart from oversights. From the equation of the Maia of the Letters with the May of the Amarna tomb, Albright and Campbell have made large deductions.

Unfortunately, they have overlooked a number of serious objections to their thesis. The name Maya is one of the commonest at this period and could apply to one of several men,[42] least of all to the owner of the Amarna tomb who held high administrative rank in the army and had several stewardships in Heliopolis. He was not, however, a King's Envoy which would have been a necessary title if he had exercised power as the King's Deputy abroad. It is clear from the Letters that Maia was on the spot in Palestine discharging his duties and it is difficult to see how he could have carried out other responsibilities, including important Court functions *in absentia*. In any case the fact that the tomb of May was still incomplete before Year 9 at the latest is of no significance. Precisely the same criteria could be used to prove that Ay died before the Pharaoh whom he served, whereas it is known that he survived Tut-ankh-Amun. Lastly, as we have already emphasised, the dating of Amarna monuments by the number of princesses represented in the train of the Royal Family can be thoroughly discredited (see p. 64).

Plate 120

The imposing edifice erected by Albright thus largely crumbles; and it remains doubtful, in default of fresh evidence from elsewhere, whether the Amarna archive will ever be sorted into its proper chronological sequence; and whether a study of the letters from the vassal princes can ever produce any solid results in view of the extremely flexible limits within which they can be dated on a relative basis. Those who have pursued such investigations have had to make a number of assumptions during the course of their studies in order to reach any firm conclusions. It may be time, therefore, to approach the problems from another direction.

All the investigators who have examined the problems of the Amarna correspondence have accepted without any question that it is a truly Egyptian archive, used as a serious tool by the Pharaoh and his advisers.

Plate 118

The name of the building where the letters were found, 'The House of the Correspondence of Pharaoh,' more commonly rendered as 'The Records Office,' has helped to drive the idea home that they were found in a repository of state documents, and the fact that such important records were left behind has been used as an illustration of the panic haste in which Akhet-Aten was abandoned, or else to show that there was some uncertainty in official quarters as to whether the City was being relinquished temporarily or for ever. Other scholars have argued that what was left behind was a collection of out-of-date letters belonging to previous reigns and of no significance to Tut-ankh-Amun, who when he moved from Amarna took all the live correspondence with him. The existence of one certain and two possible letters dating to his reign they explain as oversights.

Both these assumptions need very careful probing. The idea that these clumsy lumps of clay, impressed with outlandish signs expressing an esoteric diplomatic jargon, were part of the Egyptian State records, requires to be dismissed at once. It presupposes that whenever the king or an official required to refer to previous records he had to call for a translator to search out the appropriate tablet and read it off. This is so unlikely as not to warrant much consideration. It must be emphasised that the Pharaoh, unlike medieval Europeans kings, was literate. His training included the education of a scribe, though he had secretaries to do much of his work for him. This tradition of the educated king was of great antiquity in Egypt and the Pyramid Texts of *c.* 2400 BC speak of the Pharaoh acting after death as the scribe of the gods. It is in fact unthinkable that the god incarnate would not have been instructed in the magic arts of reading and writing presided over by Thoth, the god of wisdom: and it is almost certain that he would peruse all important state documents. After the cuneiform despatch had been read and glossed by the appropriate messenger, it would then doubtless be translated for any subsequent reference and filed away in the 'House of Correspondence.' It is the translation that would form part of the Egyptian records, composed in a more convenient and portable form than cuneiform tablets. It is virtually certain that copies of the foreign correspondence would have been kept on rolls of papyrus, all carefully dated in the meticulous manner of the Egyptian scribe. The Egyptians had had their own method of keeping records and their own tradition of office procedure since the dawn of history and were not likely to change them to suit the cumbersome system employed by barbarians and vassals. Translations of the cuneiform despatches would be accompanied by the replies that had been sent by the king or his officers. It is records of this kind that would have to be consulted by advisers of the king, such as the Chamberlain Tutu, or the Private Secretary Ay, whenever a reply was to be drafted, particularly as it is clear from the Letters themselves that replies were sent a long time after their receipt. The process of turning the king's words into Akkadian would be left to the cuneiform clerks of the 'House of Correspondence,' who after the bureaucratic manner of their kind duly filed the incoming letters as

Plate 72

soon as they had been translated. When the Court moved from Amarna a
golden opportunity was presented for discarding this useless lumber and it
was left behind, though there is evidence for thinking that a hole had been
dug below the foundations of the Records Office in which to bury it, since
unlike papyrus it could not be destroyed by burning.

That the cuneiform tablets represented a system of communication that
the Egyptians had to accept with resignation in the case of the Asiatic
princes, whose use of the system had its own traditions, is shown by the
circumstance that not a single draft despatch has survived addressed to any
of the Egyptian commissioners and garrison commanders in Palestine or
Syria. These officers would have received their instructions written in
Egyptian on papyrus; and model letters from Ramesside times exist to
show the form they would have taken. That these cuneiform letters were
not part of the Egyptian records is shown by the extreme paucity of any
copies of the replies from the Egyptian Court to the many letters it received.
Apart from nine draft replies, we have no means of telling what the Pharaoh
said to his correspondents.

We can surely dismiss from consideration, therefore, that any cumbersome cuneiform letters were brought to Amarna from earlier reigns for
reference purposes, or such letters were removed when the Court departed.[43] The Egyptian Foreign Office must have come to Amarna and
left it with its records on sheets and rolls of papyrus contained within
light portfolios or cabinets. It is not unreasonable to suggest, therefore,
that the letters found at Amarna were those received when the king was in
residence there from the time of its occupation to its relinquishment. As it
was his chief seat after Year 6 of the reign, it is probable that the bulk of
the foreign correspondence of this period has been found there. But it is
also likely that similar despatches were received at Memphis, Heliopolis
and Medinet el-Ghurab where there were royal palaces to which the Court
repaired on occasions. Whether tablets were sent for storage to a central
depot at Amarna after being formally read and translated is doubtful.

Plates 116, 117

Copies (Kn. Nos. 23, 27) were made of at least two tablets received at
Amarna before they were sent on to Thebes where the king was officiating
at the time. But where the originals were kept is not known, presumably
in the Malkata palace at Thebes. On the whole it seems most likely that the
despatches were brought to wherever the Court was residing, and after
translation were stored in an office of the local palace. The central archive,
kept on compact and portable papyrus, as we have suggested, would
doubtless be in charge of officials in the king's retinue, for it is a mistake

to believe that the Court remained rooted to one spot, or that Akhenaten shut himself up in Amarna and never ventured beyond its confines.

Since Amarna was occupied about Year 6 of Akhenaten and abandoned probably soon after Year 1 of Tut-ankh-Amun, the correspondence received during that time must stretch over a period of some dozen years and not the wider extent that has been postulated by some scholars. It is true that the letters of Ribaddi of Byblos have been used as an argument for thinking that a considerable portion of the total archive is still lacking since the despatches from this prince far outnumber those of any other correspondent, suggesting that by chance his letters have survived practically intact, whereas those of his contemporaries must be represented by about one fifth of their original number. It should be remembered, however, that some of Ribaddi's letters are duplicates sent off by different messengers when he was beleaguered, in the hope that one at least would get through. Byblos, too, was an important port of call and despatches could be sent quickly and conveniently by ships on the Byblos run. Moreover, he was an indefatigable letter-writer and the Pharaoh had to complain of the volume of correspondence with which he was inundating the Court.

This is but one example of the imponderables that result from considering the letters from the vassal princes, and in view of the meagre chronological rewards to be gleaned from them and the uncertainty about the Pharaohs to whom they were addressed, in the absence of any name in the superscriptions, we shall ignore them in our examination in favour of the letters from foreign royalty.

This group consists of despatches from Kadashman-Enlil I and Burnaburiash II of Babylonia, Ashur-uballit I of Assyria, Tushratta of Mitanni, Tarkhundaradu of Arzawa and Suppiluliumas of Hatti. We exclude the letters from Alashia (Cyprus?) in this group since they are addressed to the Pharaoh by title and not by name. It will be noted that no great power in the Near East is unrepresented in this dossier, a fact which encourages the belief that the 'royal' letters form a proper statistical sample; and this view is reinforced by the Pharaohs who are named therein, including as they do Amenophis III, Akhenaten and Tut-ankh-Amun, all resident from time to time at Amarna according to our opinion. Smenkh-ka-Re's name is missing from the tally unless he is the *Khuri(a)* of Letter Kn. No. 41 to whom Suppiluliumas writes. This, however, is unlikely, especially as the context speaks of the Pharaoh succeeding his father, or father-in-law. In view of the strong probability that Smenkh-ka-Re exercised no independ-

Plate 116

ent rule, it is virtually certain that during his co-regency, foreign kings wrote to Akhenaten rather than to him, since it is probable that they were unable to appreciate the peculiar Egyptian system of dual control, and continued to correspond with the same Pharaoh up to the time of his death. It may also be that this continuity was preferred by the Pharaohs since their younger partners might die and have to be replaced during their life-times. It is at least clear than Amenophis III received letters up to his thirty-sixth regnal year.

If we now examine the letters in this 'royal' group in which the Pharaohs are unequivocally named, we shall find that ten (*viz:* Kn. Nos. 2–4, 17, 19–24) were received by Amenophis III and an equal number by Akhenaten (*viz:* Kn. Nos. 7, 8, 10, 11, 15, 16, 25, 27–29). One letter (Kn. No. 9) was sent to Tut-ankh-Amun, and another (Kn. No. 26) to Queen Tiye. The drafts of letters sent by named Pharaohs are few, but two (Kn. Nos. 1 and 5) were sent by Amenophis III and one (Kn. No. 14) by Akhenaten. The allocation of the royal letters almost equally between Amenophis III and Akhenaten suggests that the rest of the correspondence should be divided roughly in the same proportion.

If our contention is right, that no letters from an earlier period were brought to Akhet-Aten because the Egyptian records were not kept on cuneiform tablets written in a language obscure to all but a few initiates, it follows that the despatches sent to Amenophis III must have been received at Amarna during his reign; and this reinforces the view that he was alive when Akhet-Aten was built and was ruling with his son as co-regent. Akhet-Aten began to be occupied by the official classes from Year 6 of Akhenaten's reign, which according to our reckoning corresponds with regnal year 33/4 of the older king. This means that letters were reaching Akhet-Aten for the first five years of its existence during the reign of Amenophis III and for its next five or six years during the reign of Akhenaten. If the volume of correspondence remained constant one would expect a similar number of letters to have been received during these two periods and this is in fact what we do find in respect of the ten despatches received by each Pharaoh in this particular 'royal' group.

It also means that the events mentioned in the correspondence which belongs to Akhenaten should refer only to the last years of his reign and not to his first twelve years of rule. An examination of the contents of the letters addressed to him reveals that this is also the case. There is no mention of Queen Nefert-iti who played such an important part in affairs during the greater part of his reign, but the Crown Princess Meryt-Aten is referred to under her pet-name of Mayati in several letters in the archive. She is named not only in the vassal letters by Abimilki of Tyre, whose city appears to have been dedicated to her, though it almost certainly would have belonged to Nefert-iti earlier, but also by Burnaburiash of Babylon (Kn. No. 10). There is some doubt too whether it is she or her sister Ankhes-en-pa-Aten who is the subject of a complaint by Burnaburiash in another letter (Kn. No. 11) that 'the mistress of Pharaoh's house' did not raise his head when he was distressed. In any case, the grumble must have been received late in the reign when Meryt-Aten and Ankhes-en-pa-Aten were important figures at the Egyptian Court.

Of the four letters sent to Amarna by Burnaburiash definitely during the reign of Akhenaten, two (Kn. Nos. 10 and 11) clearly refer to events of the Pharaoh's last years; and the other two (Kn. Nos. 7 and 8) make no reference to any incident that can be recognized as belonging to the first twelve years of the reign. On the contrary, the Babylonian envoy, a caravan leader, mentioned in letter Kn. No. 7 is the same merchant Salmu who acts as a messenger in Kn. No. 11, a circumstance which suggests that the two letters are separated from each other by a gap of a few years only. Of the total of six letters received from Burnaburiash, one (Kn. No. 6) seems to refer to his accession to power and may have been sent to Amenophis III, though the name of the recipient is missing; and another (Kn. No. 9) was sent to Tut-ankh-Amun, the successor to Akhenaten. The four or five relevant letters in this part of the archive, therefore, can hardly be spread over the seventeen years of Akhenaten's reign, but they might cover five years of it since Letter Kn. No. 7 reveals that the journey between the two countries was very long, hazardous from bandits and bad weather the and the Babylonian messenger had been detained long at the Egyptian Court. In the last five years of his reign Amenophis III, too, received only four letters from the King of Babylon.

The correspondence from Mitanni is no less significant. In this dossier, eight letters are addressed to Amenophis III, four to Akhenaten and one to Queen Tiye. The series begins with a letter (Kn. No. 17) from Tushratta to Amenophis III in which he recalls the circumstances which have brought him to the throne and he seeks the Pharaoh's friendship and support. This is apparently the first letter not only from Tushratta but also from the state of Mitanni to be received at Akhet-Aten and suggests, therefore, that Tushratta came to the throne about regnal year 33 of Amenophis III.[44] The rest of the correspondence during the reign of the older Pharaoh is largely concerned with negotiations for the marriage of

Tadukhipa, the young daughter of Tushratta, to Amenophis III and the fixing of a suitable bride-price. The princess was despatched with a rich dowry; and had followed her aunt Gilukhipa into the Pharaoh's harim by his regnal year 36. Tushratta in letter Kn. No. 23, dated to this year by a hieratic docket, sends greetings to her as the wife of an Egyptian king.

Letter Kn. No. 27 is the first despatch from Tushratta to the new Pharaoh Akhenaten; and the fact that there is no break in the sequence of events is shown by his sending with the letter his special envoys, Pirizzi and Pupri, to represent him at the State funeral of the old king, and reminding Akhenaten that the presents which Amenophis III had promised, apparently as a further instalment of the dowry of Tadukhipa, had not been received. This is the letter which bears the controversial date which we prefer to read as Year 12, to which point in Akhenaten's reign it naturally belongs according to the argument exposed above. The rest of the correspondence from Mitanni is almost entirely concerned with Akhenaten's failure to honour his father's alleged promises. According to Tushratta, before his death Amenophis III had undertaken to send him additional presents including two statues of solid gold; but when the gifts, reduced in number and value, arrived in Mitanni during the first months of Akhenaten's reign, it was found that inferior statues of wood overlaid with gold had been substituted. Tushratta was exceedingly angry at what he regarded as despicable chicanery on the part of the Pharaoh and his indignation is repeated in all his subsequent correspondence with Akhenaten. But however mean the deception, the incident could surely not have rankled for the entire seventeen years of Akhenaten's reign and must have been confined to the last five. If it be objected that four letters from Tushratta are too few to cover even this shorter span, especially in view of the eight received by Amenophis III in a similar period, it should be remembered that Tushratta also complains of the length of time his messengers are detained at the Egyptian Court; and it could be argued on the evidence that during the reign of Akhenaten there appears to have been a coolness between the Egyptian and the Mitannian Courts, despite the marriage alliance, perhaps as a result of an armed excursion which Mitanni made into Syria about this time in order to check the growing pretensions of Hatti.

Letter Kn. No. 26, addressed to Tiye, in which Tushratta replies to a communication from the dowager queen asking him to continue to send his embassies to her son, the new Pharaoh, and his advice to Akhenaten in letters Kn. Nos. 28 and 29 to consult his mother Tiye, are generally taken

Plate 116

Plate 117

as an indication of the youth and immaturity of Akhenaten at his accession, since he still required the practised hand of his mother to guide him in statecraft. This apparent lack of experience is one of the arguments of those who deny that the new king can have been anything more than a mere youth at the time of his accession; and who therefore regard as out of the question a co-regency, especially one lasting as long as eleven or twelve years. It also seems to refute our contention above that the letters to Akhenaten are concerned entirely with events in the last five years of his reign.

A careful reading of the despatches in question, however, does not support the view that Tiye was the adviser of her son. Tushratta is so vexed that he should have been cheated out of his gold statues and the other gifts promised by Amenophis III that he uses every means in his power to make Akhenaten honour his father's word including the enlistment of Tiye's support for his case. He also refers Akhenaten several times to Queen Tiye for the truth of the claim he is making that her husband before he died promised to send massy, chased, gold statues and other gold to Mitanni.

The argument that the mention of Tiye in the letters from Mitanni must refer only to the early years of Akhenaten's rule thus falls to the ground; and nothing conflicts with the view that the despatches addressed to Akhenaten belong to the last five years of his reign. The whole of the Amarna archive, in the writer's view, represents little more than a decade in the history of Egypt's foreign relations from the last regnal years of Amenophis III to the first regnal years of Tut-ankh-Amun.

XII The Reign of Akhenaten, 1378-1362 BC

IN THE LIGHT of the lengthy discussion in Parts I and II of this book, we may now be in a position to put together what has been learned about Akhenaten. But first we must utter a word of warning. We may with a fair degree of probability be able to plot the progress of the Amarna age as nodal points upon a small-scale map. We may even at times be able to fill in some of the detailed topographical features, but the character, colour and appearance of the entire landscape can hardly be known to us. Too many critical pieces of the chart are missing and likely to remain lost. In particular we lack any indication of the sequence of events in Akhenaten's last years, and without this information the history of his time must remain a matter for greater speculation. Because biographies, memoirs, histories and commentaries were practically never written by the Ancient Egyptians, we have to rely on evidence that is often only circumstantial. This is unavoidable and to complain of its frailty is useless. It will have to serve until better material is found to modify its claims in whole or in part. Working hypotheses are common in the field of science where finality is seldom reached except in limited spheres; but the Egyptologist has tended to reject them for fear of turning the writing of history into the writing of historical novels. If the danger is recognized, however, there is every chance of avoiding the pitfalls.

On the death of the first-born son, the Prince Tuthmosis, some time between regnal year 16 and 27 of Amenophis III, the eldest surviving son, Amun-hotpe, by the Chief Wife Tiye, became the heir-apparent. The youth appears to have been of sickly constitution, and Gardiner has pointed out that the epithet he so constantly applied to himself, 'Great in his Duration,' with the meaning of 'The Long-lived,' is possibly an expression of wishful thinking, since in youth he may not have been expected to live long. At his accession as King, he was represented as a normal man in the idealistic style of Egyptian art; but soon afterwards he had himself represented in a grotesque manner as though on reaching manhood he had developed a chronic endocrine disorder, or had chosen to be shown in such a pathological condition.

Plates 42, 45
Plates 43, 47

210

He was almost certainly brought up at Memphis where the royal princes were trained in the war-like arts, and in the desert vicinity of which they hunted lion, wild ass, gazelle and other creatures of the wild. Whether Prince Amun-hotpe indulged in such athletic exercise is doubtful. He is not represented in the tombs at Amarna as taking part in the chase or other field sports so beloved of the Pharaohs of the Dynasty, but we should not expect his prowess as a warrior or hunter to be exhibited in a private tomb. There is, however, evidence for thinking that destroyed temple reliefs at Amarna and Karnak showed him hunting wild animals, but these probably conveyed only an ideal picture of the sporting Pharaoh.

Plate XV

It seems more likely that Prince Amun-hotpe had a keener taste for the polite arts. His Chief Sculptor claimed to have been instructed in his craft by the Prince himself who is generally accredited on fairly plausible grounds with the composition of the Great Hymn to the Aten (see p. 187) though it may have been in many respects a pastiche of other religious literature of the time.

Plate 79

At the brilliant Court of his father, Prince Amun-hotpe must have come under the influence of the prominent men of his age, chief among whom was Amenophis-son-of-Hapu noted as a skilled administrator, who disposed of the manpower of the country in such enterprise as recruitment to the army for the protection of the frontiers of Egypt, particularly at the Nile mouths, open then as in Homeric times to sudden descents from marauding pirates. He also undertook the supply and organization of the labour force required for the grandiose building schemes of the King, including the hewing and transport of colossal hard-stone statues from the quarries near Memphis and Aswan. He was noted as a scholar and sage, his learning still being treasured a millennium after his death when he was deified. His king appreciated his extraordinary talents so much that he paid him the unprecedented honour of erecting for him a mortuary temple among the row of such buildings that lined the west bank at Thebes, the Southern Residence, the birthplace of the Dynasty and the city to which the kings were brought for burial in the tombs they had made for themselves in the Biban el-Moluk. In his old age, Amenophis-son-of-Hapu was appointed High Steward of the estates of Amun-hotpe's eldest sister, the Princess Sit-Amun, and allowed to instal statues of himself, the gift of the King, near the IXth Pylon that the King was founding at the Great Temple of Amun-Re in Karnak.

Plate 20

Plates II, III

Plate 17

Close relatives of Amenophis-son-of-Hapu held high positions in the state, a cousin, also called Amenophis, being the High Steward of Memphis,

Plate 19

Fig. 2

Plates 15, 16

Plates 18, 62, 63

while the latter's half-brother Ramose was soon to attain the office of Southern Vizier with his seat in Thebes.

Another influential family was more intimately connected with the royal house. Its doyens were Yuya and Tuyu, the maternal grandparents of Prince Amun-hotpe. Yuya was probably also the uncle of Amenophis III, and his sons held important positions at Court. One of them, the Army Commander Ay, was to exercise great influence in the state and eventually to attain the throne.

The family appears to have originated from Akhmim, a town in Upper Egypt, the capital of the Ninth District, where they had property; but they may also have inherited some foreign blood, since they had a striking physiognomy which has been described as more commonly found in Europe than Africa. As they held the offices of Master of the Horse or Lieutenant of the Chariotry, for three generations at least, it is probable that they had an Asiatic *maryannu* as an ancestor, since such skilled chariot warriors had introduced their Asiatic fighting machines into Syria, Palestine and Egypt; and formed a military aristocracy all over the Near East at this particular time, influencing considerably the new social structures of the older civilizations.

Near Memphis lay Heliopolis, the centre of the worship of the cycle of sun gods, Atum, Re, Khepri and Herakhty, and it would be surprising if Prince Amun-hotpe did not early come under the influence of the sun-religion. The worship of Re, the sun-god, had undergone a great expansion in its influence since the Middle Kingdom. This was doubtless due to the intellectual qualities of its priesthood who had overhauled its beliefs and revised its teaching to such effect that most of the local gods of Egypt had hastened to become solarized, attaching the name of Re to their own pristine forms. This was but one aspect of the universality of the new doctrine which sought to slough off many of the primitive concepts it had inherited from prehistoric days; and while retaining much of the old liturgy had explained its no longer intelligible utterances by up-to-date glosses and exegeses. The trend of thought was all in the direction of a monotheism which, however, did not exclude the old gods but attempted to embrace them all in a comprehensive henotheism. Re was the force that actuated the perpetual motion of the universe. He was born in the redness of dawn, when he recreated the universe, prevailed during the day and died in the redness of sunset. At night the dead god, now bearing the name of Flesh, underwent a series of transformations until by the next daybreak he had achieved the form of Khepri and was ready to give birth to the new sun. This doctrine was expressed in the new religious books that had replaced the *Pyramid Texts* and *Coffin Texts* of previous ages, though much of these old writings had been incorporated in the new funerary literature after extensive revision and editing.

The most ancient of these books to which Egyptologists have given the names of *The Book of What is in the Underworld* and *The Litany of the Sun* appear first in the tombs of the earlier kings of Dynasty XVIII and are concerned with the various transformations of the sun-god of whom the king was the offspring and to whom he returned on death. In *The Litany of the Sun*, Re, the sun-god, is invoked under his 'seventy-five names which are his bodies and his bodies are the gods.' He was also Re of the Solar Disk invoked as 'supreme power who makes the Earth to become visible, he who illumines the Westerners (*i.e.* the deceased), he whose active forms are his forms-to-be when he assumes the aspect of his great Aten'. This Aten or sun-disk, which illumines the world of the dead as well as the living and brings both to life, is the constant element in these transformations, and the power that motivated it, Re, is the supreme god. But already during Dynasty XVIII there is warrant for believing that the appearance had been accepted for the reality and the disk itself had become a sun-god in its own right under the name of Aten. This deity makes its first unequivocal appearance in the reign of Tuthmosis IV when on a large scarab it is described as a great universal god whose exalted position in the sky entitles it to rule over the empire of all that it shines upon. In the reign of Amenophis III it had acquired even greater prominence, being attached to the name of the King's barge, to that of his palace, and to those of some of the Royal Family. Conditions were therefore favourable for his son to imbibe the new teaching, and he proved an apt pupil who soon outstripped his teachers and became the one to whom revelation was vouchsafed and the innovator of change. From the first he followed the worship of the sun under a name which was his profession of faith: 'Re-Herakhty, rejoicing on the Horizon in his manifestation of the Light which is in the Sun-Disk (or Aten).' It is hardly surprising that in a land where the Pharaoh was regarded as the latest incarnation of the primal creator god who had been the first king of Egypt, his entourage should have followed Akhenaten's doctrines, or the gloss he put upon ancient dogmas, with enthusiasm.

When he came to manhood in regnal year 28 of his father, he was made co-regent and inducted as Pharaoh. The main ceremonies would have been celebrated at Memphis, the traditional centre for the coronation of the king since the time of Menes, the first Pharaoh. But before the crowning

Plate II

Plate 25

Plate 42

took place, he would have accompanied his father on a triumphal tour of his kingdom, to be presented to the populace in all the main centres and to be accepted as their true son by the local deities. No doubt the visitations were made to coincide with the great festivals of the town gods, such as the Feast of Opet at Thebes during the second month of inundation, when the god Amun, in whose honour the prince had been named Amun-hotpe ('Amun-is-content'), was carried in his tabernacle amid great rejoicing among the people. In reliefs and statuary in each local shrine, the appropriate deity would be shown as affixing the crown to the head of the King, though that ceremony was actually conducted only at Memphis by the special chamberlains in charge of the royal regalia, and doubtless in the presence of Amenophis III who would wish to see his son 'crowned in splendour while he lived.' As King the prince retained the name of Amun-hotpe as his *nomen* adding to it, however, the epithet 'Divine Ruler of Thebes;' and some Egyptologists have called him Amenophis IV to distinguish this earlier phase of his reign. For his *prenomen* he was given the name Nefer-kheperu-Re, Wa-en-Re ('Fair of forms like Re, the Only one of Re'), and he added the epithet 'The Long-Lived' at the end of his titulary.

Plate 17
Plate VIII

Plate 79

With the establishing of a second Court, a completely independent household would have been set up for the new king, who was for some reason not married to his sister, the heiress Sit-Amun, but to his cousin, the daughter of Ay, Nefert-iti. In addition, of course, he would have been supplied with a separate harim. The sons of his father's officials were appointed to similar posts at the new Court. Thus Bek, the son of Men, the Chief Sculptor of Amenophis III, was created Chief Sculptor to Amenophis IV. Pa-ren-nefer, too, the son of the Court Goldsmith and Chief Craftsman Apuia, held a similar office under Amenophis IV, being made his Chief Craftsman, and so winning the King's esteem as to be made his cup-bearer. Ramose was appointed his chief official with his seat at Thebes as the Southern Vizier. The young king's father-in-law Ay, became Master of the Horse and his private secretary, and in the latter capacity must have been responsible for taking down much of the King's decrees and thoughts. In the address to posterity which Ay left in his tomb at Amarna, he declares: 'My Lord taught me, and I carry out his instructions.' Nevertheless, we may suppose that as a man of riper years and experience his judgement may have been there to temper with advice the opinions on which the oracular decisions of the King were founded. His wife, Tey, had been the nurse of Nefert-iti, by which we are probably to understand that she was her step-mother, and had brought up the Queen, probably after the death

Fig. 2
Plate 62

Plate 119

of her true mother, and was held in high regard. Ay had a second daughter, Mut-nodjme, but whether she was a full sister or a half-sister of Nefert-iti is not known. She was, however, an important figure in the Queen's entourage and is distinguished by having two dwarf attendants in her train, like the princesses of seventeenth-century Spain.

Fig. 4

The first important decision of the new reign was to open a quarry at Gebel Silsileh for the extraction of sandstone for the construction of a great Temple to the Aten at Karnak to the east of the temple of Amun. There was probably a small shrine already on this spot known as 'The Mansion of Aten' but Amenophis IV decided to enlarge it very considerably. A stela commemorating the event was set up at Gebel Silsila and originally showed the King making an offering to Amun. It speaks of Amenophis as being the High Priest of Re-Herakhty, rejoicing on the Horizon in his manifestation of the light that is in the Sun-Disk, and the Court officials as being the directors of the quarry service for which all the workmen from one end of the country to the other were mustered. The temple was in process of being built under the name of 'The Aten is found in the House of the Aten', when an event occurred which even today has a revolutionary appearance. The name of the new god was enclosed in cartouches and given a titulary like that of a Pharaoh celebrating his Jubilee. He now became '(Re-Herakhty, rejoicing on the Horizon) (in his manifestation of the Light that is in the Sun Disk), Aten, the Living, the Great, Who is in Jubilee, Lord of Heaven and Earth.' At the same time he lost his anthropomorphic or theriomorphic form and instead of being shown as a falcon or falcon-headed man bearing the sun-disk on his head, he is represented by an abstract symbol, the elaborated glyph for sunlight, a disk encircled by a uraeus with an *ankh* life-sign depending from its neck and having a dozen or more rays ending in hands.

Plates 45, 110

Plate 5

The transition from orthodox art forms to this new revolutionary style can be seen most effectively in the tomb-chapel of the Vizier Ramose, where the royal pair appear at the Window of Appearances, or the State Balcony, of their palace while the Aten shines upon them. At the same time, the King and, to a lesser extent, the Queen are no longer represented idealistically as perfect beings, larger and more handsome than real life, but in a curious deformed way. The King wears a loose robe more like a woman's and the fluttering streamers at the back of his crown have become very long and feminine. This is the new fashion in which the Royal Family was now to be represented and which their followers hastened to copy as far as they could. The traditional pose assumed by the courtiers in the

Plate 43

Plate 50

Fig. 2

presence of royalty also changes and instead of a mere deferential inclination of their heads or bodies, they now bend themselves double or prostrate themselves before the King and his Chief Queen.

This epiphany of the Aten in its developed form seems to have taken place in the second regnal year of Amenophis IV when his father was celebrating his First Jubilee after a thirty years' period of rule. What special factors caused the young king to develop such ideas are not yet known. Whether he underwent some religious experience, some revelation, like Caligula, as a result of illness, can only be surmised. What is clear is that only he can have been responsible for specifying the grotesque style in which the Royal Family was to be represented and insisting on the divinity incarnate in him before which all mortals must abase themselves. That he was worshipped Plate 49 seems evident from the relief at Cambridge where he is shown followed by his own prophet, implying that he was revered as a god.

The new teaching and its forms of expression made their appearance while much of the temple of the Aten was in process of construction at Plate 45 Karnak, and apart from some blocks, presumably from the sanctuary, the Plate 48 decoration of the monument is in the extreme style of the new art. The curious distortions are seen at their most uncompromising in the colossal Plates 2–4 figures from its peristyle court, where the 'expressionist' management of form, unparalleled in any civilized art until modern times, still has a haunting power to move the spectator with some echo of its inner spiritual disturbance.

The Aten, however large and impressive his temple might have been built, could only have been a squatter in the City of Amun; and the King was soon fired with the desire to found a new capital solely for the Aten 'as his place of origin which he had made for himself.' The site selected lay about halfway between Memphis and Thebes, at the modern Tell el-Plate 112 Amarna where the cliffs on the east bank recede from the river to form a vast amphitheatre about eight miles in diameter and three in depth.

cf. Plate 6 The King recounts on the earlier Boundary Stelae that were carved in the rocks at the North and South extremities, how in his regnal year 4(?) he mounted a great state chariot plated with electrum on the chosen day of demarcating the site which he called Akhet-Aten (the Horizon or Seat of the Aten); and while all nature and mankind rejoiced, set a course for an altar which had been set up and where a huge oblation was made to the Aten. Then the courtiers, high army and state officials were led into his presence, prostrating themselves before him, while he affirmed that it was the Aten himself who had revealed the place to him: and that it was found

89–91 Three bracelet plaques apparently found among rubbish near the entrance to the tomb of Amenophis III in the western branch of the Biban el-Moluk, where they had been dropped by thieves who tore them from their gold settings: the present mounts are modern. They were doubtless made for one of the King's jubilees to which the scenes carved on them refer.

Above, a dark sard plaque, worked *à jour*, showing a winged female sphinx wearing a cap similar to that favoured by Nefert-iti (*cf.* Plate VIII) surmounted by a plant motif, like the example carved on the side of the throne of Mut-nodjme (*cf.* Plate 57). The sphinx receiving the name of the king may represent the lion goddess Tefnut who accepts the king's name in certain coronation scenes

Left, a carnelian plaque carved in relief with figures of Amenophis III and Tiye seated on thrones upon the jubilee palanquin and receiving emblems of an eternity of life and rule from two of their daughters, who also shake sistra

Below, a carnelian plaque carved in relief with figures of Amenophis III wearing jubilee robes and different crowns within the twin Pavilions of the Festival. He receives the emblems of an eternity of life and rule from Tiye wearing tall plumes upon her crown

92 The Second Shrine which surrounded the sarcophagus of Tut-ankh-Amun: 4.1 m. long, 3.5 m. wide and 2.45 m. high. It is made of wood covered with gesso modelled in relief and overlaid with thin sheet gold. The exterior walls are inscribed with an unknown and esoteric cosmological text concerned with the creation of the solar disk during the night. The shrine consists of 16 parts, *viz*: 2 roof sections, 4 cornices, 4 corner-posts, 3 panels (two sides and a back), 2 doors and a threshold, which are tenoned together. Some of the tenons are of copper, the rest are wood. Precisely the same construction was used for the shrine found strewn about the corridor and chamber of Valley Tomb No. 55 (Plates 94–96, 102), which was also about the same size

93 Panel from a casket-lid carved on a veneer of stained ivory, with some details in gold leaf, > showing Queen Ankhes-en-Amun in a bower handing her husband, Tut-ankh-Amun, a bouquet of flowers and mandrake fruits, or love-apples, which the maidens are picking in the garden below (*cf.* Plate 9). The features of the young King with his somewhat snub nose and firm, chubby chin are distinctive. The Queen is in elaborate dress and wears her long braided tress caught with two jewelled clasps

94–97 Tomb No. 55 in the Biban el-Moluk as it appeared to the excavators in 1907. *Above*, the approach corridor soon after the removal of a half-demolished sealing at the entrance. The passage is filled with limestone chips to within three or four feet of the roof, and wedged between the walls is the long side of a gilded wooden shrine on which has been thrown one of its doors (*cf.* Plate 92), decorated with a scene in low relief of a queen worshipping the Aten. Inscriptions gave her name as Tiye. The poor state to which the woodwork had been reduced by water entering from the crack in the ceiling can be readily seen. The excavators positioned the planks on the right to enable them to crawl over the obstruction without damaging it. *Below*, the gilded back panel of the shrine lying on the floor of the main chamber of just beyond the ramp of chippings which extended from the corridor. A drawing of this appears in Plate 102. Queen Tiye is shown in low relief before an altar pouring a libation to the Aten. She is preceded by her son Akhenaten whose figure has been adzed out of the scene. Stones fallen from the roof have increased the damage. Other parts of the same shrine lean against the east wall. Wherever the woodwork lay

horizontal the modelled gesso and gold leaf were still intact and the scenes and inscriptions preserved; but of the parts leaning against the wall only one still retained part of its overlay; the rest had slid in fragments to the floor. *Above*, view in the main chamber showing the recess in the south wall, probably the beginning of an attempt to hew a second chamber. Within the recess can be seen two of the four Canopic jars leaning in the left-hand corner. The adjacent wall has lost much of its coat of plaster, and the parts of the shrine leaning against the east wall are mostly denuded of their gilded gesso. On the floor below the recess can be seen the lid of the coffin illustrated below and on Plates 98 and XIV. *Below*, a close-up view of the lid of the wooden coffin inlaid and gilded, and split from neck to feet in its fall when the lion-headed bier supporting the coffin rotted and collapsed. The lid, which was presumably lying loose on the shell, was jerked clear. The gilded bronze uraeus on the brow is intact, but the gold mask has been ripped from the face. By the side of the lid and partially obscured by it, is the shell containing the decayed mummy covered with thin gold sheets which formed the lining of the lid but which were detached by damp before the bier gave way

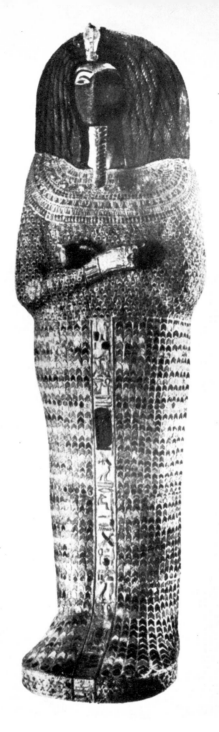

98, 99 *Left* restored lid of the coffin shown in Plates XIV and 97. It is decorated with the usual feather pattern of royal coffins of Dynasty XVIII. The name has been cut out of the inscribed band, which also has a spelling belonging to the early years of Akhenaten. The uraeus, however, bears the later form of the Aten's name showing that it was added subsequently to a coffin not entitled to bear such a protective emblem. *Right*, Canopic coffinette of gold inlaid with coloured glass, one of four, which held the embalmed viscera of Tut-ankh-Amun. It resembles the larger coffin in design, but shows the upper part enfolded in the wings of the vulture, Nekhebet, and the King wearing the royal head-cloth in place of a secular wig. Inscriptions inside reveal that it was originally made for Smenkh-ka-Re

100, 101 Two of four magic bricks found in the chamber of Tomb No. 55, made of sun-dried clay, inscribed with spells to protect 'the Osiris King Nefer-kheperu-Re' (Akhenaten) and originally fitted with amulets. *Left*, the Southern Brick from under the bier, with the stump of its torch intact. *Right*, the Northern Brick from the north-west corner, its wooden statuette missing. Two other fragments made of a different mud hastily inscribed in hieratic were found in the recess and along the eastern wall

102 Drawing made by Harold Jones of the back-panel of the shrine shown in Plate 95 while it was still *in situ* in the tomb. The copy is to scale but no dimensions are given. From two greatly denuded planks exhibited in the Cairo Museum it can be seen that the width is about two metres between the corner posts. The inscriptions show that the shrine was made by Akhenaten for his mother late in her reign

103–105 Drawings by Norman Davies of scenes in the private tombs of Amarna. *Above, left and right*, two reliefs in the tomb of Huya, the Steward of Queen Tiye (*see also* Plates 52, 53) who was granted his tomb late in the reign of Akhenaten. Those scholars who dismiss all juxtapositions of the names and figures of Amenophis III with those of Akhenaten as examples of posthumous filial piety make no such reservations in the case of Queen Tiye and her son; they are generally agreed that she visited Akhet-Aten, or resided there, after the death of her husband, though they do not explain why such an event is not portrayed till after Year 9. The scene *above* shows, left, Tiye with her daughter Beket-Aten beside her chair drinking wine within the palace by lamp-light, since the Aten has now set and its rayed arms do not reach them. Opposite her sit Akhenaten and Nefert-iti with two of their daughters. None of the girls is old enough to be allowed wine, but they are plied with fruit. The High Steward Huya is reduced to a minute ministering figure even on his own tomb walls. *Above opposite*, Akhenaten leads Tiye by the hand through the outer pylon on the right into her 'sunshade' temple at Amarna, followed by a retinue consisting of Beket-Aten carrying a bouquet and attended by nursemaids, chamberlains and ladies-in-waiting carrying fans. Another diminutive figure of Huya bowing low precedes them. *Opposite below*, an early but restrained example of the classic scene of the Royal Family offering to the Aten, from the tomb of the Steward Ipy who discharged his duties at Memphis. In this relief, at the entrance portal, Akhenaten and Nefert-iti offer elaborate unguent-containers inscribed with the name of the Aten, while their three eldest daughters rattle their sistra behind them. The Aten, its name enclosed in two large cartouches, and displaying a titulary like a king's, shines upon an altar piled with flesh, wine and bread and burning incense, and decorated with a tiny kneeling figure of the King offering a loaf (*cf.* Plate 49). Nefert-iti stands before a smaller altar. Inscriptions praise the Queen with flattering epithets and give the pedigrees of her daughters in the usual detail

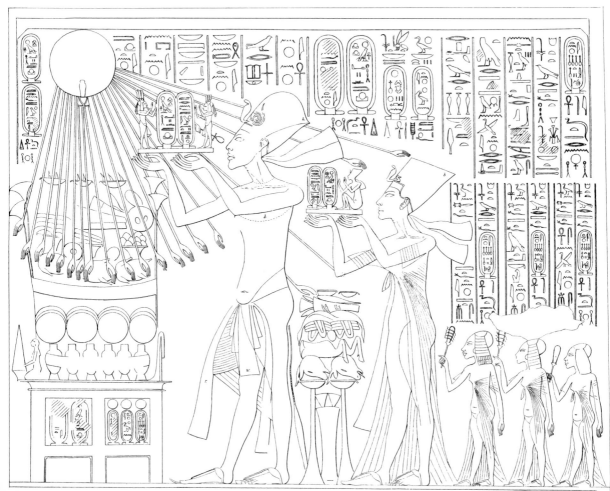

106–108 Fragments of royal shawabti-figures from Amarna, probably all from the Royal Tomb (*cf.* Plate 73). *Above left*, red-granite head of Akhenaten wearing the *nemes* wig-cover. *Below left*, part of a limestone specimen with cartouches bearing the King's *prenomen* and *nomen* Nefer-kheperu-Re, Wa-en-Re, and Akhenaten. *Below*, lower part of calcite shawabti of the King's Chief Wife, Nefer-neferu-Aten Nefert-iti, perhaps a 'stray' from the clearances in the Royal Wadi at Amarna in 1931–32, but acquired from a dealer in Cairo in the latter year

109 Part of the cache of jewellery alleged to have > been found in or near the Royal Tomb at Amarna about 1882 (*see also* Plate XII). In the centre are parts of a collar of Amarna type (*cf.* Plate 7) made of hollow gold flower petals, a mandrake fruit and poppy-seed heads. Surrounding this is a necklace arbitrarily strung with carnelian and glass beads and faience figurines of the godling Bes playing his tambourine, a characteristic Amarna amulet. Also shown are, left, a gold sequin in the form of a marguerite; right, a carnelian *wedjat*-eye mounted in a gold finger-ring; a gold-mounted scarab bezel from a ring and a gold spacer-bead

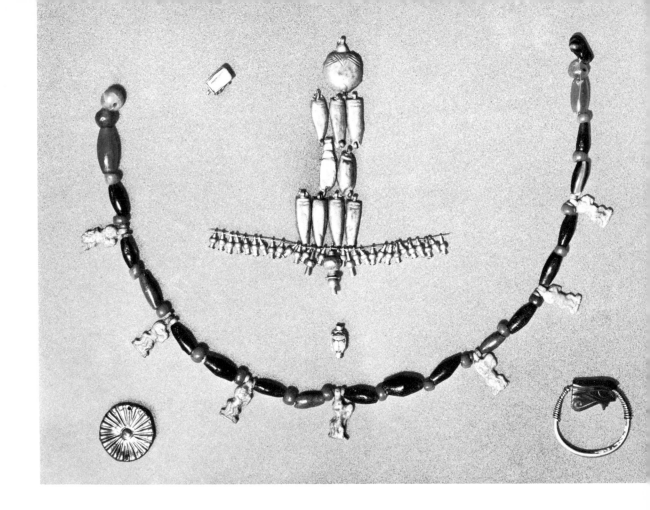

110 The Canopic chest of Akhenaten restored from the shattered fragments found in the Royal Tomb. The four guardian goddesses of tradition (cf. Plate III) have been replaced by the falcon of Re-Herakhty so prominent in Akhenaten's first two regnal years. The heads of the four stoppers of the internal compartments have been broken off and are missing, but were probably similar to the example shown in Plate 67

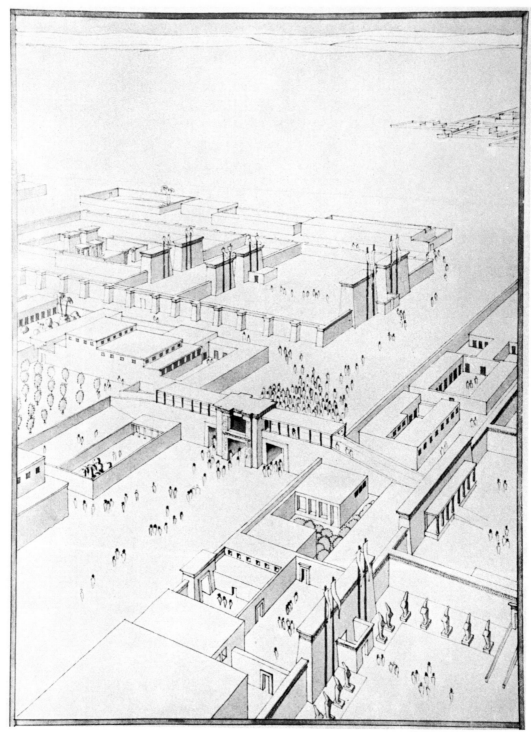

III Reconstruction by Ralph Lavers of the central area of Akhet-Aten. In the foreground,
running north and south, is 'Kingsway' spanned by a bridge connecting the Great Palace with
the King's House. South of the latter is the smaller temple, the 'Mansion of the Aten'. In the
lower right-hand corner is the Broad Hall of the Palace with its colossi, and the other state apartments separated by a stone wall from the private quarters. The King's House contained a terraced
garden, a lake and private suites for the King, Queen and six Princesses, and extensive magazines

112, 113 Aerial views of Amarna taken in 1932. *Above*, looking north, the Nile on the left, and the eastern cliffs approaching the river on the sky-line. The dark patches are the cultivation: running parallel with it is 'Kingsway'. The remains of the bridge are seen in the middle distance connecting the then unexcavated Great Palace with the King's House. South of this lies the 'Mansion of the Aten', its sanctuary white with chips from its destroyed stonework. *Below*, looking east, the Palace in the foreground, lying mostly under the cultivation, its vast hypostyle hall on the right. Part of the extensive south and west temenos walls of the Great Temple are visible on the extreme left. Mounds marking the site of the Records Office area lie immediately above the King's House

114 Court in the unique Northern Palace at Amarna, looking towards the eastern cliffs as they approach the Nile at the northern extremity (*cf*. Plate 112). This palace appears to have had a large pool and a zoo as two of its special features. In the north-east corner was the sunken garden, seen above, surrounded by a colonnade on three sides. Behind the row of stone column bases at the rear can be seen the remains of mud-brick rooms, perhaps aviaries. One of them still had its mural paintings partly preserved and was decorated with a frieze of waterfowl in a papyrus marshscape

115 View in the house of the Vizier Nakht at Akhet-Aten soon after its excavation in 1922, looking south from the great Central Hall to an inner reception room with its stone lustration slab and splash-back. The floors and walls were built of mud-brick, limewashed and painted in bright colours. The circular stone bases supported red-painted wooden columns that, in the Central Hall, rose two stories above the domestic quarters to support a blue-painted ceiling. Lighting was by means of small grilled windows or openings placed near the roof-line

116–118 Two slabs of clay impressed with cuneiform signs, part of the hoard of over 350 such tablets dug up at Amarna in 1887 and now known as the Amarna Letters. They have found their way mostly to museums at Berlin, Cairo, London and Oxford and are still being intensively studied. They proved to be communications from foreign rulers to the Pharaohs at Akhet-Aten. *Left*, a tablet (Kn. No. 23) in the British Museum from Tushratta of Mitanni to Amenophis III announcing that the goddess Ishtar of Nineveh has been sent on a visit to Egypt. A docket written in hieratic by the Egyptian filing-clerk gives the date the original was received at Thebes in Year 36 and indicates that this was a copy. *Centre*, left–hand edge of a tablet (Kn. No. 27) in Berlin from Tushratta to Akhenaten with a hieratic docket giving a date, the beginning of which is broken at the right-hand end. *Below*, the site of the Records Area during excavations in 1933, looking east. The house where the tablets were found lies 50 yards to the right of the picture in the south-west corner of the mounds shown in Plate 113

119, 120   The tomb of Ay at Amarna,
right, was intended as the finest in the
necropolis but little more than the left-
hand half of its main hall has been
hewn and only the first four columns
of its central aisle have been completed. The east wall has been carved with
reliefs, though not finished in colour.
The entrance portal has also been
sculptured and on the right-hand
reveal of the doorway appeared the
famous hymn to the Aten (*see* pp.
187–9) which, since it was uncovered in 1884, has been largely destroyed. The reliefs in the east wall, *above*,
are concerned with the Investiture
Scene. Ay and Tey, loaded with the
gold collars of honour (*cf.* Plates 50,
77), bow beneath the Window of
Appearances, while the Royal Family
throw down yet more gifts—collars,
vessels, rings, fillets and gloves. Ay's
servants caper behind him in their
excitement. In the background the
other dignitaries, soldiery and foreign
and native onlookers raise their hands
in praise and wonder

to be virgin ground that belonged to no god, goddess, nor indeed to anyone. The Court in reply assured him that the Aten would disclose his wishes only to him and that all the nations of the earth would come to Akhet-Aten bearing tribute to the Aten by whom they lived. The King then lifted his hand to the sun-disk in the heavens and swore an oath, declaring that he would make Akhet-Aten for the Aten, his father, in that precise spot and nowhere else; nor would he hearken to the Queen nor anyone who tried to persuade him to build Akhet-Aten elsewhere. He went on to name the buildings which he was erecting or proposed to erect in the new town—a House of the Aten, a Mansion of the Aten, a Sunshade of the Queen, a House of Rejoicing for the Aten in the Island 'Aten-distinguished-in-jubilees,' and other necessary works for the Aten, the Apartments of Pharaoh and the Apartments of the Queen. The ruins of some of these buildings have been uncovered and identified during the present century. Plates 112, 113, 118
The Mansion and the House of the Aten are the Smaller and Great Temple respectively. The Island appears to be the central portion of the City in which these buildings have been found. Plate 111

The more legible parts of the stelae conclude with the arrangements that the King has made to cut his tomb in the eastern mountain and for his burial to be made in it and also that of Nefert-iti and her daughter Meryt-Aten. Moreover, he specifies that if any of them were to die in any town elsewhere, he or she was to be brought to Akhet-Aten for burial. His officials were to be rewarded with tombs there, and the interment of the Mnevis bull of Heliopolis, an incarnation of the sun-god, was also to be made in the same mountain range. In making this provision, the King was preserving a rite of very ancient origin which is in curious conflict with his tendencies towards an abstract and intangible conception of god-head. It does suggest, however, that he was transferring to Akhet-Aten the ritual of sun-worship which had been hitherto observed at Heliopolis, despite his interest in that town, where he had a palace and a temple to the Aten.

The other Boundary Stelae at Amarna are dated to the sixth regnal year Plate 6
on the second anniversary of the founding of Akhet-Aten, when Amenophis IV, having now changed his name to Akhenaten, again mounted a great state chariot, and proceeded to fix the exact boundaries of the city by means of the great stelae cut in the surrounding cliffs. Having established his southern limit on the east bank, he was able to decree where the point should be fixed for the southern limit on the opposite bank, the corresponding northern points and the extreme eastern and western boundaries midway between. In each case he vows that he will not pass beyond the boundary

he has made for ever; and this oath is still construed to mean that Akhenaten shut himself up in his new-built city and never ventured outside it again. This interpretation is certainly wrong and contradicts his statement about being brought back from other towns in Egypt for burial at Akhet-Aten. It is also refuted by a codicil dated two years later mentioning that Royalty was then in Akhet-Aten to inspect the Boundary Stelae—an entirely otiose statement if Pharaoh had never moved out of the city. In so highly organized a state as Egypt, where every field was minutely recorded in ledgers and cadastral surveys, and its potential and actual yield noted, it was extremely important for taxation purposes that the area of the land which the King was bestowing upon the Aten should be strictly defined; and this the rest of the text of the stelae proceeds to do, even to the extent of declaring that Akhet-Aten stretched from the southern stela to the northern landmark on the east bank a total of 6 *ater*, $^3/_4$ *khe* and 4 cubits (nearly eight miles) and exactly the same distance on the western bank. It would be difficult to specify a more precise measurement. Akhenaten states categorically that the area within these bounds is Akhet-Aten in its entirety, and it all belongs to Father Aten—its mountains, deserts, fields, various arable lands, new lands, water, men and women, cattle, fowl, groves and everything that Father Aten produces. The phrase about not going beyond the city limits, therefore, merely means that Akhenaten proposed to keep within the demarcated area all the territory that was dedicated to the Aten.

Plate 31

There is some doubt about the exact date of the founding of Amarna, but the provision that is made for the burial of the eldest princess only may indicate that the idea occurred to Akhenaten very early in his reign. The date on the first stelae to be erected at the north and south extremities of the city is damaged, though the Year 4 is suggested by internal evidence. The dates on the stelae, of course, do not necessarily reflect the situation that prevailed at the time they were completed, since they must have taken several months to carve. Dated wine-jar dockets from the ruins of Central Amarna are relatively few before Year 5 and this has suggested that the city began to be occupied by the official classes about Year 6, when Akhenaten paid a state visit for the purpose of establishing the city bounds more precisely, following the earlier occasion when the site had been demarcated and dedicated. By that time a number of buildings had been erected and were ready for occupation.

In the same year, which seems to coincide with Year 33/4 of the reign of Amenophis III, when he celebrated his Second Jubilee, the Aten underwent a change in its titulary being called, 'The Father Divine and Royal, who is

in Jubilees and is in the House of the Aten at Akhetaten.' At the same time
Amenophis IV changed his name to Akhenaten and inflated the name of
Nefert-iti by the addition of Nefer-neferu-Aten ('Fair is the Goodness of
the Aten'). A letter dated to Year 5 of his reign still gives his *nomen* as
Amenophis, whereas on the stelae of Year 6 it is Akhenaten, which he now
substituted for the old form on his earlier monuments though there were   Plates 46, 49
the usual oversights.

A damaged reference in the earlier text of the Boundary Stelae has been
generally interpreted as suggesting that Akhenaten left Thebes because of
a violent conflict of opinion with the priesthood of Amun, and on his
hejira to Akhet-Aten in his Year 6, began a persecution of the Theban
cults, having the names and figures of such gods as Amun and Mut excised
wherever they appeared. We have dealt with this theory above (see p. 195)
and advanced reasons for thinking that at this stage of his career, a studied
neglect of the older cults on the part of Akhenaten is more probable than
an active persecution. While the old king Amenophis III lived, the worship
of Amun was still observed, and work on building-schemes at Thebes still   Plate IV
went ahead, probably engaging the older and more traditional of the royal
craftsmen.

At Akhet-Aten, on the other hand, operations proceeded with feverish
haste, despite the lack of skilled workers and experienced overseers, as is
seen all too plainly in the condition of the tombs which Akhenaten bestowed
upon his faithful followers. Nearly all their tomb-chapels are unfinished,   Plate 120
often with the chambers only partially hewn, and walls left blank or with
scenes sketched in and still awaiting the sculptors' chisels. Two of them,   Plate 55
those of Huya and Any, are sufficiently complete to have been used for
burials; but there are no traces of such deposits which presumably were
taken elsewhere when Akhet-Aten was officially abandoned. As soon as
one tomb was partially excavated, the stone-masons were diverted to
another enterprise, while the draughtsmen moved in to decorate what walls
were available and were followed in turn by sculptors and painters. Even
so wealthy and influential a person as the king's father-in-law, Ay, who
began a tomb which was designed as the finest and largest in the necropolis,
has managed to get only half his main hall excavated and one wall decorated.   Plate 120
Of fourteen sepulchres whose owners can be identified, nine were started
and left incomplete before regnal year 9.

While all these tomb-chapels follow the architectural pattern of contemporary tombs at Thebes, according to the pretensions of their owners,
they differ radically from them in the decoration of the main walls, which

are in relief originally intended to be painted. The Aten religion had banished from the repertoire of funerary subjects all reference to the elaborate Osirian ritual and prayers, and replaced the scenes in which the tomb-owner officiates as a principal by others in which the chief actors are the King and Queen with members of their family. In such representations as

Plates 105, 119
Plates 103, 104
Plate 44

'The Investiture from the Palace Balcony', 'The Royal Family Worshipping the Aten,' 'The Visit to the Temple,' 'The Royal Family at Table,' or 'The Reception of Tribute,' the figure of the tomb-owner has been relegated to a very minor position and size, and may even be entirely excluded. This is in conformity with the Atenist doctrines which had displaced the gods of burial in favour of Akhenaten as the patron of the dead as well as the living. The most striking feature of the decoration of these tombs, however, is the unity of subject matter that replaces the former miscellaneous extracts from the designers' pattern-books, assembled according to the tastes of the owner. At Amarna each tomb wall carries a single composition designed to fill the entire area: indeed, in a chamber of the Royal Tomb, the composition spreads over two adjacent walls. This space-concept is peculiar to the Amarna period and reflects the same intellectual approach to picture-making that in other spheres produced a monotheistic conception of god-head and a more rational and consistent cosmogony.

For the construction of the Royal Tomb in a wady among the eastern mountain range, and private tombs in the foothills, part of a corps of specialized craftsmen and their labourers were removed from their village on the west bank at Thebes and housed apart in walled barrack-like quarters near the scene of their main labours. Other workmen were employed continuously on building the city of the living. Akhet-Aten was laid out

Plate 112

on an untouched site on the east bank where agricultural land was scanty and confined to the river verges. The initial planning was on a somewhat lavish scale with the estates of the wealthy fronting on to two or three main

Plate 111

thoroughfares, one of which even today is known as the *Sikket es-Sultan* (Kingsway). Behind them, the less important officials built in vacant lots; and the hovels of the poor, usually sharing a common courtyard, were squeezed in haphazardly wherever there was space. No system of drainage is evident and rubbish was dumped in pits and middens outside the house precincts. As the city grew and its population increased, it spread northwards and was still in process of being built when it was abandoned.

The South City, which was one of the first portions to be laid out, housed most of the important officials, such as Pinhasy, the Chief Servitor

Plate 115

of the Aten, and the Vizier Nakht who had succeeded Ramose on the latter's death before the move to Akhet-Aten. There was also in this region a Maru-Aten or pleasure palace of the King with a lake and basins, gay with painted pavements and coloured inlays. Here were the kiosks, known as 'sunshade temples,' one belonging to the Queen and another to one or more of the princesses.

The Central City contained the great official buildings, such as the immense Palace which extended for nearly eight hundred yards along the west side of 'Kingsway' and ran westwards down to the river bank. Its northern boundary was the Great Temple set within an enclosure over eight hundred yards long and two hundred and fifty yards wide. In addition there was a smaller temple or Chapel Royal adjoining the Palace on its south side and covering an area of about twenty-five thousand square yards. Near at hand were government offices such as the 'House for the Correspondence of Pharaoh', the Office of Works and the Police Barracks. This part of the city shows evidence of being carefully planned.

Half a mile downstream lay the North Suburb containing the smaller houses of the merchants and lesser officials rubbing shoulders with the slums of the poor. It is probable that the main quays of the city were situated here and received the produce brought over daily from the richer and more extensive cultivation on the west bank. This suburb began to be occupied about the middle of the reign and was still being developed when Akhet-Aten was abandoned. Beyond it to the north was the North City which has not been fully excavated and published. It contained other palaces and official quarters.

All the domestic building was in mud-brick, coated with plaster in the case of the better houses, and decorated in colour. The mansions of the wealthy had stone thresholds, doorposts and lintels, column bases and window-grilles, and wooden columns and doors. Bathrooms were fitted with stone lustration slabs and soak-aways. The decoration of palace and temple walls was often carried out in coloured stone inlays, and in glazed tiles or glass applied in a kind of mosaic. The temples and the official part of the palace, however, were built of more durable limestone, apparently quarried locally, but certain portions were of hard alabaster, quartzite and granites. A great deal of mud-brick whitewashed to imitate limestone was also used, particularly in the initial building, and was later replaced by stone.

The temples follow the distinctive pattern of the Heliopolitan sun-temple in being open to the sky. The transition is not, as in the usual Egyptian temple, from the bright sunlight of the forecourt, through the increasing gloom of the intervening halls, to the pitch darkness of the innermost

Plates III, 113

Plate 118

Plate 114

Plate 47

Plate III

Plate IV

237

sanctuary. Instead, the officiants moved through airy, spacious roofless courts to the altars which themselves were open to the life-giving rays of the Aten. Here was the Mansion of the *Ben-Ben;* at Amarna not the pyramidal stone of Heliopolis, but a great round-topped stela showing the Royal Family at worship.

Building in the city was continuous and modifications were made to the Palace and the Great Temple and other structures to reflect changes in doctrine or political events throughout the period of occupation. Thus when Queen Nefert-iti disappeared from the scene and her place was taken by her eldest daughter, the inscriptions and portraits in her sun-shade in Maru-Aten were altered in favour of the Princess Meryt-Aten. Most of the construction of the South and Central sections of the city was completed before Year 9, when another event occurred affecting the official dogma. About this time the name of the Aten was changed to ('Re, the Living, the Ruler of the Horizon, who Rejoices on the Horizon) (in his manifestation of Re-the-Father, who returns as the Sun-Disk') and an epithet was altered to show that he was now 'Lord of Jubilees.' The exact date of this change is not recorded but it is known to have fallen somewhere between year 8 and 12. It is generally taken to have occurred in Year 9; and the writer has sought to show that it indicates that the Aten had celebrated yet another jubilee coinciding with the Third Jubilee of Amenophis III in his thirty-seventh regnal year. By this time the senior monarch was probably residing for part of the year at Akhet-Aten since several buildings associated with him are known from jar-dockets from the site; others belonged to Queen Tiye and her young daughter Beket-Aten. Despatches from foreign powers addressed to him were being received at Akhet-Aten in his thirty-sixth regnal year at least. It would be a mistake to think that both kings resided in one particular spot whether at Akhet-Aten or Thebes. They probably moved about the country with their retinues like the courts of medieval kings. A travelling harim is known from a later reference, but it was probably even then a venerable institution. There were royal palaces at several towns in Egypt, though the main residence appears to have been at Memphis; and it is from beneath the foundations of a later palace here that a statue-head of Nefert-iti has been recovered.

Amenophis III probably died in the third month of inundation in his thirty-ninth regnal year and the twelfth of Akhenaten. His funeral arrangements doubtless took the statutory seventy days, after which he was buried in the large tomb he had prepared, but not finished, for himself in the western branch of the Biban el-Moluk. At these ceremonies Akhenaten appears to have officiated as custom demanded, for it was while he was in Thebes at this time that he received a despatch from the King of Mitanni at the hands of special envoys who had been sent to condole with him on the death of his father.

Plate 117

A little later, however, Akhenaten was in Akhet-Aten for the great reception of tribute that marked his accession to sole rule, and his recognition by foreign powers as the successor of Amenophis III. For this ceremony, he and the Queen were carried in their state palanquins to their thrones under a great gilded baldachin set upon a parade ground; and there with the six princesses and their retinue behind them they received the envoys from Asia and Africa, introduced by the Vizier and other high officers of State, bearing rich gifts for the new divine lord whose blessing they begged.

Plate 44

This was perhaps the golden hour of Akhenaten's reign. From this distance of time it looks as though his accession to sole rule was the beginning of a series of troubles for him. In his father's reign, the situation in Syria and Palestine was in its usual endemic state of internecine squabbling. The Egyptian position there was ostensibly strong, the fissile nature of local politics rendered a sustained coalition of petty states against Egyptian hegemony virtually impossible, and such an alliance was the only force that could challenge the well-organized armies of Pharaoh. The Egyptian district commissioners had only to divide in order to rule, and it is quite possible that they encouraged some of the local shifts of allegiance and manoeuvrings for power in order to serve Egyptian ends. The operations of the marauding Hapiru imposed more of a threat, but as they were sporadic and at this time unco-ordinated, they could be contained by police action. Where Egyptian interests were directly menaced was in the lands that bordered the powerful states to the north and north-east of Syria. Here the schemes of the local vassals could be integrated by the ambitions of such powers as Mitanni and Hatti and a challenge issued to Egyptian pretensions. Such a policy appears to have been followed by Mitanni in the early days of the Dynasty, when her power reached its climax and the whole of northern Syria came under her sway. In subsequent reigns, however, a *modus vivendi* with Egypt was achieved. The real threat to Mitanni came from the Hittites to the north-west, and a see-saw struggle developed between the two powers. In these circumstances, Egyptian aid, or at least neutrality, was sought by both nations. Hatti had already benefited by Egyptian pressure on Mitanni and sent gifts (or tribute) to Tuthmosis III at least twice during his reign; and a treaty was established between the two kingdoms. Egyptian claims in

Syria were also recognized by Mitanni and the two powers concluded an alliance by the marriage of Mitannian princesses to the Pharaohs.

By the later years of the reign of Amenophis III, however, the vassal states of Hatti had shifted their allegiance to Mitanni; and neighbouring Anatolian peoples had made disastrous incursions into Hittite territory, even sacking its capital, Hattusas. At this crisis, when Hittite power seemed in total eclipse, a palace revolution brought the able young prince Suppiluliumas to the throne; and under his vigorous political and military direction the fortunes of Hatti began to revive, despite some reverses. By the time Akhenaten achieved sole rule, Suppiluliumas had recovered much lost ground and was ready to carry war into the enemy territories.

The advent of this new actor on the Syrian scene inevitably produced unrest in the Egyptian border states, some of whom began to consider whether a change of allegiance would not be profitable, while others sat on the fence until it was clearer where their best interests lay. The moment was therefore ripe for a parade of force by the Pharaoh in person. At the head of his chariotry and infantry, with his Nubian shock-troops, archers and auxiliaries, he ought to have taken the field, suppressed the overtly rebellious, replaced those who were plotting treachery, rounded up some of the local footpads and bedouin, encouraged the waverers, rewarded the faithful, and removed as hostages to the Egyptian Court the sons of those princes whose reliability was not wholly assured. The campaign could then have been concluded by a grand hunt in the chief trouble spot to exhibit the prowess of the Pharaoh; and on his return to Egypt, the expedition could have been represented as a famous victory, with its lists of rich plunder and rebels slain or captured.

Plate 13

Amenophis III had made such an expedition to Sidon early in his reign; and referred to himself as 'Conqueror of Shinar' in North Syria; but in his corpulent middle age he left campaigning to his generals and contented himself with conducting diplomacy by means of widespread marriage alliances. Nevertheless, when firm action had to be taken, trouble-makers were removed from the scene, as when a task-force of marines killed the arch-intriguer Abdi-ashirta of Amurru.

Akhenaten continued this more passive policy of his father; but while Tadukhipa, the daughter of Tushratta of Mitanni, whom Amenophis III had married by his regnal year 36, now became his responsibility, there is no evidence that he opened negotiations for marital ties with foreign dynasts, though he did apparently inherit some unfinished business concerning a marriage that his father was negotiating with the daughter of the King of Babylon.[45] A visit, if only an armed reconnaissance, by the Pharaoh in Palestine and Syria was long overdue to raise the morale of the vassals by listening to their complaints and settling differences on the spot; perhaps also by removing corrupt Egyptian commissioners. Such an expedition, however, would almost certainly have led to an armed clash with the new-won vassals of Hatti, and perhaps with the Hittites themselves. Whether treaty obligations, both with Hatti and Mitanni inhibited the Egyptians from taking any decisive action, or whether they believed that conflict between Hatti and Mitanni would neutralize both states to the advantage of themselves will never be known. The Pharaoh's withdrawal from the northern field of action at this time led eventually to the extinction of Mitanni, and more immediately to the loss of Amurru which became a vassal of Suppiluliumas. Nevertheless, some punitive measures against the recalcitrant appear to have been taken. Aziru, who had replaced his father Abdi-Ashirta, was summoned to Egypt to give an account of himself; and the troublesome Labayu of Shechem was killed in a skirmish. Forces and supplies were evidently being marshalled for a serious Asiatic expedition at the end of Akhenaten's reign; and indeed such a campaign in the region of Gezer may have been mounted.

Though no claim has survived that Akhenaten was the all-conquering war-lord who campaigned successfully abroad, there is equally no evidence for the 'pacifist' principles in the conduct of his foreign policy that some modern apologists have accredited to him. High-ranking army commanders were prominent in his immediate entourage. His military bodyguard, and the soldiers that figure in the Amarna tomb reliefs as spectators on the side-lines have given one observer the impression that Akhet-Aten was an armed camp. Akhenaten's state barge and the pylons of his temples at Thebes and Medamud showed him in the traditional pose of slaughtering the helpless foe. Though his physique may have been far from athletic, he was evidently not averse to being represented as the happy warrior. The set-backs in Syria and the loss of influence among the vassal states, must have led to unrest in other sectors of the Egyptian sphere of influence in Asia. Such reverses were probably inevitable after the unparalleled success of Egyptian arms since the days of Tuthmosis III, but it was a misfortune for Akhenaten that the ebb of Egyptian power in Asia should have set in at the time when his new god the Aten had assumed charge of the welfare of Egypt and its dependencies.

Other troubles affected Akhenaten's personal relationships. Some time after Year 12, and probably soon after, the Princess Meket-Aten, the

Plate 119

Fig. 1

Plate 51

Plate 87

second daughter of Nefert-iti died, and was buried in a subsidiary suite of rooms in the Royal Tomb at Amarna, where reliefs show the Royal Family mourning over the dead girl on a bier. The presence of a nurse-maid suckling an infant outside the death chamber has been interpreted to mean that Meket-Aten had died in childbirth, in which case the father of her child is likely to have been Akhenaten, who also had daughters by Meryt-Aten and Ankhes-en-pa-Aten (see, however, p. 137).

It must have been soon after this event that Nefert-iti too died. In recent years it has become generally accepted that after the death of Meket-Aten, Nefert-iti fell into disgrace and her place was taken by her eldest daughter, Meryt-Aten. The evidence for this is very thin and rests largely upon the discovery at Maru-Aten that the sunshade temple of the Queen had been taken over for Meryt-Aten, her name being carefully erased from the inscriptions and that of Meryt-Aten cut over it. Nefert-iti's distinctive attributes had also been blotted out with cement, her features re-cut and her head enlarged into the exaggerated skull of the Princess Royal. It was, however, not an unusual occurrence in Egypt for certain monuments of one generation to be 'usurped' by the next, for reasons which are imperfectly known. In this particular case, such a personal monument as the sunshade of Nefert-iti, which appears to have had as its function the daily renewal of the Queen's powers, would have had no use after her death, and its transfer to her daughter may therefore be regarded as an act of economy, not enmity. If Nefert-iti had been disgraced, it is unlikely that her name would have been transferred to the young co-regent Smenkh-ka-Re. On the contrary, it would have been excised everywhere, together with her figure. Still less is it likely that her portrait bust and other studies of her would have been retained in the sculptors' workshops at Amarna.

Plates 7, VIII

Plate 114

Again, the excavators of the north palaces at Amarna claim to have found objects bearing the name of Nefert-iti in conjunction with those of Tut-ankh-Aten and the Princess Ankhes-en-pa-Aten; and have surmised that it was the Queen's fanatical belief in Atenism that kept the young couple faithful to the new religion and to Akhet-Aten, until with her death all opposition to a return to orthodoxy was removed. Unfortunately, the excavation of the north palaces has not been fully published, and it is therefore difficult to interpret half-reported results; but the writer understands from Professor H.W. Fairman that no object was found bearing the names of both Nefert-iti and Tut-ankh-Aten. All the evidence would seem to show, therefore, is that a palace was occupied for a while by Nefert-iti and soon afterwards by Tut-ankh-Aten and his Consort, but there is nothing to prove that all were living there together at the same time.

The writer is disposed to interpret the very scanty and ill-recorded data as favouring the view that soon after the death of Meket-Aten, Nefert-iti died and was buried in the Royal Tomb at Amarna according to the promise made on the earlier Boundary Stelae. Professor Fairman who was in the expedition that re-excavated the Royal Tomb in 1932, but failed to publish a full report, has declared that he found the name of Nefert-iti prominent in the main burial hall on the pillar fragments and walls, and has since wondered whether the tomb was not in fact hers.[46] The so-called 'well' has been cut in the tomb-corridor; and this is generally thought to have been done after a burial had been made. A fragmentary shawabti figure of Nefert-iti, which may have come from the Royal Tomb, is now in the Brooklyn Museum.[47] Lastly, in 1882 some natives illicitly digging in the central wady at Amarna first uncovered the Royal Tomb and evidently found in it, or near it, a cache of jewellery which had probably been overlooked, or abstracted, hidden away and never retrieved, during the transfer of the royal burials to another place. The hoard includes a massive gold ring of Nefert-iti, gold ear-plugs and gold, glass and faience beads of typical Amarna type. An intrusive Coptic burial was probably also found at the same time, for gold-work of that period was mixed with the hoard by the time it was acquired *en bloc* by the Royal Scottish Museum in 1883. It may have been such a later mummy with its wrappings torn to shreds which was subsequently found outside the Royal Tomb by officials of the Antiquities Service when they came to investigate in 1891–2, and which has given rise to the persistent rumour that a rifled corpse, torn to pieces, was all that remained of Akhenaten, whereas it is certain that all burials in the Royal Tomb were removed elsewhere when the town was abandoned and the necropolis guards withdrawn. It is not possible to say whether the gold hoard came from the burial of Meket-Aten or Nefert-iti, or from both.

On the death of Nefert-iti, her place was taken by Meryt-Aten, referred to in the Amarna Letters, as 'your daughter Mayati' by Burnaburiash of Babylon writing to Akhenaten. It would appear that she was the mother of a Princess Meryt-Aten-the-Less, from an unpublished inscription, but without fuller details it is not possible to say who the father was, though the inference seems to be that it was Akhenaten. Certainly Meryt-Aten was married to the next king, Smenkh-ka-Re who appears to have been

Plate 108

Plates 109, XII

Plate 9

Plate 68

a younger brother of Akhenaten and was made his co-regent some time after regnal year 12, probably in the following year. The position of this ephemeral monarch is ambiguous. A date in his third regnal year is known from a graffito in the tomb of Pere at Thebes, and this is usually taken to be his last on no sure grounds. But if he died at the age of twenty (see p. 147), it is unlikely that he ruled for more than four years assuming that he was appointed co-regent on reaching manhood. He was evidently preparing a tomb for himself at Thebes for the graffito speaks of his mortuary temple as being in the 'House of Amun,' and there are no signs of any tomb of his at Amarna. Like his father he was presumably an adherent of Amun as well as Aten. Some of his funerary equipment was

Plate 99
Plate 98

taken over for the burial of Tut-ankh-Amun and bears texts of orthodox pattern; yet he was buried in a coffin carrying inscriptions of Atenist type which belonged to one of the royal women, probably his wife while she

Plate 113

was still a princess. A great extension, including a large hypostyle hall, was built for him at the Royal Palace at Amarna, perhaps for his coronation. The evidence of the wine-jar dockets tends to support the view that his reign was wholly contained within that of the senior co-regent Akhenaten, since 'Year 1', which on one docket is written over 'Year 17' must belong to Tut-ankh-Amun, the successor of Akhenaten[48]. That Smenkh-ka-Re came to the throne before the death of Akhenaten is clear enough from

Plate 82

several monuments in which the younger king is shown with the elder in situations which do not suggest a posthumous relationship. Of such scenes, the most startling is that which appears on an unfinished stela in

Plate 81

Berlin and points to homosexual relations between these two rulers. Such a perversion appears to be emphasised by the epithet 'Beloved of Akhenaten' which Smenkh-ka-Re incorporated into both his cartouches, and by his adoption of the name Nefer-neferu-Aten which Nefert-iti had borne since Year 6.

On the marriage of Meryt-Aten to Smenkh-ka-Re at his appointment as co-regent, the next eldest surviving princess, Ankhes-en-pa-Aten, rose to importance at her father's Court, and she may be the 'Mistress of thy House' to whom Burnaburiash promised a present of lapis lazuli seal rings in his last letter to Akhenaten. She, too, bore a daughter who was called after her; and though the father is not explicitly stated, it has been inferred that he was Akhenaten from the proximity of his cartouche in the incomplete and damaged inscription. The fate of this child is unknown to us; neither do we hear anything more of the children of Ankhes-en-pa-Aten's elder sisters: they presumably all died in early infancy.

The end of the reign of Akhenaten is even more scantily documented than the earlier part and the situation appears to be confused. Smenkh-ka-Re's tenure of power was short-lived: he died after a reign of three or four years, probably late in Akhenaten's fifteenth regnal year. It is highly probable that Queen Meryt-Aten had predeceased him. It may be that it was at this point that Ankhes-en-pa-Aten assumed her more important role in the State, since she can hardly have been born much before Akhenaten's first three years on the throne and could not have reached an age to bear children before the end of his regnal year 15. The dowager Queen Tiye was also important at Akhet-Aten where a sunshade temple was bestowed on her by her son. Her steward, Huya, was granted a tomb in the northern group in which the tribute of Year 12 is represented. The award of this tomb to her steward almost certainly shows that Queen Tiye had taken up her main residence at Amarna, after the death of her husband, and she is known to have had an estate or house there. It also suggests that it was at Amarna rather than Thebes that her burial was to be made. The discovery of fragments of a sarcophagus bearing her name and that of Akhenaten points to her having been buried in the Royal Tomb at Amarna or at least destined for interment there, perhaps in a subsidiary suite of rooms hewn off the main corridor, but in the absence of any published details it is fruitless to speculate. What is certain is that about this time Akhenaten provided some handsome burial furniture for her though what fragments have survived are in a wretched condition. In the last five years of his reign, Akhenaten must have suffered almost continual bereavement, the deaths, among others, of Meket-Aten, Nefert-iti, Tiye, Meryt-Aten and her daughter, and Smenkh-ka-Re, not to mention the younger daughters of Nefert-iti and those of Ankhes-en-pa-Aten following one after the other.

Plate 104

Plate 44

Plates 95, 102

What is difficult to fix is the date of the iconoclastic fury that Akhenaten unleashed against the other cults of Egypt, particularly that of the Theban Amun. The writer is inclined to place it near the end of his life. Until this outburst it would seem that the older religions had been simply ignored by the King after the first five years of his reign. Their revenues had probably been diverted on an ever-increasing scale to Amarna to help maintain the enormously expensive cult of the Aten, with its lavish offerings on behalf of the dead as well as the living, and also to pay for the grandiose building schemes of the Court. Some idea of the shortage of treasure which such ambitions caused in the State can be seen in Akhenaten's defalcations in the supply of gold which his father had promised to foreign potentates before he died. The priesthoods had been largely dispersed or absorbed by the new faith. Although Smenkh-ka-Re built his mortuary temple in the precincts of Amun at Thebes, it is very doubtful whether this involved any large-scale patronage of Amun, or a rapprochement between Akhenaten and an alienated priesthood of that god, as is so often claimed by those Egyptologists who see the Amarna revolution as a struggle between the King on one side and various priesthoods on the other, right from the start of his reign. It seems to the writer very unlikely that Smenkh-ka-Re would have attempted to worship Amun of Thebes against the wishes of Akhenaten, or that the latter would have sanctioned any compromise with a cult which, according to some interpreters, he had earlier proscribed with remarkable vindictiveness, particularly as the progress of his thought in so far as it can be traced, was all in the direction of an unyielding monotheism.

Plate II, *Fig. 5*

It would seem that the edicts that resulted in the destruction of the statues of Amun and the erasure of his name and those of his consort, Mut, and other gods, were promulgated after the death of Smenkh-ka-Re. They were certainly carried out with great thoroughness from one end of the kingdom to the other. Even the cartouches of Akhenaten's father were not spared; and such small objects as scarabs received the same attention as colossal monuments like the temple of Luxor. It seems likely that it was at this moment, when the other gods were suppressed and their existence denied, that Akhenaten also gave orders for the plural form of the word for 'god' to be erased wherever it appeared. This campaign of excision and suppression was the last great act of Akhenaten's reign and may reflect a mental collapse on the part of its author whose health, judging from the appearance of his physique, can never have been very robust. Soon after the grape harvest of his seventeenth regnal year, he died in circumstances that are totally obscure to us and likely to remain so.

XIII

The Amarna Aftermath, 1362-1319 BC

THE WINE-JAR DOCKET already alluded to which has the Year 1 written over that of 17 indicates that the successor of Akhenaten came to the throne only at his death or a few months before it. Of the two alternatives, the former seems to the writer the more likely. The new king, Tut-ankh-Aten, was the next surviving son of Amenophis III, probably by Queen Tiye, and as he was aged only nine or ten, had not reached official manhood. But he may have been nominated the heir-apparent on the death of Smenkh-ka-Re, if not crowned as co-regent. He was already sufficiently important to figure in reliefs, since a fragment of wall, still unpublished, has come to light at Hermopolis, naming him as a 'King's son, of his loins.' His claim to the throne was consolidated by his marriage to the heiress Princess Ankhes-en-pa-Aten. At Amarna they resided in the Northern Palace but their main seat was at Memphis, where his coronation was doubtless held. The motive force of the Atenist movement had lost its momentum with the death of its guiding spirit, prophet and incarnation. Nevertheless, the young pair still carried on the cult of the Aten, as their names suggest and the decoration of the royal thrones testifies.

Plate 10

The entourage of Akhenaten appears to have vanished with their lord, but this may be illusory and the result of our incomplete knowledge of the personalities surviving at the end of the reign. The Vizier Nakht, the Cupbearer Pa-ren-nefer, and the Great Chamberlain Tutu are not heard of again. Their tomb reliefs, however, remain un-desecrated, so it would appear that they were not dishonoured before or after their departure from office. It is probable that their sons obtained appointments at the new Court. One official, however, the fan-bearer and factotum May suffered the excision of his figure and name from the sculptured walls of his tomb (see p. 202), a sign of disgrace which is usually accredited to his fall from favour under Akhenaten, though it may have been due to later vindictiveness.

There was one important official, at least, who kept his position under the new King and even improved it. This was the Master of the Horse, Ay, who as the King's uncle and the Queen's grandfather had an influential

Fig. 3

247

voice in the affairs of state, particularly as the Pharaoh was still a young boy. His appointment as Vizier and Regent[49] may date to the advent of Tut-ankh-Aten when the new officers of state, took up their posts.

Plate 73

Plates 63, 65

Other members of the Ay family appear to have gained eminence in the entourage of the young King. The General and Fanbearer, Nakht-Min, who was to donate five shawabtis for the burial of his lord is believed to have some close connection with Ay and may have been his son. Another general, Har-em-hab, who rose to be the King's Deputy, a post he could

Plate 56

expect to hold until the King had begotten a son and heir, was married to Mut-nodjme, a daughter of Ay and sister of the late Queen Nefert-iti. This marriage may have been instrumental in first raising him from a position of comparative obscurity to the immediate circle of the royal family[50].

The period between the death of one king and the crowning of his successor was always a critical time, when it was believed that the forces of evil and disorder had triumphed over the rule of righteousness. The death of Akhenaten must have been generally regarded as an especially dangerous moment in the fortunes of Egypt. Abroad, it had just suffered losses in North Syria where intriguing vassals had fallen under the sway of the Hittites. In Palestine unrest threatened the Egyptian position in the key centre of Gezer. At home, the age-old shrines lay abandoned; and while doubtless the common people still clung to their household gods, all organized religious activity was in confusion. In the world of the Late Bronze Age this would have been a most serious cause of anarchy and a crisis of confidence. All motivation would have been lost: a blight would be thought to have settled on everything and all enterprises large and small would seem ill-fated. The temples and their staffs performed important administrative and economic functions in the State in the absence of anything like an organized civil service, and when they ceased to operate, the whole business of life for many sectors of the populace would also come to a halt. The Egyptians, like other peoples of the Ancient World were directed largely by magic, by a faith in the supernatural that generally worked for a beneficent end by giving them a confidence and discipline which enabled the odds of adversity to be overcome. Often a hazardous enterprise, the outcome of which was uncertain, achieved success when an oracle of a god had instigated it and promised it good fortune. Similarly, in all the many little undertakings of daily life that had to be met with fortitude and patience, the will to overcome set-backs, or to surmount obstacles was lacking when once the view took root that the gods were offended and had withdrawn their support. Without the gods, in fact, all was in vain, as so many mottoes engraved on scarab-shaped amulets expressed it. Such a general breakdown of morale seems to have been the chief legacy of Akhenaten's religious experiment; and his successors had the task of getting Egypt back on the well-trodden paths that over the centuries had led to prosperity.

The situation which prevailed when Tut-ankh-Amun came to the throne is clearly outlined in the great Restoration Stela which he erected at Karnak, probably in his fourth regnal year:

> Now when His Majesty appeared as King, the temples from one end of the land to the other had fallen into ruin; their shrines were desolate and had become wildernesses overgrown with weeds; their sanctuaries were as though they had never been; their precincts were trodden paths. The land was in confusion for the gods had forsaken this land. If (an army) was sent to Asia to widen the frontiers of Egypt, it met with no success. If one prayed to a god to ask things of him, he did not come. If one supplicated a goddess, likewise she did not come either. Their hearts were enfeebled so that what had been made was destroyed.

The picture is traditionally over-drawn, but probably less than usual. The stela goes on to recount the measures that the King was devising to restore his peoples' confidence. They included the fashioning of statues and cult-images of the gods in gold and precious stones; the re-habilitation of the sanctuaries; the re-filling of their treasuries and the allocation of property and slaves to them so that their daily offerings could be maintained. He also inducted priests from notables of each district, 'one whose name is known.' The male and female slaves, temple-singers and dancers were consecrated from the Palace personnel and their subsistence charged to the King. The economic fall-out from this activity must have been substantial. Certainly a great deal of reconstruction and restoration of the former temples were undertaken during the reign of Tut-ankh-Aten, and the epithet that is applied to him on one of the seals of his tomb, 'who spent his life in fashioning images of the gods,' might well serve as his epitaph.

Plate XVI

In conformity with his policy of a return to orthodoxy, the proscription of the other gods was rescinded, and the worship of the Aten, as distinct from Re-Herakhty was quietly dropped. The King changed his name to Tut-ankh-Amun while his Queen became Ankhes-en-Amun. He attempted to pick up the reins of government where his father Amenophis III had dropped them, completing his unfinished monuments as at Sulb and Luxor and making a tomb for himself perhaps very near to where the old king was resting in the Western Branch of the Biban el-Moluk. It was probably early in his reign that the decision was taken to abandon Akhet-Aten as an unlucky site for a Residence City and to make Memphis his chief seat. It was from his palace at Memphis that the decree on the Karnak Restoration Stela, quoted above, was promulgated. The official classes moved away from Akhet-Aten with the Court, the wealthy abandoning their fine houses, though removing from them anything of value such as the precious wooden columns and other fittings before bricking them up. The clerks of the Records Office packed their rolls of papyrus documents into their portfolios; and before they left, took care to bury a mass of unwieldy cuneiform despatches from Syria, Palestine, and elsewhere in Asia, under the floor, ignoring one or two broken tablets and sign-lists left strewn about the houses of their quarter. Squatters soon moved into the vacated residences and some kind of life still continued in the town, mostly centred around the faience and glass works attached to the Great Palace.

The burials of those who had died at Amarna were transferred by their pious relatives to the family burying-grounds elsewhere. The withdrawal of the police and necropolis guards would have invited wholesale pillaging of the wealthier burials; and a decision was therefore taken to re-inter the bodies of late members of the Royal Family in the traditional cemeteries of their Dynasty at Thebes. Tombs suddenly had to be found for Tiye, Nefert-iti, Meket-Aten, Meryt-Aten, Smenkh-ka-Re and Akhenaten himself, as well as some of the other royal children and retainers whose names and fates are unknown to us. We do not know whether Smenkh-ka-Re's burial had already been made by Akhenaten before his own death, but it seems probable. There was apparently no intention of burying Akhen-

Plate 110

aten in the Royal Tomb at Amarna, for his shattered Canopic chest in the main chamber bears no tell-tale stains to show that it has been used. How much of his funerary furniture was retained for his interment can never be

Plate 100, 101

known. He would have begun to prepare his tomb equipment from his first months on the throne, but with the increasing austerity of his mono-theistic ideas, it is doubtful whether he retained the traditional Osirian paraphernalia. The burial arrangements at Thebes, should have been the direct responsibility of the Southern Vizier, perhaps Ay; and under the circumstances, it is probable that small tombs were hastily cut in the various burying grounds at Thebes designed to hold more than one occupant. In

Plate 94

one of these in the Biban el-Moluk, Tiye, Akhenaten and Smenkh-ka-Re were interred with such equipment as Tut-ankh-Amun was prepared to supply or consider appropriate. In another cache it is tempting to believe that Nefert-iti and her daughters and perhaps grand-daughters were laid to rest. At the funerary ceremonies Tut-ankh-Amun and his Queen would, of course, have had to officiate and there was no question of any mean and dishonoured burials, though they may have been less opulent than the deceased had planned for themselves.

These measures for the re-habilitation of the land and the return to orthodoxy can hardly have been the sole decision of a child of nine or ten and we shall probably not be far wrong in attributing most of this policy to Ay, the chief adviser of the King. His ascendancy, however, can be over-emphasised and a fragment of embossed gold foil on which Tut-ankh-Amun is shown slaughtering the traditional foe has been consistently misinterpreted to mean that the King was shown performing this ritual act *before* Ay. The apparent *volte face* that Ay now performed in returning so swiftly to the *status quo* has given him the reputation among Egyptologists of being at best a trimmer and at the worst a sinister intriguer. Such views, however, ignore completely the character of government in Ancient Egypt, though similar radical changes of opinion have been observed in modern authoritarian states ruled by semi-divine 'personalities,' when the leader has been replaced by another. The god incarnate who ruled Egypt could not be regarded as less than inspired except in retrospect, when the policy he had pursued was seen as a whole and found to be disastrous. There was always a time-lag before rulers such as Queen Hat-shepsut ceased to be venerated and became execrated, and when they were dismissed as not having been the true sons of Re who ruled with *maet*. But there is no reason to believe that Ay was any less sincere under Akhenaten than he was under Tut-ankh-Amun.

Fig. 3

The Restoration Stela, however, shows that Tut-ankh-Amun early acknowledged that cardinal errors had been made by his predecessor, perhaps through failings of personality as much as policy. The homosexual aberrations of Akhenaten must have seemed ill-omened to his subjects, who took to the tomb with them among the Declarations of Innocence that they expected to recite before the Mercy Seat of the God of the Dead, the asseveration that they had never indulged in such perversions. Only the more ribald folk-yarns accredited Seth with such vices and he was the god of violence and evil. It is probable, therefore, that soon after his death, the reign of Akhenaten was regarded as an unfortunate interlude, like that of Hat-shepsut's, when the rule of *Maet* had been overthrown. His heresy was quickly dropped by his successors as a prime error that had brought upon Egypt nothing but ill-luck.

On the strength of heavily damaged architraves found in the Second Pylon at Karnak, it has been claimed for Ay that he acted as Tut-ankh-Amun's co-regent. This, however, is based upon a misinterpretation of the fragmentary texts and a misunderstanding of the institution of co-regency[51]. As long as he lived, the hope remained that the King would father a son on one of his wives, preferably the Chief Queen, to become in time his co-regent, but in this he was disappointed. Two human foetuses bearing his name were found in his tomb and are accepted by most Egyptologists to have been his children born prematurely and subsequently buried with him according to a practice that was common in the case of royal burials in the Biban el-Moluk. They both appear to have been female children and when their father died in his tenth regnal year, there was no one of the line of Amosis to succeed him: the glorious Dynasty XVIII had ended.

At the death of the Pharaoh, it was necessary that his successor should ascend the throne at the following dawn; and when this could not occur, Egypt was threatened with a crisis in the whole of nature as well as the affairs of man. The death of Tut-ankh-Amun coincided with a defeat in North Syria when the Hittites, in defiance of their treaty obligations, twice invaded Egyptian territory between the Lebanon and Anti-Lebanon and took back captives and spoil. It was at this juncture, as we learn from the Hittite archives, that Queen Ankhes-en-Amun wrote to Suppiluliumas, the King of the Hittites, asking for one of his sons whom she could marry and so make King of Egypt, since she had no son of her own who could be crowned Pharaoh. The reasons for this extraordinary request will probably never be satisfactorily explained. It may be that, as she confessed, marriage to one of her subjects was abhorrent to her, and only a man of royal blood, even if a foreigner, was suited to become the new god incarnate. It may be, on the other hand, that events in turbulent Asia made a marriage alliance with the rising power of Hatti a very desirable stroke of foreign policy. Whatever her motives were, they struck Suppiluliumas as being exceptional, and he thought it advisable to despatch a chamberlain to Egypt to obtain a first-hand account of the situation. On his return Prince Zennanza was sent, but was murdered while making his way to Egypt.

All this diplomatic activity must have taken place within the statutory seventy days between the death of the King and his entombment, and it is difficult to see how the negotiations could have been conducted without the knowledge of Ay; yet it was Ay as the next Pharaoh who officiated at the burial service for Tut-ankh-Amun, and is shown in the tomb-painting performing the last rites. He can only have come to the throne by the same

Plate XVII

means as were offered to Zennanza; and that Ay married his grand-daughter Ankhes-en-Amun seems inescapable, especially as their names appear side by side on the bezel of a finger-ring once seen in a dealer's shop and now lost to view. We hear no more of Queen Ankhes-en-Amun; and in his tomb in the Western Branch of the Biban el-Moluk, Ay is shown indulging in the marsh sports in company with Queen Tey, the same wife who, thirty years earlier, had been described as the nurse and tutor of Nefert-iti.

Ay buried his predecessor not in the large hypogeum he had probably planned for himself, but in a small tomb in the main valley of the Biban el-Moluk, almost opposite the place where Akhenaten, Tiye and Smenkh-ka-Re had been laid to rest some nine years earlier. It has been suggested that this tomb (now numbered as 62) was actually made for Ay, who however usurped the tomb that Tut-ankh-Amun was preparing in the Western Branch (No. 23), and this in turn had been usurped from Smenkh-ka-Re, who may have taken over the incomplete tomb that Akhenaten began to cut at Thebes during his very first regnal years. Unless foundation deposits come to light, it is impossible to test the truth of this theory. It has been suggested that Ay buried Tut-ankh-Amun in Tomb No. 62 rather than Tomb No. 23 because the latter was difficult to guard properly in the remoter Western Branch. Since he subsequently decorated it for his own occupation, however, we are to infer that other reasons dictated the exchange of tombs. Tut-ankh-Amun may well have been buried in Tomb No. 62 in order to be near other members of his immediate family in Tomb No. 55.

Despite the small size of the tomb of Tut-ankh-Amun, which had to have some of its steps, a lintel and jambs cut back to allow the larger objects to be taken into it, the burial furniture was exceptionally rich. A comparison with the wrecked remains of similar objects from other royal tombs at Thebes will show that Tut-ankh-Amun was provided with gold-covered statues and cult-images where other kings made do with resin-coated wood. He probably fell heir to most of the burial furniture of both Akhenaten and Smenkh-ka-Re, neither of whom was given a full Osiride burial. Certainly the half-obliterated name of Smenkh-ka-Re can be seen under the cartouches in the interior of the Canopic coffinettes; and the writer suspects that some of the wooden statues were originally made in the early years of the reign of Akhenaten for that king's burial. Tomb No. 62 also housed chariots, palace furniture and other objects used by the late King during his lifetime, as well as heirlooms of his family, including a state flabellum with the name of Akhenaten untouched.

Fig. 6

Plates 62, 119

6 Faience ring bezel

Plate 99

Plate 10

Plates 71, 72

The reign of Ay was short and is ill-documented, regnal year 4 being his highest known date. Tut-ankh-Amun had apparently begun a mortuary temple for himself, probably near to his father's great edifice at Medinet Habu, though its remains have not been identified. Ay also built his mortuary temple in the vicinity at the southernmost end of the row of such structures on the Western Plain at Thebes; and incorporated in its precincts a palace used during the religious festivities. The entire complex, however, was taken over and extended by his successor who usurped the work, including some statues which Ay had in turn usurped from Tut-ankh-Amun, probably because they were incomplete and uninscribed at the latter's death.

Plate 63

Ay also built a rock-chapel to Min and other local gods at Akhmim the family seat. As mentioned above, he had begun to decorate the large Tomb No. 23 in the Western Branch of the Biban el-Moluk, but no trace of his burial has been found in the debris-strewn chambers, though his stone sarcophagus has been smashed to pieces, mostly in recent times.

Plate 56

Plate 77

He was succeeded by the General Har-em-hab who had held high office as the King's Deputy under Tut-ankh-Amun. It was during this time, while the Court was at Memphis, that he had constructed a magnificent tomb for himself in the nearby necropolis of Sakkara, from the ruins of which were extracted in the early nineteenth century, reliefs which grace the museums of several European capitals. Of late the opinion has found favour that some kind of struggle developed between Har-em-hab and Ay for the possession of the crown, on or after the death of Tut-ankh-Amun, and that the older man somehow forestalled the King's Deputy in attaining supreme power by marrying Ankhes-en-Amun. Har-em-hab, in his turn, when he came into his own on the death or disappearance of Ay, with the support of the priesthood of Amun, wreaked a 'terrible vengeance' on his predecessors, usurping their monuments where he did not deface them, and striking out from the archives all record of their reigns. Ay was never buried in the tomb he had made for himself and his name and figure were desecrated throughout its decoration.

It need hardly be said that the evidence for such a highly-coloured romance is minimal.[52] If Har-em-hab rose to high position under the young Tut-ankh-Amun, it could only have been with the approval, if not the active promotion of Ay, whose daughter he had married. As for the Amun priesthood, it owed its re-habilitation and prosperity entirely to the Post-Amarna kings, and in fact a nephew of Ay held high sacerdotal positions at Thebes including the office of Second Prophet of Amun during his reign

Plate 66

at least. Har-em-hab, we may be sure, continued to enjoy royal favour under Ay, and 'The Weepers' relief in Berlin appears to date to this period of his career.[53] The best proof that Har-em-hab's accession was the result of a smooth transfer of power is to be found in the statement on his coronation statue at Turin. Here he details the steps in his career that led to his promotion to high office under former kings, until the god of his natal city, Horus of Hnes, eventually singled him out for the Crown. If Har-em-hab had seized supreme power by a palace revolution or a military coup, we should have been treated to a totally different account of his induction to kingship. Then he would have described how he had overcome evil and illegitimacy in the land by his superior right and the possession of *maet*, in much the same way as the accession of Set-nakhte, the first king of Dynasty XX, is described in the Great Harris Papyrus. It is in fact highly probable that in default of any living heirs, Ay associated Har-em-hab on the throne with him before he died; and the coronation statue, now in Turin, was made on the occasion of the appointment of Har-em-hab as co-regent when a visit to Thebes during the feast of Opet would be included in his grand tour of the realm.

Plate 78
Plate 57

It is true that Har-em-hab does not appear to have buried Ay in the tomb he had prepared for himself; but a thorough clearance may turn up evidence to show that this interpretation is wrong. It seems odd that Har-em-hab should have left a large and expensive tomb unoccupied when it could easily have been adapted for his own sepulchre, particularly as he has been accused of the wholesale usurpation of his predecessors' monuments. The writer's view is that Ay was almost certainly laid to rest in Tomb No. 23,[54] but his burial may have been desecrated later as part of a systematic campaign of vilification of the Amarna kings.

It is also a fact that Har-em-hab usurped some of the monuments of his immediate predecessors; but then, so did Ay, and so did most Pharaohs, or their officials on their behalf. So far from instituting a policy for the systematic destruction of the Atenist monuments with which he is usually accredited, Har-em-hab appears to have built at Amarna, and it is fairly certain that it was his officials who tidied up the tomb of Tut-ankh-Amun and resealed it after it had been robbed by metal thieves during the troubled times that he inherited earlier in his reign.

Har-em-hab had a long reign of at least twenty-seven years during which he had to contend with lawlessness at home, an aftermath of the breakdown of the machinery of state at the end of the reign of Akhenaten, and increasing pressure from the Hittites abroad. His success in dealing with these problems can be gauged by the strong, united and prosperous state which he seems to have left to the ambitious and aggressive Ramessides of the next dynasty.

It was they who began the vindictive persecution of the memory of Akhenaten and his successors. It was a tenet of the totalitarian rule in Ancient Egypt that the kings of a new dynasty should regard their immediate predecessors as illegitimate in order to enhance their own divine right. Ramesses I had lived under the Atenist Kings and probably held high office under them, but with Sethos I and particularly with Ramesses II there came to the throne Pharaohs who knew not Akhenaten, and who probably were not attracted by the legend he had left behind him, and were determined to efface all his memorials and those of his immediate successors. The official buildings at Akhet-Aten were dese-

Plate XI

crated and later demolished and the stone used for the foundations of temples that Ramesses II built on the opposite bank at Hermopolis. The name and figure of Akhenaten were hammered out wherever they appeared, though thanks to the carelessness of the workmen there were many oversights. The king-lists were amended to exclude the successors of Amenophis III up to Har-em-hab, and their regnal years were added to those of the latter monarch. If any unavoidable reference had to be made to the former reign of Akhenaten, he was referred to under a circumlocution as 'that criminal of Akhet-Aten.' The monuments of Tut-ankh-Amun and Ay had their inscriptions altered to apply to Har-em-hab. Lastly, the

Plate 98

tombs of the 'heretic' kings were sought out and their burials desecrated. Why Tut-ankh-Amun's was left unmolested is a mystery. Probably after at least two ransackings it had been resealed and hidden under a great mass of chippings and debris, and its exact location had been lost.

It is ironical that Ramesses II, the Pharaoh who was most active in this persecution of his predecessors was himself deeply indebted to many of Akhenaten's innovations for the more modern language of his official utterances, for the large-scale compositions that covered his temple walls and for the egomania that made him the most bombastic of all the divine Pharaohs.

Epilogue

Akhenaten and the Historians

THE READER WHO HAS had the diligence to plod thus far will realise that the view of Akhenaten presented in the foregoing pages differs somewhat from the standard accounts which fall into two or three well-defined categories. One tradition sees the Amarna Period as an early example of that struggle between Church and State which characterized much of the politics of nineteenth-century Europe. Akhenaten then emerges as the liberal, the free-thinker, even the scientist, who defied the encroaching and reactionary power of the priesthood, particularly that of the wealthy god Amun-Re of Thebes. His failure led to increasing sacerdotalism in the State, culminating in the alleged take-over of the kingship by the priests of Amun at the end of Dynasty XX, thus celebrating the triumph of superstition and reaction over progressive rationalism.

Another interpretation springs from American Non-conformist liberalism and sees Akhenaten as representing a stage in the evolution of Man from benighted savagery to the Declaration of Independence. In the development of religion and thought, Akhenaten stands out against the momentum of traditional religion as the instigator of ideas which were in advance of his time. As such, he seems the world's first individual and the world's first idealist. Associated with this viewpoint is the concept of Akhenaten the internationalist; and at a further remove, the pacifist.

More recent theses follow Marxist lines of thought. The Amarna Period was not merely a religious upheaval, but a social and political revolution as well, the result of class struggle. Akhenaten becomes one of those leaders who appears to mark a stage in the progress of Man from savagery to socialism. He joined forces with the workers or common people, *i.e.* his 'new men,' with whom he replaced the old ruling families of hereditary slave-owning magnates, and challenged their ideology with new ideas about internationalism and the equality of men. He was defeated, however, by an alliance of reactionary clerics and the army, who under Tut-ankh-Amun were able to restore the old conservative landed gentry to power. In the reign of Har-em-hab, the priesthood triumphed over the Amarna revolution and consolidated their power and privileges at the expense of the King's supreme authority.

When viewed in its own context of Late Bronze Age Egypt, however, the Amarna Period has a less modern look and a less revolutionary appearance. The idea of a struggle between an enlightened and progressive king on the one side and a reactionary and scheming priesthood on the other, simply will not stand up to closer scrutiny. In matters of doctrine, a mere nuance separated the theology of Akhenaten from that of Amun-Re, as Alexandre Piankoff has convincingly argued: 'It (the Sun-disk) is the visible image of godhead that the devotees of the Amarna reform wished to adopt for their cult, without however denying that the motor, the active and activating force is Re, as is clearly expressed in the name of Akhenaten's god. The adversaries of the reform insisted, on the contrary, on the primacy of that activating and invisible force, which according to them was the godhead itself.'[55]

The grateful kings of Dynasty XVIII had created the wealth of the temples and they could as easily have transferred their endowments elsewhere if the idea had ever occurred to them. Their administrative ascendancy was not in doubt. Both Tuthmosis IV and Amenophis III appointed Overseers of Priests of Upper and Lower Egypt, and the latter king kept the position within the royal ambit by making the young Prince Tuthmosis such a sacerdotal overlord. The idea of a separation of functions between the priesthood and the administration is, in fact, a modern concept; and in Egypt during the New Kingdom, these two aspects of government were as indissolubly linked as they had ever been. All the high priests in the various temples of Egypt were mere surrogates of the king; and the supremacy of his position is seen in the ease with which Akhenaten was able to reduce the wealthy priesthood of Amun to complete impotence and to disperse it in a very short time. The subsequent proscription of the Amarna kings was not decreed by priests, though they joined in the rejoicing at the downfall of a heretic, but by the Pharaohs of Dynasty XIX, to prove their own legitimacy.

The ideas that Akhenaten disseminated so far from being in advance of their time had a strong antiquarian flavour, and attempted to restore the supremacy of the Pharaoh to what it had been in the early Old Kingdom. The Pharaoh had had international status from the time of Menes who was proclaimed a divinity ruling over foreigner and Egyptian alike, the Master of a Universe that was bounded by the circuit of the sun's disk.

The pacifist interpretation of Akhenaten's foreign policy by a former generation of scholars has arisen from too naive an acceptance of the claims of the Pharaohs that they ruled unchallenged over a sort of Empire in Asia, instead of exercising claims over a sphere of influence. The anarchy and internecine strife revealed in the Amarna Letters then seemed exceptional instead of typical. Akhenaten was not averse to being represented in the traditional pose of the conquering Pharaoh, and there is nothing to show that under him Egyptian influence suffered any wholesale collapse. The claim in the Restoration Stela of Tut-ankh-Amun, that under his predecessor military operations in Syria met with no success, is tendentious and exaggerated. If we are to believe the Hittite accounts, there were even severer set-backs under Akhenaten's successors.

The Marxist arguments are based upon equally flimsy premises. Akhenaten's 'new men' were the old men writ large. The evidence that exists all points to the belief that Akhenaten's 'common people' were the sons of his father's officials. They claimed to have been advanced by the King in order to flatter him according to an old convention, but it was no more than a polite acknowledgement that he had appointed them to their posts. In Egypt in the fourteenth century BC the number of educated persons able to work the elaborate paperbound administrative machine was a very small percentage indeed of the population, and it would have been impossible to find substitutes for them if they had all been eliminated. The army was as much in favour under Akhenaten as it had been in the days of his predecessors. It figures prominently in the scenes of the Amarna tombs; and of a score of high officials who have left their monuments at Amarna, half a dozen were staff officers. There was no conflict between Akhenaten and his army; in fact the edicts of Akhenaten were probably put in force by the army in default of former temple administrators.[56]

The 'reforms' of Akhenaten had resulted in the sequestration of temple revenues and their diversion to the treasury of the Aten and therefore of the King. With the restoration of the old machinery of government, it could not but happen that the process would be reversed. The king's officials had become corrupt and extortionate through the delegation of too much power, and when Har-em-hab, like Tuthmosis III before him, sought to correct their abuses it was inevitable that they should lose authority to the new temple administrators.

It must be confessed that, damaged though they were by his detractors, Akhenaten's memorials have on the whole bequeathed him a favourable reputation, and a recent student has found his personality 'attractive.' His unashamed family life, the poetic sentiments of his Great Hymn to the Aten, the loss of the temple reliefs in which he would be shown as the slaughtering superman and the beauty of his wife have created for him

259

a legacy of good-will. We have no Egyptian Suetonius to describe for us an earlier Caligula. If Akhenaten wrought any evil it has been interred with his bones.

In our study, we have found nothing of the revolutionary in the political and social character of his reign. In the artistic field his innovations were of a strictly limited type and their initial mannerism had changed to something more traditional by the latter part of his reign. In the sphere of religion, while he accepted much that was orthodox, whether it was the shawabti-figures of the Osiride cult, or the spirit incarnate in the Mnevis bull of ancient superstition, or the henotheism evident in the reformed sun-worship of the Dynasty, there was one aspect in which he was wholly original, and that was his insistence upon a true monotheism, the worship of one god only, whose incarnation he was, to the exclusion of all else. Where this idea came from in the world of the fourteenth century BC, which widely recognized so many different manifestations of godhead, is not known; but his own identification with the Aten probably provides the key. Nurtured as he was in an environment in which the Pharaoh had achieved such a degree of exaltation that his father worships himself as a god, and his son worships him too, an egocentric megalomania could only see Divinity as the giant shadow cast by a Pharaoh. The Aten is a heavenly king who had a similar titulary to his earthly counterpart, who bore his names in similar double cartouches, who celebrated royal jubilees, and above all, like the Pharaoh, was unique.

It would be surprising if this cataclysm in the affairs of Egypt had not left some mark upon the folk-memory of its inhabitants, and what appears to be a dim recollection of the great event of Akhenaten's reign is transferred to the time of Kheops and 'his brother' Khephren, the builders of the two larger pyramids at Giza, in the fanciful story recorded by Herodotus: 'Egypt was excellently governed, so the priests said, until Kheops succeeded to the throne, and plunged into all manner of wickedness. He closed the temples and forbade the Egyptians to offer sacrifices, compelling them to labour in his service ... Khephren imitated the conduct of his predecessor ... Thus the affliction of Egypt endured for the space of one hundred and six years, during which time the temples were shut up and never opened. The Egyptians so detest the memory of these kings that they do not much like even to mention their names.'

In the end it was Akhenaten's intolerance of other gods and the closing of their temples that disorganized the machinery of government in Egypt, and brought his innovations to an inglorious end.

Egyptian chronology is still based on Manetho who in the third century BC wrote his *History of Egypt* which now exists only as corrupt extracts preserved in the writings of Josephus and some Christian chronographers. In these writings the Pharaohs are listed under Greek versions of their names, a practice which is followed here (thus *Amenophis* for Amen-hetep, Amun-hotpe, etc.). Only the ghost of a proper king-list survives for Dynasty XVIII in the copyists of Manetho but most of the reigns appear to have been given their correct length. Fortunately data from the monuments during this period are sufficiently voluminous to provide useful controls, and one or two celestial phenomena which have been recorded can be dated by astronomical calculations. Thus a mention of the rising of Sirius in Year 9 of Amenophis I has been put at 1537 BC, though in the absence of any precise details as to where in Egypt the observation was made, this date has now been questioned. A lunar date in the reign of Tuthmosis III and another in the reign of Ramesses II have enabled the accessions of these kings to be fixed at 1490 BC and 1304 BC respectively. An alternative date for the latter is 1290 BC which is not accepted here in view of the evidence from comparative cuneiform sources (M. B. Rowton: *Journal of Near Eastern Studies* 25, pp. 240–58) and since the Sothic era of Menophres appears to fall at 1320 BC in the reign of Ramesses I (J. Cerny: *Journal of Egyptian Archaeology*, 47, pp. 150–2). Finally in the light of his views on co-regency and jubilees, the writer has suggested below a greater overlapping of reigns than is generally accepted (C. Aldred: *Zeitschrift für Ägyptische Sprache* 94, 1–6).

ARCHAIC PERIOD		MIDDLE KINGDOM	
Dynasties I–II	*c.* 3100–2686 BC	Dynasties XI–XIII	*c.* 2060–1674 BC

OLD KINGDOM		SECOND INTERMEDIATE PERIOD	
Dynasties III–VI	*c.* 2686–2181 BC	Dynasties XIV–XVII	*c.* 1674–1559 BC

FIRST INTERMEDIATE PERIOD		NEW KINGDOM	
Dynasties VII–X	*c.* 2181–2040 BC	Dynasties XVIII–XX	*c.* 1559–1085 BC

DYNASTY XVIII

(Each name and figure within brackets indicates a suggested equivalent in Manetho and his regnal years from his coronation to the appointment of a co-regent or successor.)

Amosis	(Amosis, 25 yrs, 4 mths)	1559–1531 BC
Amenophis I	(Amenophis, 20 yrs, 7 mths)	1534–1504 BC
Tuthmosis I	(? Chebron, 13 yrs)	1514–1502 BC
Tuthmosis II	(?Mephres, 12 yrs, 9 mths)	1504–1489 BC
Tuthmosis III	(Mephramuthosis, 25 yrs, 10 mths + 21 yrs, 9 mths	1490–1436 BC
Hat-shepsut	belonging to 'his sister, Amessis')	1489–1469 BC
Amenophis II	(Amenophis, 30 yrs, 10 mths)	1444–1412 BC
Tuthmosis IV	(Tuthmosis, 9 yrs, 8 mths)	1414–1405 BC
Amenophis III	(? Orus, 28 [also 36 and 38])	1405–1367 BC
Amenophis IV } Akhenaten }	(? 'his daughter Acencheres', 12 yrs, 5 mths)	1378–1362 BC
Smekh-ka-Re	(? ———)	1366–1363 BC
Tut-ankh-Amun	(?Rathotis, 9 yrs)	1362–1353 BC
Ay	(? Armesis, 4 yrs, 1 mth)	1353–1349 BC
Har-em-hab	(? Harmais, 5 yrs)	1349–1319 BC

DYNASTY XIX				DYNASTY XX
Ramesses I	1320–1318 BC	Ramesses II	1304–1237 BC	1200–1085 BC
Sethos I	1318–1304 BC	and six other rulers to 1200 BC		

261

Abbreviations

The following conventional abbreviations are used to refer to the Egyptological journals most frequently cited in the notes and bibliography.

ASAE   *Annales du Service des Antiquités de l'Égypte*, Cairo.

CAH²   *Cambridge Ancient History*. Second Edition, 1961 –.

JARCE *Journal of the American Research Center in Egypt*, Cambridge, Mass.

JEA   *Journal of Egyptian Archaeology*, London.

JNES   *Journal of Near Eastern Studies*, Chicago.

ZÄS   *Zeitschrift für Ägyptische Sprache und Altertumskunde*, Leipzig and Berlin.

Notes

CHAPTER I

1 It would seem that Mineptah (1237–1219 BC) sent grain to relieve famine among the Hittites. G. A. Wainwright, *JEA* 46, pp. 24 ff.

CHAPTER II

2 At the death of Tuthmosis II both his daughters by Hatshepsut were mere infants, suggesting that their mother had been married to the Pharaoh when she was a child at his advent.

3 Following Charles F. Nims, *ZÄS* 93, pp. 97 ff., who has sought to show that Hatshepsut's monuments were not desecrated until after the forty-second year of his reign.

CHAPTER III

4 Apart from Tent-Amun, Tuthmosis IV is known to have had three other daughters represented in tombs of his officials, *viz.*: Amun-ipet, Tia and Sit-Amun. The Princess Pihy as well as Tia is known from labels found in the debris of a tomb of royal children dated to Year 27 of Amenophis III, but there is nothing to indicate exactly when they died (Birch: *Rhind Papyri*, Pl. XII, 1, 3–5).

5 Their tomb (Biban No. 46) was sealed with the 'necropolis' stamp only, suggesting a re-sealing, since tombs of members of the royal family apparently also bore the seal of the reigning king. *Cf.* A. H. Rhind: *Thebes*, pp. 83 ff.

6 I have followed W. C. Hayes (*CAH²*, Fasc. 10, Pt. 2, p. 29) in identifying *Shetep* as the Wady Keneh, but with reservations (*cf.* G. W. Fraser, *Proceedings of the Society of Biblical Archaeology* 21, p. 157).

7 Jean Yoyotte, *Kemi* 15, pp. 23–33. *Idem. Comptes rendus du groupe linguistique d'études chamito-sémitiques*, 8, pp. 77–78.

8 The reference *Kn.* is to the edition of the Letters prepared by J. A. Knudtzon and his successors from 1907–14 under the title of *Die El-Amarna-Tafeln*.

CHAPTER IV

9 T. Säve-Söderbergh: *Four Eighteenth Dynasty Tombs*, pp. 39–41. Surero presents a pectoral to the King during the festival celebrations and new furniture and statues for consecration in various shrines.

CHAPTER VI

10 Apart from Mut-em-wiya, there are Mut-nodjme, the sister of Nefert-iti; and Mut-em-nub, the sister of Queen Tey. The finger-ring from the Royal Tomb (Plate XII) also bore the name of 'Mut, Lady of Heaven'.

11 J. Cerny, *JEA* 43, p. 33, note 1. It is noteworthy that Queen Tiye is never referred to by the more expanded version of her name – Nefert-ari.

12 Three queens at least of Tuthmosis III bore foreign names. H. E. Winlock: *Treasure of Three Princesses*, pp. 41 and 47.

13 C. Aldred: *JEA* 54, pp. 100–106.

14 A. R. Schulman: *JARCE* 4, p. 63, discusses proposed restorations to the text, but his suggestion of 'King's Son of Kush' seems less likely in view of Reisner's careful tally of the Viceroys (*JEA* 6, p. 73, note 1). H. W. Helck's restoration, 'the King's Son N(akht-Min)', is also possible.

15 For the restoration of the scene from various fragments, see *JEA* 7, pp. 1 ff.

A fragment giving the earlier name of the Aten dates the composition to before Year 9 (*ibid.* p. 5).

16 The case for an independent reign for Smenkh-ka-Re is, however, very weak. I follow Professor H. W. Fairman in considering it wholly contained within that of Akhenaten: *cf. City of Akhenaten* III, pp. 157–9.

17 The resemblance has been stressed by S.R.K. Glanville: *JEA* 15, p. 8, note 2. Tut-ankh-Amun also resembled Queen Tiye (see p. 99 above) who, however, according to our thesis was a cousin of her husband and doubtless shared certain facial characteristics, *cf.* Plates 22, 59 above).

CHAPTER VII

18 A. H. Gardiner: *JEA* 31, p. 28.

19 C. Aldred: *ZÄS* 94, Pt. II, p. 6. See also *Chronology* on p. 261 and *cf.* J. A. Wilson, in J. B. Pritchard *Ancient Near Eastern Texts*, p. 245, note 1.

20 A. H. Gardiner: *ZÄS* 43, pp. 27–47.

21 I suspect that Si-Mut was a relative of Anen but can furnish no supporting evidence. The re-discovery of his lost tomb in the Dra Abu el-Naga area might throw light on his family connections.

22 A. Erman: *ZÄS* 27, p. 63.

23 G. Möller: *Paläographie* II, No. 632 (Gurob). This was pointed out to me by the late William C. Hayes.

24 The Amenophis who ruled for 30 years, 10 months as given by Josephus, may be Amenophis II (since he must have reigned for about that length of time) and not his grandson, despite the identification with Memnon in Syncellus.

CHAPTER VIII

25 I have no details to show whether the inscription gives the name of the mother of Meryt-Aten-ta-sherit, and whether it is enclosed in a cartouche.

CHAPTER IX

26 I have had access to the unpublished diary of Mrs Emma B. Andrews, a copy of which is in the Metropolitan Museum of Art. Mrs Andrews acted as hostess to her cousin, Theodore Davis, on his *dahabiyeh* and her careful daily jottings, unpretentious and private, are fully reliable in showing the true sequence of events.

27 These gold bands were stolen by one of Elliot Smith's laboratory attendants and have never been recovered.

28 G. Elliot Smith: *Westminster Hospital Gazette*, 4, p. 25 ff.

29 The roundels were of three kinds. Two of bronze gilt were of a size and pattern similar to those found on the pall of Tut-ankh-Amun. A smaller disk was of gold stamped in relief with the design of a five-pointed star, a pattern of particular significance for sewing on a pall. A fourth disk, only a third of the size of the largest roundel but similar in design, probably came from chariot harness.

CHAPTER X

30 A. Piankoff: *Bulletin de l'Institut Français d'Archéologie Orientale*, 62, pp. 207–18, also *idem, op. cit.* pp. 121 ff.

31 *E.g.* the Prince Tut-ankh-Aten and the Princess Bek-et-Aten.

32 C. Aldred: *JEA* 45, pp. 28–31.

33 The noun 'Akh', when translated as 'effective spirit' or 'glorious state' has the connotation of 'a transformation' perhaps a virtual incarnation, since its determinative can be a human figure. *Cf.* A. H. Gardiner: *Tomb of Amenemhet*, p. 100; W. Federn: *JNES* 19, p. 253.

34 G. Roeder: *Urkunden zur Religion*, pp. 4 ff. J. A. Wilson in J. B. Pritchard: *Ancient Near Eastern Texts*, pp. 365–7.

35 J. Cerny: *JEA* 34, p. 121.

36 F. J. Chabas: *Revue Archéologique* 14, p. 307.

37 See note 30.

38 *Cf. W.* Helck: *Verwaltung*, p. 300, note 7.

39 P. Newberry: *JEA* 14, pp. 8–9 and 117. It should be noted that the slab illustrated in Plate 9 above evidently came from the Memphis area.

40 A further argument for those who accept a long coregency between Akhenaten and his father is the absence of any deliberate mutilation or alteration of the name of Amun in that of Amenophis III in Biban Tomb No. 22. This suggests that the iconoclasm did not occur until after Year 12.

CHAPTER XI

41 W. F. Albright: *CAH*[2], Fasc. 51, p. 4.

42 The King's Envoy to Foreign Lands, May, on a statue in the British Museum has been suggested by W. Spiegelberg. A better candidate in my view is the King's Envoy to Foreign Lands and Master of the Horse, May, represented in Theban tomb No. 55. (N. de G. Davies: *Ramose*, pl. VIII.)

43 My argument also disposes of the assumption that copies were made in later reigns for reference purposes as H. W. Fairman has suggested in the case of Letter No. 27 (see K. A. Kitchen: *Suppululiuma*, p. 7, note 1).

44 K. A. Kitchen (*op. cit.* pp. 33, 39) argues that the account is retrospective because the daughter of Tushratta would not have been of marriageable age before twelve to fourteen. I see nothing to support the assumption that child marriages could not be negotiated in ancient time for political reasons, especially as Tadukhipa was evidently espoused to Amenophis III to maintain the marriage alliance between Egypt and Mitanni after the death of her aunt (*ibid.* p. 24, note 2).

CHAPTER XII

45 See Kn. No. 11, lines 5–21, 14–18.

46 Elizabeth Thomas: *Royal Necropoleis*, pp. 88–9.

47 This was bought from a dealer in Cairo soon after the clearance in the Royal Tomb during 1931–32.

48 See note 16.

CHAPTER XIII

49 A. R. Schulman has pointed out that Ay also bears the title of 'crown-prince designate' or 'regent' claimed by Har-em-hab and had a prior right to the throne after the death of Tut-ankh-Amun without issue. (*JARCE* 4, p. 58.)

50 C. Aldred: *JEA* 43, p. 41. R. Hari, however (see following note 51), argues that Har-em-hab did not espouse Mut-nodjme before he became King. I find his reasoning somewhat forced.

51 Robert Hari, *Horemheb et La Reine Moutnedjemet* p. 177 disposes of this misinterpretation. The publication of Hari's thesis anticipates so many of my own conclusions on the reigns of Ay and Har-em-hab that I have been able to abridge this part of my argument. I part company with Hari, however, in his view of an independent interregnum for Mut-nodjme and troubles at the end of Har-em-hab's reign. His study suffers from too traditional a view of the power of the Amun priesthood and of the importance of Thebes. His

identification of the Vizier Pramesse with Ramesses I has to be abandoned now in view of H. Goedicke's study (*Chronique D'Egypte* 41, p. 23 ff.).

52 *Cf.* R. Hari: *op. cit.*, pp. 58, 144–5.

53 This relief is generally dated to the reigns of Tut-ankh-Amun and the leader of the procession is identified as Har-em-hab. A. R. Schulman *ibid.* p. 64 has suggested that he may rather be Nakht-Min. As the burial is of a high-priest of Ptah of Memphis, the chief mourner is more likely to be Har-em-hab who held his important offices in the north while Nakht-Min discharged his similar duties in the south. See also R. Hari (*op. cit.* pp. 62–4).

54 In 1907 T. Davis found in pit-tomb No. 58 in the Biban, a box containing pieces of gold foil engraved with designs taken from objects belonging to Ay as king and also as a private person (*cf. Fig.* 3). I have now discarded my former suggestion that this tomb may have been the last resting-place of Ay.

EPILOGUE

55 A. Piankoff: *op. cit.* p. 218: *idem: The Shrines of Tut-ankh-Amon* (1962 edn.) pp. 12–13.

56 A. R. Schulman: *JARCE* 3, pp. 52, 58, 67.

Excavations and Surveys

ALDRED, C. The Tomb of Akhenaten at Thebes. *JEA* 47, pp. 41–65.
— Two Monuments of the Reign of Horemheb. *JEA* 54, pp. 100–106.
BOURIANT, U., Legrain, G., and Jéquier, G. *Monuments pour servir à l'étude du culte d'Atonou* I. Cairo, 1903.
BRUNNER, H. Eine neue Amarna-Prinzessin. *ZÄS* 74, pp. 104–8.
CARTER, H. *The Tomb of Tut-ankh-Amen*. 3 vols. London, 1923–33.
COONEY, J. D. *Amarna Reliefs from Hermopolis*. Brooklyn Museum, 1965.
DAVIES, N. DE G. Akhenaten at Thebes. *JEA* 9 pp. 132–52.
— *The Rock Tombs of El Amarna*. 6 vols. London, 1903–8.
— *The Tomb of the Vizier Ramose*. London, 1941.
DAVIS, T., MASPERO, G., *et al. The Tomb of Queen Tiyi*. London, 1910.
— *et al. The Tombs of Harmhabi and Touatankhamanou*. London, 1912.
ENGELBACH, R. The So-called Coffin of Akhenaten. *ASAE* 31, pp. 98–114.
FAIRMAN, H. W. A Block of Amenophis IV from Athribis. *JEA* 56, pp. 80–82.
— Once Again the So-called Coffin of Akhenaten. *JEA* 57, pp. 25–40.
FAKHRY, A. A Note on the Tomb of Kheruef at Thebes. *ASAE* 42, pp. 449–508.
GARDINER, A. H. The So-called Tomb of Queen Tiye. *JEA* 43, pp. 10–25.
HABACHI, L. Clearance of the Tomb of Kheruef at Thebes. *ASAE* 55, pp. 325–50.
HAYES, W. C. Inscriptions from the Palace of Amenhotep III. *JNES* 10, pp. 35–56, 82–112, 156–83, 231–42.
HORNUNG, E. and PIANKOFF, A. Das Grab Amenophis' III. *Mitteilungen des Deutschen Archäologischen Instituts Abteilung Kairo* 17, pp. 111–127.
KEES, H. (*ed.* T. G. H. James). *Ancient Egypt, A Cultural Topography*. London, 1961.
PEET, T. E., WOOLLEY, C. L., FRANKFORT, H., PENDLEBURY, J. D. S. *et al. The City of Akhenaten* Parts I–III, London, 1923–51.
PETRIE, W. M. F. *Tell el Amarna*. London, 1894.
PIANKOFF, A. *The Shrines of Tut-ankh-Amon*. New York, 1962.
QUIBELL, J. E. *The Tomb of Yuaa and Thuiu*. Cairo, 1908.
THOMAS, ELIZABETH. *Royal Necropoleis*. Princeton, 1966.

Historical Studies

ALDRED, C. The Beginning of the El-Amarna Period. *JEA* 45, pp. 19–33.
— The End of the El-Amarna Period. *JEA* 43, pp. 30–41.
— Year 12 at El-Amarna. *JEA* 47, pp. 41–60.
— Two Theban Notables during the Later Reign of Amenophis III. *JNES* 18, pp. 113–20.
BREASTED, J. H. Ikhnaton, The Religious Revolutionary. *The Cambridge Ancient History*, 1st edn. Vol. II, Chap. VI. Cambridge, 1924.
EDGERTON, W. F. The Government and the Governed in the Egyptian Empire. *JNES* 6, pp. 152–60.
ENGELBACH, R. Material for a Revision of the History of the Heresy Period. *ASAE* 40, pp. 133–84.
GARDINER, A. H. *Egypt of the Pharaohs*, Oxford, 1961.
— The Coronation of King Haremhab. *JEA* 39, pp. 13–31.
GUNN, B. Notes on the Aten and His Names. *JEA* 9, pp. 168–76.
HARI, R. *Horemheb et la Reine Moutnedjemet*. Geneva, 1965.
HAYES, W. C. *The Scepter of Egypt*, Part II, New York 1959.
— Egypt: Internal Affairs from Tuthmosis I to the Death of Amenophis III. *CAH²*, Fasc. 10, Pts. 1 & 2, 1962.
HELCK, H.-W. *Der Einfluß der Militärführer in der 18. Ägyptischen Dynastie*. Leipzig, 1939.

JAMES, T. G. H. Egypt: From the Expulsion of the Hyksos to Amenophis I. *CAH*², Fasc. 34, 1965.

NEWBERRY, P. E. *Scarabs*. London, 1906.

— Akhenaten's Eldest Son-in-Law. *JEA* 14, pp. 3–9.

— King Ay, the Successor of Tutankhamun. *JEA* 18, pp. 50–52.

PENDLEBURY. J. D. S. *Tell el-Amarna*. London, 1935.

PFLÜGER. K. *Haremhab und die Amarnazeit*. Zwickau, 1936.

SCHULMAN, A. R. Some Observations on the Military Background of the Amarna Period. *JARCE* 3, pp. 51–69.

— The Berlin Trauerrelief and Some Officials of Tutankhamun and Ay. *JARCE* 4, pp. 55–69.

SEELE, K. C. *The Coregency of Ramses II with Seti I*. Chicago. 1940.

SIMPSON, W. K. The Sed Festival in Regnal Year 30 of Amenemhet III. *JARCE* 2, pp. 59–63.

Religion ANTHES, R. Die Maat des Echnaton von Amarna. *Journal of American Oriental Society, Supplement No. 14*, 1952.

CERNY, J. *Ancient Egyptian Religion*. London, 1952.

DRIOTON, E. Trois Documents d'Époque Amarnienne. *ASAE* 43, pp. 15–43.

FRANKFORT, H. *Kingship and the Gods*. Chicago, 1948.

— *Ancient Egyptian Religion, An Interpretation*. New York, 1948.

KEES, H. *Der Götterglaube im alten Ägypten*. 2nd edn. Berlin, 1956.

PIANKOFF, A. Les Grandes Compositions Religieuses du Nouvel Empire. *Bulletin de l'Institut Français d'Archéologie Orientale* 62, pp. 207–18.

SCHÄFER, H. *Amarna in Religion und Kunst*. Leipzig, 1931.

Studies in Pathology ALDRED, C. and SANDISON A. T. The Pharaoh Akhenaten: A Problem in Egyptology and Pathology. *Bulletin of History of Medicine*, 36, pp. 293–316.

DERRY, D. E. Note on the Skeleton Hitherto Believed to be that of King Akhenaten. *ASAE* 31, pp. 115–19.

HARRISON, R. G. An Anatomical Examination of the Pharaonic Remains Purported to be Akhenaten. *JEA* 52, pp. 95–119.

SMITH, G. E. *The Royal Mummies*. Cairo, 1912.

WEIGALL, A. The Mummy of Akhenaten. *JEA* 8, pp. 193–99.

The Amarna Letters ALBRIGHT, W. F. The Amarna Letters from Palestine. *CAH*², Fasc. 51, 1966.

CAMPBELL, E. F. *The Chronology of the Amarna Letters*. Baltimore, 1964.

HELCK, W. *Die Beziehungen Ägyptens zu Vorderasien im 3. und 2. Jahrtausend v. Chr.* Wiesbaden, 1962.

KITCHEN, K. A. *Suppiluliuma and the Amarna Pharaohs*. Liverpool, 1962.

KNUDTZON, J. A. *et al. Die El-Amarna-Tafeln*. 2 vols. Leipzig, 1908–15.

MERCER, S. *The Tell el Amarna Tablets*. 2 vols. Toronto, 1939.

Chronology ALDRED, C. The Second Jubilee of Amenophis II. *ZÄS* 94 pp., 1–6.

HORNUNG, E. *Untersuchungen zur Chronologie*. Wiesbaden, 1964.

KITCHEN, K. A. On the Chronology and History of the New Kingdom. *Chronique d'Egypte* 40, pp. 310–322.

PARKER, R. A. The Lunar Dates of Thutmose III and Ramesses II. *JNES* 16, pp. 39–48.

ROWTON, M. B. The Material from Western Asia and the Chronology of the Nineteenth Dynasty. *JNES* 25, pp. 240–58.

List of Illustrations

Acknowledgement is made by the author and publishers to the following for permission to use their photographs for the plates: B. V. Bothmer, IX, X, XI; Trustees of the British Museum, VI, 19 24, 25, 26, 80, 116; Peter A. Clayton, I, III, IV, XII, XIII, XIV, XV; Martin R. Davies, II; Egypt Exploration Society, 6, 42, 43, 44, 52, 53, 55, 103, 104, 105, 111, 115, 118, 119, 120; Syndics of the Fitzwilliam Museum, Cambridge, 49; Griffith Institute, Ashmolean Museum, Oxford, 10, 70, 71, 72, 73, 74, 92, 93, 99; Professor Max Hirmer, VIII, XVII, 11, 12, 14, 20, 39, 75, 76; Professor H.W. Müller, 48, 65; Dr Charles Nims, 40; William Stevenson Smith, 114. Plates V, VII, XVI and 13 are by the author, and those of objects not otherwise acknowledged above are by kind permission of the relevant museums cited.
The present location of the objects is indicated and the following abbreviations used: BM. British Museum, London; CM, Cairo Museum; MMA, Metropolitan Museum of Art, New York; SMB, Staatliche Museen zu Berlin.

Figures

Index *Numbers in italics refer to plates*